Oliver Ransford was born in Bradford, Yorkshire, in 1914 and was educated at Bradford Grammar School. He began studying medicine at Leeds Medical School, and later moved to the Middlesex Hospital where he qualified in 1936. He subsequently became MD (London), FFA, RCS (England), DA. He joined the British Colonial Medical Service and then took up private practice in Bulawayo in 1947. He has won a considerable reputation with his many books on Southern African history, which include *Livingstone's Lake: the Story of Nyasa; The Battle of Spion Kop; The Rulers of Rhodesia*; and *The Slave Trade: the Story of Transatlantic Slavery*.

'Oliver Ransford ... has now turned his attention to the Great Trek of 1834–5, one of the most dramatic as well as the most important events of South African history. ... Mr Ransford writes well, while the romance and colour of the story he tells lend vigour to his telling of it and help make his book eminently suitable to the general readership at which it is directed.'
British Book News

'The merit of Mr Ransford's work is that for those who speak no Afrikaans, it gives some insight into the Afrikaaner mind.'
The Economist

For Penny

THE GREAT TREK

Oliver Ransford

CARDINAL edition published in 1974
by Sphere Books Ltd
30/32 Gray's Inn Road, London WC1X 8JL

First published in Great Britain
by John Murray (Publishers) Ltd in 1972
Copyright © Oliver Ransford 1972

This book is set in Intertype Lectura

Printed in Great Britain by Cox & Wyman Ltd,
London, Reading and Fakenham

ISBN 0 351 17949 6

CONTENTS

	Introduction	11
1	Trekboers	13
2	The Afrikaner Debate	27
3	The Voorste Mense	43
4	Potgieter	66
5	Vegkop	76
6	Pillar of Smoke by Day	89
7	Serpent in Eden	106
8	The Great Murder	124
9	Blood River	136
10	Natalia	160
11	The High Veld	180
12	Fulfilment	196
	Epilogue	205
	Notes on Text	209
	Glossary	229
	Bibliography	231
	Chronological Table	233
	Index	237

LIST OF ILLUSTRATIONS

1 Zulu warriors, from a coloured lithograph by G. F. Angas*

2 Voortrekkers (Reproduced by courtesy of South African Railways)

3 The mighty rampart of the Drakensbergs (Reproduced by courtesy of Department of Information, Pretoria)

4 Trek wagons crossing a river, from an etching by W. H. Coetzer*

5 Andries Hendrik Potgieter (Reproduced by courtesy of Mr Ivanoff of the Vaderland, Johannesburg)

6 Piet Retief, an imaginary portrait*

7 Battle of Vegkop, from an engraving by an unknown artist*

8 Trekking through the hills, from pen and ink sketch by H. Lea

9 Trek wagons descending a hill, from an etching by W. H. Coetzer*

10 Dingaan, a contemporary drawing, from *Journey to the Zoolu Country* by A. Gardiner*

11 The seizure of Piet Retief and his men, from a drawing by John F. Campbell*

12 The Bloukrans massacre, 1838, from an oil painting by Thomas Baines*

13 Sir Harry Smith, from an engraving by D. J. Pound, *c*. 1859*

14 Andries Pretorius, from a photograph*

15 Attack at Blood River, from an etching by W. H. Coetzer*

16 The battle of Blood River, a drawing by A. A. Telford after W. H. Coetzer (Reproduced by courtesy of Mr A. Telford)

17 The Retief Stone (Photo: the author)

18 Reconciliation of Pretorius and Potgieter, 1852*

* Reproduced by courtesy of the Africanna Museum, Johannesburg

MAPS IN TEXT

The expansion of the Trekboers from Cape Town   24

The trek of Louis Tregardt and J. Van Rensburg   50

The Great Trek   92

Routes of Piet Retief and Wen Commando   110

The Great Murder   131

Diagram of the battle of Blood River   148

The Trekker Republics   182

The Thirstland Trekkers   206

ACKNOWLEDGMENTS

I have been constantly astonished and at the same time deeply touched by the number of kindly people who have come to my aid and provided me with information about the Great Trek. I cannot mention all of them by name but at the same time am unable to refrain from mentioning my thanks to the following: Messrs H. E. Beyer, G. A. Chadwick, S. J. Cilliers, W. H. Coetzer, A. Colenbrander, T. H. Cooke, E. A. Galpin, N. Johnson, C. E. More, Mrs C. Minchin, Dr Norwich, Prof J. J. Oberholster, Dr W. Punt, Mrs C. Rheinallt Jones, Mrs P. Siebert, Miss Anna Smith (and her two assistants Mrs L de Wet and Mrs H. J. Bruce), Prof. F. J. du T. Spies, Mr R. W. Stacey, and Dr L. B. Thompson. I must express too my special obligation to Mr and Mrs Charles More for their valuable counsel and advice.

My greatest debt of gratitude is owed again to my wife who joined me in seeking out information about the Voortrekkers and the historical sites with which they are associated, and then kept guard at home while the midnight oil was burning.

INTRODUCTION

'Their adventures and exploits form one of the most singular chapters of modern history, and deserve a clearer record than has yet been given to them.' So in 1875 wrote the brilliant English historian James Anthony Froude of the South African Voortrekkers.

Since that date many fine accounts of the history of the Voortrekkers have been written, notably by M. Nathan and E. W. Walker. But the story needs retelling for the general reader's benefit if only because the Great Trek led to the development of the Afrikaner nationalism which so concerns Black Africa today.

The Great Trek was an abrupt bound into the continental interior by settlers mainly of Dutch origin living in Cape Colony at the beginning of the Victorian era. Within the space of twenty years their advance had doubled the area of effective white occupation of South Africa, and by thrusting themselves among the Bantu the Voortrekkers had greatly increased the sub-continent's race problem.

The march into the wilds was made by a few thousand men armed with muskets and Bibles, together with their women and children. It was opposed by the two most powerful military empires in southern Africa: together they constituted a far more formidable obstacle than the Red Indian nations which impeded the contemporary advance of the American frontiersmen towards the Pacific. Yet Hollywood has still to chronicle the struggles of the trekkers, perhaps because in the past cinemagoers have been conditioned to see nothing discreditable in dispossessing Sioux, Cherokees and Seminoles of their land, yet keen with pity over the injustices of Black Africa.

The central fact which gives structure to the inception and course of the Great Trek was the Dutch colonists' insistence on continuing to live according to the pattern established by their immediate colonial forebears. Its design prescribed three fundamental requisites:

each burgher was entitled to 6,000 acres of grazing land: governmental control must be minimal; and (most important of all) the Divinely appointed gulf which separated white Christian people from coloured heathens should be maintained. When these points were challenged by the British who took over Cape Colony during the Napoleonic wars the Dutch settlers became determined to detach themselves from the Colony and seek their *lebensraum* in the African interior.

Most accounts of the exodus of the Afrikaans-speaking colonists from the Cape have laid emphasis on their struggle for possession of Natal, which in the end was won by British imperialism. To my mind the trekkers' successful occupation of the South African high veld is of far more significance. For on the high veld was bred the Afrikaner nationalism which plays so large a part in African politics today, and, since the territory turned out to be the richest parcel of real estate in the world, it provided the Afrikaners with the means to dominate the remainder of the sub-continent.

This book about the Great Trek has been written in the belief that a sound knowledge of this central episode in the South African past will enable the reader to understand the strange necessities which drove the Afrikaners to their present racial attitudes. In its course I have deliberately dispensed with detailed references and text notes, but all source material has been listed in the bibliography.

I

Trekboers

By the end of the eighteenth century a new breed of men had evolved in South Africa – the trekboers. No people quite like them had ever existed before. Descended from white colonists who had settled at the Cape of Good Hope after 1652 when the Dutch East India Company established a staging post there, they had quickly espoused themselves to their strange new environment and became an integral part of Africa. The earliest colonists were of Dutch stock, but many settlers of German origin had joined them later, and after the revocation of the Edict of Nantes in 1685 *De Kaap* had accepted a considerable infusion of French Huguenot refugees. By 1800 the white colonists numbered rather less than 40,000, and were so connected by marriage that they more resembled a gigantic family living on its ancient estate than a polyglot community scraping a livelihood from one of the world's most out-of-the-way places.

The first colonists dug in at the Cape, hemmed in on one side by the sea and on the other by tiered rows of mountains which divided them from an unknown continental interior; rather uneasily they realised that it must stretch all the way to Egypt and the Mediterranean. In their bridgehead at the butt end of Africa they felt themselves to be hostages not only to the tribesmen and savage animals which they knew must inhabit this interior, but also to the whims of their masters, the Council of Seventeen, who, from Amsterdam, governed the far-reaching empire of the Dutch East India Company.

The Seventeen ruled their subjects despotically. The rank and file of the white settlers at *De Kaap* were employed only as soldiers and producers of fresh fruit and vegetables from the Company's gardens to supply the crews of its merchantmen. They were excluded from all responsible and professional positions which the Seventeen invariably filled with Hollanders. At the completion of their contracts very few men could afford to pay their passage back to Europe, and after taking their discharge there was at first little hope of these 'free burghers' finding employment except as tradesmen and tavern keepers. But in 1657, since difficulty was being experienced in obtaining supplies of grain from the local Hottentots, the Council at the Cape allowed a handful of settlers to set up as farmers (Boers in the Dutch tongue) along the Liesbeeck stream which ran into Table Bay beside the infant village of *De Kaap*.

This was a start; a few burghers could now cherish some form of independence and the number grew when the Administration presently found it expedient to encourage stock-breeding too among the Boers in order to supply passing ships with meat. And the cattle-Boers soon found it paid them to push beyond the immediate confines of the Dutch settlement in search of pasture.

For ground in the hinterland could be legally obtained from the Company which operated a system of quit rents; stock bred quickly here and there was always a market for fresh meat at *De Kaap*. Moreover, little capital was required to set up as a grazier; cattle could be bought inexpensively (usually for brandy) from the Hottentots. Hottentot labour was cheap and they made excellent herders, while an income could always be augmented by hunting. And the stock-breeders found it gloriously refreshing to be free from the petty regulations of the Company officials at the Cape.

But penetration of the hinterland was blocked by a series of formidable mountains rising up in gigantic steps, beautiful to look at but menacing in their immensity. And beyond the mountains lay lands which were the reliquary of all sorts of displaced peoples, animals and flora, and filled accordingly with unknown dangers. Only along the coast, both to the north and east of *De Kaap*, was there easy access to new grasslands, but on one side the graziers were soon led to arid regions and on the other, the east, to trackless forest lands.

The problem facing the cattle-Boers could thus be solved only by finding passes through the mountain barriers, and the more venturesome among them accordingly yoked double spans of oxen to their great wagons, explored the valleys and kloofs which ascended succeeding escarpments, and broke at last into a new world. They came to a vast inland plateau which, although bounded on the west by the Namaqua Desert, appeared to extend indefinitely towards the north.

14

It was true that areas of this high plain – the Great and Little Karoos – were mere herbages of scanty plants dependent on less than ten inches of rain each year and uninviting to stock farmers, but for the most part the plateau was luxuriant with the sweet grass which provided ideal grazing for cattle. There was little shade to be found there to be sure; a combination of deliberate grass burning, strong winds and dry cold winters did not encourage tree growth, but this disadvantage was more than off-set by the pasture's quality and the scarcity of human inhabitants. There were only scattered settlements of Hottentots and Bushmen living on the vast plains, and they could offer little resistance to the invasion of their lands by white men. Both races were yellow-skinned and spoke a click language suggesting a common origin, but whereas the Bushmen relied on hunting and food-gathering for their sustenance, the Hottentots were culturally more advanced, possessing large herds of cattle and sheep, and, perhaps because of better nutrition, they were generally of larger stature than the tiny Bushmen hunters.

The white pioneers on the high veld were preceded by big game hunters and gangs of outlaws who plundered the indigenous people's herds, but for the most part the newcomers were farmers with their families who preferred the adventures of a roving life to the mannered, candle-lit world of *De Kaap* or the lush orchards of Paarl.

Although at first the Boers had not clearly distinguished between the yellow-skinned people with whom they made contact, it took the pioneers little time to discover that the Hottentots were prepared to trade with them while the Bushmen were not. Essentially the Hottentots had led nomadic lives, constantly moving their stock in search of better pasture. Now they were inclined to settle round the white farmers' camps, bartering their cattle for beads, guns, tobacco and brandy, and to find some security in return for their services as herdsmen and domestics. The Bushmen on the other hand would have nothing to do with the Whites. Their inclination was to withdraw before them into the more inaccessible parts of the interior. Yet their presence was always felt and it was always a malevolent one, for they were quite incapable of resisting the temptation to raid the European pastoralists' stock. In general then the inter-reaction of the colonists with the Hottentots was peaceful, whereas that with the Bushmen was hostile.

The breakthrough by Europe into the hinterland of the African

15

sub-continent exerted a profound psychological effect on the Dutch pastoralists. Here before them lay an apparently limitless homeland, a suddenly revealed heritage, whose freedom of space released them from physical and spiritual immobility. More and more Boers followed the pioneers into the interior where conditions suited them so well that they experienced a minor population explosion and formed the nucleus of a new nation. They were as nomadic as the Hottentots, or as the antelope they hunted. Trekking for them became a way of life. 'The whole of Africa,' sighed the Governor at the Cape in 1699, 'would not be sufficient to accommodate and satisfy' the trekboers, but a year later he was notifying the Seventeen with more satisfaction that 'The Cape promises to grow by the increase of its own people, who, not knowing another fatherland, will not ... again depart.'

By the beginning of the eighteenth century thousands of trekboers were living permanently on grazing farms in the interior, some of them temporarily migrating each winter to the coast, so that their cattle might enjoy its sweet grass, but generally moving farther into the plains when their land was exhausted or when their journeys of exploration had revealed more attractive grazing or water. These people rarely put up permanent dwelling places; their homes were the wagons parked by a water point on the 'loan places' they had registered with the Company. Their farms usually approximated to the conveniently-managed size (for Africa) of 6,000 acres, and they generally marked out this area in a rough and ready manner by trotting a horse from the wagon along all four points of the compass for half an hour.

The trekboers' livelihood depended primarily on stock-breeding, but where the ground was suitable they grew grain. They were not especially devoted to one particular farm; their attachment was reserved for the stock they owned and for the virgin land as a whole which Providence had opened up to them. Trekking was in the blood of these land Vikings; it lay in the very core of their nature. For they were possessed by a restless spirit which is called the *trekgees* and it drove them on continuously in search of new territory. They would move if they were annoyed by wild animals or hostile natives or by tax collectors, but more often they trekked for no more reason than a quenchless hope that better pastures lay beyond the next horizon. 'Myn vrouw, wy moet trek', a Boer patriarch would say to his wife,

16

and then their possessions were packed, the oxen put to the yoke again, and the wagons jolted slowly forwards with the axles groaning as the whip cracked over the oxen's straining backs. So common were these miniature migrations or *trekkies* that everyone in a Boer family exactly knew his task: the men would ride ahead to find the easiest going for the wagons and locate water for the night's resting place, the children and servants would lead the oxen as *voorlopers*, while the womenfolk took their ease in the wagons, looking out from under the tilts at the changing scenes of Africa. And every day the party would be five or ten miles farther away from Cape Town.

Reading the pages of official records at the Cape and the rarely published reminiscences of the trekboers themselves one begins to take note of the slow adjustment of these cattle-farmers to their surroundings, and the growth of a certain expertise in enabling their herds to overcome local pestilences and grow prolific. They became particularly skilled in using and maintaining their key possessions – guns and ox wagons – and, spending much time in the saddle, they became the most competent horse-masters in the world. It would be entirely wrong to regard the trekboers as members of an exotic civilisation transplanted to the South African interior: these new-comers had become as much a part of Africa as its indigenous people and as the Bantu who, all unknown to them, were at the same time migrating southwards down the continent. As though to signify their allegiance to their new homeland the Boers began to speak of themselves as Afrikanders and then as Afrikaners, and thus distinguished their people from the townsmen who lived at the Cape. These Afrikaners of the interior were already remarkably isolated and self-sufficient. Every year, it is true, they would journey to *De Kaap* to renew their grazing licences, to arrange and contract marriages to buy essentials which they could not produce themselves, like gunpowder, cloth, coffee, liquor and agricultural implements, and to sell the products of their stock-farming and hunting – horses, cattle and sheep on the hoof, skins and hides, soap, beeswax and ivory.

But for the remainder of the year the Boers were cut off from all organised society; inevitably they became self-reliant and, it must be conceded, somewhat refractory to law. Because of their special circumstances these people grew increasingly resentful of the somewhat feeble attempts made by Company officials to impose their regulations on them. The instinct of these pioneers, who anyway could never see a mountain range without being certain that Paradise lay beyond, was to move farther and farther away from irritations of this sort, and in the course of four generations the trekboers, as family units or in small groups, advanced slowly and without co-ordination through the mountains and around the Great Karoo to all the lush pastures of the high veld south of the great Orange river. Here in the wilds they could enjoy the *lekker lewe*, the free and independent lotus life, which they so much cherished. It released them, for all intents and purposes, from the necessity of physical labour since they employed Hottentot hirelings as field workers, shepherds, herdsmen and domestic servants. It is true that some of the trekboers felt distress at being deprived of the regular religious ministrations of more settled communities, as well as of easy trading facilities, but at the more accessible farms at least even these needs might be catered for by itinerant pastors and by pack pedlars – the *smouse* of South African history – who carried in their donkey packs not only guns but needles, threads, buttons and all the multitudinous piece-goods which are the common denominator of Western civilisation.

The fabric of the Afrikaners' life and their character too were governed and developed by the soil and climate of South Africa, by the look and feel of the ground they farmed, by the gentle colours and contours of the veld, by the dark table-topped koppies which were dotted over it, and by the cordilleras of smoky-blue mountains that stared at them from the distance. Their life-style took on a special quality of its own. They made little attempt at comfort, much less at elegance. The huts they inhabited when a settled period allowed them temporarily to abandon the cramped quarters of an ox-wagon, were rough and unsubstantial, the so-called *hart bees houses* of pioneering South Africa. These were usually three-roomed; the floors were made of a mixture of clay and cattle dung, the walls of mud, the roofs of thatching-grass and reeds. Yet these edifices, which today would be condemned by any health authority, accommodated whole families: two or three men and their wives would crowd into a single house and in it would bring up a host of children. Furniture was of the simplest kind: seats and beds were no more than a wooden framework strung with unplaited *riempies* and covered with a rough mattress and karosses, while ox-skulls were used as stools on the *stoeps*. Leather proved to be the most abundant and useful of their raw materials: tents, the *riems* which replaced the ropes of Europe, their shoes and even garments were made from this most practical of a rancher's by-products. The cattle-Boers fed well. Meat was always plentiful and it was embodied in the many dishes peculiar to the Afrikaners, which are drawn from Holland, Germany and France, all of them spiced with flavourings from the east that have been culled from generations of Malay slaves at the Cape. An early lunch was taken at 11 a.m. and supper at seven in the evening, but there was always coffee standing on the *stoep* for anyone who passed by, and a bed too if required. For although an English clergyman grumbled that the Boers' 'Characters and manners are very simple, approaching to the rude', their dearest enemies could never reproach them for lack of hospitality.

The Afrikaner men impressed all visitors with their physique. The Boers, wrote one English traveller, 'living principally on gross animal food are exceedingly tall and large', and over and over again we find some reference to the sheer physical energy of these bearded giants as well as, it must be admitted, to the deplorable stoutness of their wives. Large families were the rule here in the African hinterland: it was usual for men to marry while still in their teens, and quite common for their wives to bear fifteen children. An almost biblical reverence was paid to the head of the family, and sons thought nothing odd about remaining under the patriarchal roof after marriage.

These first Afrikaners undoubtedly lived in an intellectual backwater, almost completely cut off from the flow of new ideas which were invigorating Europe during the Age of Reason. Many of them were unlettered and illiterate, but it would be wrong for us to conceive of them as being not concerned with education: on many farms *meesters* from Europe were retained to teach the children. Because they were set apart from the rest of the world, the Boers had no reason to learn any language other than their spoken *taal*, a variation of Dutch, nor did they feel themselves as lacking in mental stimulation; they had reached the happy state of living in balance with nature; the veld was their world and everywhere they could see the quiet seasons' slow wonders unfolding before them. These very circumstances bred self-reliance; their little wants from the outside world were satisfied by a *smouse* or an annual trip to the Cape; for the rest they had only to look to the products of the veld. 'These farmers,' wrote Edward Blount after visiting them, 'live without concern; for they have everything themselves; their slaves and their sons are their masons [and] their blacksmiths. . . .' Life for them had taken on a special rhythm of its own. Reaction to all problems was unhurried, something to be discussed at length. They walked slowly round their difficulties, inspecting them from every side, but once they had decided on a solution they stuck to it with rigid obstinacy.

The country which they had inherited suited them above all others. People either love the South African high veld or they avoid it, and despite all the calls it made on their fortitude, the Afrikaners were only truly happy there. When reading the accounts left by travellers in the interior at this time, one can sense the almost Rousseauesque simplicity with which these cattle-Boers lived, and can understand their descendants' nostalgia for it which they display to this day. Certainly in the trekboers it bred the tight cohesiveness of those who have lived on the dangerous frontiers of European expansion into the wilds, and this is perhaps as strong a tie as can unite any community.

For recreation the Boers had the best hunting in the world at their very doorstep. Game abounded. 'Abundant', 'excessively plentiful', 'teeming' and 'immeasurable' were the sort of adjectives used by travellers from the Cape when they described the huge herds of antelope they saw grazing the veld two centuries ago. Besides the buck there were innumerable elephants, giraffes and ostriches as well as beasts of prey like lion and leopard. Inevitably the Afrikaners became magnificent marksmen, and because ammunition was hard to come by they took care to make every shot effective. These people enjoyed the simple pleasures: when they gathered together and especially at the periodic *Nagmaal* or Communion the frontier folk revelled in music, card games, community dancing, field sports and the neighbourhood's gossip. But life was not all pleasure. The white farmers were continuously involved in coping with adverse natural phenomena like droughts or in fighting off the aboriginal people who raided their stock. To deal with the latter, loose military formations called commandos were mustered from time to time. The frontiersmen made splendid light cavalry and they suited their tactics perfectly to the vast spaces they inhabited. The commandos were able to live off the country without difficulty and would take the field for weeks at a time. The men depended on a single weapon – the flintlock or *snaphaan* which was as long as a pikestaff – and a singular style of fighting – charging their perfectly trained horses right up to an enemy group, firing from them without dismounting, retiring to reload, and then returning to repeat the attack. These tactical movements came to them almost naturally, and were developed with great skill. The reloading of guns was an especially complicated procedure: the Boers had to pour a measured quantity of gunpowder from a powder flask down the barrel of their *snaphaan*, push a plug of wadding down behind it with a ramrod, follow this with a leaden slug the size of a marble and a second plug to hold it in place; next the hammer had to be primed and only then could the flintlock be fired. Yet these men were capable of doing all this at a gallop and so quickly that they could fire several shots every minute. The spear of the Hottentot and the poisoned arrow of the Bushmen were no match for the muskets of these formidable gunmen unless they were foolish enough to get involved in hand-to-hand fighting. Discipline in the commandos admittedly was slack; there was no suggestion among the Boers of the military tautness which a modern soldier would regard as proper to a fighting unit; 'There was a commandant of the forces,' a French traveller explained after serving on commando, 'but as a matter of form only in whom no right of punishment was recognised, and whose command anyone would obey only if they thought fit.' The Afrikaners trained their servants to fight alongside them, and they could when the occasion arose muster a considerable force. In 1774 we read of a 'general commando' numbering about a hundred 'Christians' and 150 'Bastards[1] and Hottentots' which took the field against hostile Bushmen, killing 500 of them and taking 250 prisoners who were destined to become apprenticed servants to the farmers.

The Afrikaners were above all a deeply religious people. Brought up as Calvinists, they followed a rigid but vital creed which owed more to the Old Testament than to the New.[2] They believed the Bible to be the true and single medium between themselves and God; no human intermediaries were in consequence required, and the authority of each church rested upon its congregation and not on a priest. It followed that these people saw nothing wrong in criticising the preachers who ministered to them, much less the Company executives who attempted to maintain some temporal control over the

21

emigrants. Yet at the same time this closed community of farmers placed great stress on the regular and proper celebration of the Church's offices: the Boers would travel for days on end to have their children baptised or to attend the annual *Nagmaal* of their district.

The teachings of John Calvin, misconstrued though they might be, convinced the Afrikaners that the Lord had deliberately separated the peoples of the world into different races and that it was no part of their duty to attempt to bring them together. And so, although the Dutch Reformed Church, no less than their physical isolation, was a tremendously strong unifying factor, at the same time its tenets inclined to make them intolerant of the coloured people who shared their land. For did not the Bible speak of the Children of Ham who were condemned to perpetual servitude and did it not forbid them to consort with the heathen? These men and women grew genuinely into the belief that the white men were 'the highest image and likeness of the Lord' and so endowed that the creative plan of Providence intended them for the loftiest positions in the world. But these early South Africans went further: not only did they feel intensely that they of all people enjoyed a special relationship with God, but they conceived that in their daily actions they were reliving the story of the Bible. The historian, Dr George McCall Theal, put the cause of this concept very well when he wrote that each Afrikaner lived 'under such skies as those under which Abraham lived. His occupation was the same, he understood the imagery of the Hebrew writers, more perfectly than anyone in Europe would understand it, for he spoke to him of his daily life. . . .' Such beliefs might lead the Boers into harmful rigidities but they also gave them immeasurable strength as a people and allowed them to defend themselves against the rigours of their environment with all the relish of Old Testament prophets who knew that the Lord was on their side.

It took determination and great courage to overcome all the hazards which the trekboers met in the wilds, and there is something to be greatly admired in the way these descendants of a sea-faring people adapted themselves to their new land environment, especially when it stands in such vivid contrast to the fatalistic acceptance of a subsistence economy by the indigenous races who had occupied it for centuries. Inevitably their lives and a philosophy of the white man's superiority encouraged the growth of rugged individualism in the Afrikaners. They were not exactly truculent, but they became unusually impervious to reasoned argument, and side by side with this attitude there developed an obstinate resentment and contempt for all forms of governmental authority. It sometimes seemed more than fortunate that their haphazard migrations were all the time taking the trekboers farther and farther away from the Company officials at Cape Town.

The trekboers' slow advance through the extremity of Africa may have been sporadic and casual but it went on with the inevitability of an incoming tide, each individual trekker party representing a wavelet which lapped across another section of the wilds. And their expansion had a different quality from anything which had occurred before. These pioneers were not inspired by the explosion of an ambitious will, by the lure of a rich country's plunder, or by the drag of newly discovered gold. Their advance was a communal quest for increased freedom combined with a feeling for seclusion, a resentment of authority and an abiding curiosity about the veld which lay beyond the next line of hills. It went on year after year, decade after decade, through the seventeenth and eighteenth centuries. Generally speaking it was directed in two main streams. One went north close to the Atlantic coastlands and then, as the country became more arid, turned eastwards to skirt the southern limits of the Great Karoo. The second and stronger flow passed eastwards, with the water of the Indian Ocean glittering on the right hand, until the great forests round the Brak river deflected it through the Little Karoo and down the Langekloof towards the Gamtoos river, or in some cases farther inland between the folded Langebergen and Zwartbergen Mountains to fan out in fine grazing country along the reaches of the upper Sundays river. Here the two streams converged on each other, and mingled together in the country south of the great Orange river.

Progress was slow but it was steady; by 1745 the west bank of the Gamtoos was settled; in 1760 Jacobus Coetzee had ventured across the Orange in search of ivory and he was followed a little later to the great river by farmers who halted on its banks or established themselves on the Zeekoe river (this river was in 1798 officially recognised as the Cape boundary by Governor Van Plettenberg when he set up a marker there). In 1770 there was already a handful of farmers living in the Sneeuwbergen which, like the Stormberg and Nieuwveld Mountains, formed one of the scarps of the great interior plateau. Two years later the trekkers had reached Bruintjes Hoogte and were entering the valley of the Great Fish river. In a hundred years the descendants of the farmers who had been given smallholdings on the Liesbeeck stream had moved forward until some of them were living more than five hundred miles from *De Kaap*.

Then quite suddenly the migration stopped. In the north the trekkers were brought to a halt by the aridity of Namaqualand; to the north-east their progress was opposed with increasing ferocity by the Bushmen of the Sneeuwbergen region; and farther south the Boers' expansion ended because it clashed with another migratory move-

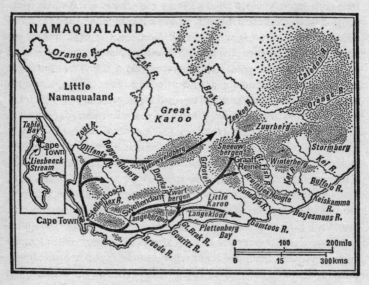

Expansion of the Trekboers from Cape Town

ment. It made contact with black men moving in the opposite direction from the forest lands of central Africa, a multitude of strong virile people which was spearheaded by the warlike Xhosa tribe. This was by no means the first meeting of white and black man in south-eastern Africa. Although travel beyond the Gamtoos was for long officially prohibited, hunting parties from the beginning of the century had pressed ahead of the trekboers towards the Great Fish river. Their men were not averse to rustling cattle from the Hottentot settlements they passed on the way, but in 1702, near the present town of Somerset East, they collided with a more formidable people, the Xhosa, who were prepared to fight to protect their herds. In 1736 there was another encounter during which these tribesmen exterminated a party of white hunters who had ridden as far as the Keiskama river. But now, fifty years later, the Bantu began to make contact with white men who had come east not to hunt but to make permanent homes for themselves on land which the tribesmen regarded as their own. The collision resulted in fighting and then in a sort of stalemate, the Great Fish river becoming a rough-and-ready frontier between white trekkers and Bantu migrants. The river was not a particularly formidable obstacle; during the dry season no more than a trickle of water flowed down it. It was an unsatisfactory boundary for another reason: dense bush grew along the river's banks and provided excellent cover for the cattle rustlers of both races. Yet it became a genuine frontier; it divided two entirely different cultures, and a traveller even today who visits the Fish river is conscious of a curious paramesic feeling, of a sense that here began the long struggle between the black and white peoples of southern Africa which still remains unresolved.

After the first clashes, when the two races settled down uneasily on either side of the Fish, periodical raiding of each other's herds occurred, the whites driving eastwards as far as the Buffalo and Kei, the blacks destroying farms even as far as Plettenberg Bay and Knysna.

But with the Orange and Fish rivers providing them with frontiers of a sort, the trekkers by the end of the eighteenth century had succeeded in establishing themselves in a territory which was larger than France. Already as a people they were moulded into a remarkably uniform pattern; they had developed the *taal* into a new language, Afrikaans, which was a simplified version of the High Dutch spoken by their forebears but with added words of German, Portuguese and Bantu origin; they had quite cut off their ties with Europe and were tending to do so with their seat of government at the Cape. The officials there, attempting to reassert their authority in the distant districts, appointed magistrates to Swellendam and Graaff Reinet, but this only increased the tension between the frontiersmen and the Company's servants at the capital. Open revolt flared up in 1795: numbers of trekboers withdrew their allegiance from the Company and set up two republics of their own. But that same year by the curious symmetry of history, Great Britain decided to occupy the Cape in order to defend the sea routes to India during the war with France. Quite suddenly the Afrikaners realised that their *lekker lewe* was threatened by a far more exacting enemy than the Dutch East India Company: it was menaced now by the needs of an expanding British empire and by the agitation for racial reform by missionaries who had followed the red-coats to the Cape.

NOTES

1 Half Breeds.
2 The books of Exodus and Joshua were particularly popular, and were to suggest to the Voortrekkers their own identification with the Children of Israel.

2

The Afrikaner Debate

As things turned out, during the first eleven years of the French revolutionary wars, the Cape Boers were governed by four separate administrations. In 1795 as we have seen, the original Dutch East India Company gave way to a British Government; after the Peace of Amiens of 1802, the Colony reverted to Dutch rule, when the short-lived Batavian Republic came into being; finally, when the war broke out a year later, the British Government decided that it must again make sure of this key to India, and it dispatched a large fleet to the Cape in 1805. During the anxious months when the battles of Trafalgar and Austerlitz were being fought, sixty-three ships sailed south-wards through the Atlantic; a combined service exercise in a style strangely predictive of the Second World War followed: after a skirmish in the dunes of Blaauwberg Strand the burghers submitted to superior arms and the second British occupation of the Cape began. From now on the Boers were ruled by a succession of governors and officials whose standards of values were utterly different from their own. They were disciplined by autocratic foreigners who made no attempt to hide their feelings that the Dutch colonists were a tiresome responsibility conferred on them by the necessity of maintaining a naval station on the way to India. And what made things worse was the way these arrogant British were far more inclined to listen to criticism and denunciations of the Boers than to sit down and hear the colonists' even perfectly legitimate complaints.

That was not all: in the wake of unsympathetic officials came a host of Christian missionaries who were determined to preach the fashionable doctrine of brotherly love and racial equality to anyone who would listen to them. With their advent the whole impact of contemporary English liberalism and Negrophilism, buttressed as it was by central authority, fell suddenly on the Boers. The mission-aries' teachings were, of course, repugnant to a white race not only convinced of its superiority to the Hottentots and Bantu, but which genuinely believed that its very existence depended on subjugating these inferior beings who had harmed them so often. And, indeed, one cannot help but feel a good deal of sympathy for the Boers on this matter, especially as the missionaries were earnest irritable men who had no experience in dealing with a multi-racial society, and who seemed to reserve all their charity for its coloured members. Many of the missionaries came from the artisan class and had re-ceived the call during the British evangelical revival: for instance, John Philip, who was particularly loathed by the Afrikaners, had been a mill hand before entering the Church, while Robert Moffat of Kuruman had begun life as a gardener. This sort of background inevit-ably led them to display a narrowness of vision which might have been avoided by a wider education, and, however praiseworthy their purpose, however splendid their new awareness of the equality of men, it is sad that the missionaries did not express their opinions about the Boer attitudes to the coloured people more tactfully, and avoided other of their more patronising criticisms. But, however badly they had been received by the Dutch Colonists, the mission-aries certainly had the ear of the Cape Government, and it was mainly due to their agitation that the British authorities in 1828 passed an ordinance which released all Hottentots from any legis-lation that enforced discrimination on account of colour. Pass laws and child apprenticeship were all abolished and there is no doubt that the Boers were correct in claiming that Hottentot vagrancy, with its concomitant evil of stock-theft, thereafter increased im-measurably. What rankled even more was the enrolment of Hot-tentots as soldiers to enforce the Colony's laws, and the way Hottentot servants were allowed – even encouraged – to make official complaints about the treatment meted out to them by their masters. In matters of this sort the Hottentots were all too often abetted by the missionaries; one of whom took credit for causing the arrest of no less than twenty white farmers for the maltreatment of their servants. We must remember, too, that to answer such a charge in court meant that a man had to leave his wife and children unpro-tected on an isolated farm for days and weeks at a time, and we can sympathise with the shocked surprise of one of them who, on receiving a summons to a distant magistracy, groaned 'My God! Is this the way to treat a Christian?'

Not all the Boers were willing to accept a summons of this sort, and during 1815 a key piece of Afrikaner history dropped into place when a Frederick Bezuidenhout ignored several warrants to appear at Graaff Reinet to answer charges of ill-treatment laid by one of his Hottentot servants. After two years had gone by Hottentot soldiers led by a white officer attempted to arrest Bezuidenhout, and killed him when he resisted. At the grave-side a few days later his brother, Johannes Bezuidenhout, swore to 'expel the tyrants from the country', but the rising he led ended rather tamely when the rebels were confronted by a posse of Dragoons at Slagters Nek. Bezuidenhout himself was killed in the skirmish and his followers surrendered; five of them were condemned to death. Unhappily the hanging was badly bungled: the ropes of four men broke and they were only executed at the second attempt. The horror of the scene at Slagters Nek, the well-named 'Butcher's Pass', which on orders from Cape Town was watched by all the district, became deeply etched into Boer folk-memory.

But it was the insecurity of the eastern frontier which nourished a more fundamental discontent. On this frontier black and white men were competing for grazing land and hunting, and trouble was continuously breaking out. Both sides were equally to blame; a Boer commando would raid kraals across the Fish river; this would be followed by a Xhosa marauding expedition, and this in turn by punitive attacks, until a state of uneasy equilibrium was re-established. But after the British take-over there was a tendency to curb the Boers' unauthorised attempts at recapturing their 'Christian cattle', and Piet Uys who was to become one of the leaders of the Great Trek spoke for many when he announced that 'I prefer living amongst barbarians, where my life depends on the strength of my arms' than being ham-strung by a British policy which regarded the Boers as being the instigators of all the troubles, and the Xhosa as invariably innocent. One of Uys's countrymen put things a little differently when he noted that although in the past his family 'had been five times clean swept out by Kafirs . . . in those old times when they were robbed they redressed themselves, but their hands were tied when the Kafirs were loose'. Certainly provocation by the Xhosa increased. Some of the high spots in the fighting that continually engulfed the frontier were dignified by the name of Kafir Wars (although a modern generation of historians prefers to refer to them as 'Frontier Wars') but none was so damaging as the sixth Kafir War of 1834–5, the so-called 'Hintsa's War', which put all the white inhabitants of the Cape's eastern province into a state of wild panic for weeks on end. The name was unfairly applied: Hintsa may in theory have been the paramount chief of the Xhosa nation, but in fact his power was limited to the eastern side of the Kei river, and he had little control over the Rabe clan of his people residing in the territory between the Fish and the Kei. This area, known as the Ciskei, paid allegiance to a rival chief named Gaika or more properly Ngqika. It was Gaika's people who at the end of 1834 poured into the Colony, killed forty white men (but spared women and children), burned the homes of 400 settlers, looted many hundreds of head of cattle and horses and, although Piet Retief (who would have another job to do before long) rallied the farmers of the Winterberg district and drove the raiders off, the Xhosa farther south laid waste country as far as Algoa Bay and Somerset East. 'Seven thousand of His Majesty's subjects,' wailed one harassed official at Cape Town, 'were in one week driven to destitution.'

Fortunately, Colonel Harry Smith was in the Colony at the time: this soldier who had distinguished himself during the Peninsular War (and would subsequently play an important part, too, in the drama of the Great Trek) was dispatched post-haste to the danger point, and he quickly drove a counter-offensive right up to the banks of the Kei. He then signed a peace with Hintsa which required the Xhosa to pay an enormous cattle indemnity and to retire across the Kei. The Ciskei was now annexed as the province of Queen Adelaide, but an unfortunate incident marred the British success: Hintsa offered himself as a hostage until the indemnity was paid and even suggested that he accompany Colonel Smith in collecting the Xhosa cattle. He was accordingly lent a 'remarkable and powerful horse' and, soon afterwards, when riding with Smith and either by accident or design, he bolted. Harry Smith tried to shoot the fleeing man but both his pistols misfired: then, giving chase, he caught hold of Hintsa and dragged him heavily to the ground. Hintsa was still full of fight. 'He was jabbing at me furiously with his assegai,' Colonel Smith recalled in his autobiography, and the chief succeeded in breaking away to cover in a near-by stream bed. There, while pleading for mercy, the top of his skull was blown off by one of Smith's officers and his body was afterwards mutilated by British and colonial troops.

It was a sad and unsavoury end to the war, and it had an unexpected result. While Smith with the backing of the Governor at the Cape was arranging to push the Colony's frontier to the River Kei and incorporating the province of Queen Adelaide, news of the war and its shabby if victorious conclusion was being wafted by sailing ship to London. Lord Glenelg, the British Colonial Secretary, who received it, was a man greatly given to worry and philanthropy, and he was deeply distressed by reports of the manner of Hintsa's death. They seemed to confirm his long-standing suspicion that these recurring unpleasantnesses on the Cape frontier were always due to the harsh intransigence of the white settlers and never to that of the defenceless Xhosa. One of his secretaries minuted that after persuing the dispatch, Glenelg was heard to say that he 'objected to the war as unjust in its origins, and cruel in its progress and impolitic in its results'. He assured someone else that 'the original justice was on the side of the conquered, not of the victorious party', and he finished up by writing a confused dispatch in the December of 1835 which was described as 'golden' by his friends in the Clapham Sect and as 'infamous' by the South African colonials whom it robbed of the fruits of victory. For the disapproving dispatch announced in somewhat ambiguous terms the revocation of the newly-won province of Queen Adelaide.

Smith received the news with deep resentment. From then on, as he recalled in his autobiography, 'Every act of the murderous Kafirs during the war was regarded as a just retaliation for previous wrong,' and at Whitehall he made no bones of his contempt for the misguided bureaucrat who had 'directed the province of Queen Adelaide be restored to barbarism'. But his indignation was as nothing compared with that of the trekboers who had regarded Smith's expulsion of the Xhosa from the Fish river as the best possible guarantee of future peace on the eastern frontier.

Although the retreat from the province was not enforced until 1836, rumours of the vacillations of the British policy had by then been circulating in South Africa for the best part of a year and were regarded as a last straw by Boers who were already disillusioned with life in the Colony's eastern province. Not only did it seem that the chronic insecurity on the frontier would now continue, but to make things worse they had been blamed by the Government for provoking an unjust war. It was time, many of them decided, to emigrate. The Colony was no place for Christian people to live.

Theirs was not a sudden decision. For some time now the farmers had been contemplating their many other grievances, and, although pinpricks compared with the ignominious abandonment of Queen Adelaide, they added up to such a sense of affront and injustice that these kindly God-fearing people were beginning to talk of either revolt or secession. Consider these grievances. Land was becoming scarce and expensive owing to the natural increase in the Afrikaans-speaking population and the advent of 5,000 British settlers during 1820. For years the eastern province had suffered from droughts which are the curse of Africa and everyone who has experienced the successive failure of the annual rains will know how disappointment will at last drive a man to leave everything he has laboured for and move off to a new country where the rainfall may be more reliable. Then there was the creeping advance of the English tongue, especially in official circles, at the expense of the *taal*. Worse was the emancipation of the slaves which had been ordained throughout the British Empire in 1833; it was accompanied by what the Boers, with a good deal of justification, considered to be inadequate compensation to the owners, and as though to irritate them more it was timed to take effect during the harvest season. There was, too, the chronic mortification at the way the Boers' actions were so freely criticised by the missionaries: indeed the explorer, Cornwallis Harris, who visited the Cape in 1835, considered that this grudge particularly rankled among the trekboers for, after enumerating all the other reasons for the farmers' unrest, he wrote, 'Far greater than these, however, are the evils that have arisen out of the perverse misrepresentations of canting and designing men, to whose mischievous and gratuitous interference veiled under the cloak of philanthropy, is principally to be attributed the desolate condition of the eastern frontier.'

But perhaps what most embittered these early Afrikaners was the official recognition of the equality between coloured men and whites. As one Boer woman, Anna Elizabeth Steenkamp, wrote later, she considered the emancipated slaves 'being placed on an equal footing with the Christians, contrary to the laws of God and the natural distinction of race and religion' and added, 'wherefore we rather withdrew in order thus to preserve our doctrines in purity'.

Thus it was that on every farm *stoep* of the eastern Cape during the 1830s, the Boer farmers were wrapped in mysterious consultations: they were discussing neither their crops nor their livestock as usual, nor yet the everlasting droughts; they were concerned with a burning desire to get away from British control. The grim choice between revolt and secession so probed and agitated their minds that people were now saying just a little more than they meant to say and urging extravagant courses, for over-statement is always the language of men suffering from long-standing grievances. The hot-heads were to be heard recommending armed revolt, but with the memory of Slagters Nek still freshly impressed on their minds the majority spoke instead of a massive migration beyond the Colony's frontiers. There was little opening on the west or east; they were hemmed in there by the sea or the Xhosa, but a mysteriously empty land lay to the north, beyond the Orange river, a land of fine pasturage in which the British showed no interest; and as little opposition could be expected from the few Griquas who lived across the river it seemed that this country might be occupied without much risk.

By this time the Boers had built up a fairly complete picture of what they spoke of as Transorangia. For ivory hunters made frequent expeditions to the north; Griquas (or 'Bastards' as the Dutch knew them) – for the most part half-breeds of Dutch and Hottentot blood – were hacking out farms there; and an increasing number of Boer farmers had grown accustomed to making seasonal migrations with their stock across the river and taking advantage of the grazing after the rains. Some Boers had even settled permanently in the triangle of country between the Orange and Caledon rivers where the town of Zastron stands today. And one restless man who had fallen foul of the law – Coenraad Buys – had trekked far away to the north with a motley collection of Bantu wives, coloured progeny and English deserters. Rumours had recently come trickling back to the Colony that the 'Buys Volk' had ended up near the Zoutpansberg Mountains in splendidly watered country. Yet clearly the Boers must find out more about these lands before contemplating their settlement, and they went about the problem by secretly commissioning three commandos – the *Commissie Treks* – to spy out the country across the Orange river. The first *Commissie Trek* went westwards into the thirstlands of what is now South West Africa, and came back with a disappointing report about its aridity. The other two, which respectively penetrated to Natal and the Zoutpansberg mountain range, however, returned filled with enthusiasm for the countries they had visited. In both places, they said, was land for the taking, land where their countrymen could set up independent states and where they could continue to live the *lekker lewe*.

It would be as well if at this point we turned to look at the country beyond the Orange reconnoitred by the *Commissie Treks* and which was to become the South African provinces of Natal, the Transvaal and the Orange Free State.

The high veld of the Cape colony which the trekboers had reached after finding their way over the successive scarps of the plateau's mountain barrier, was found to continue far beyond the Orange, rising as high as 6,000 feet and becoming progressively more fertile. On the east this open prairie is bounded by the mighty line of the Drakensberg Range,[1] pathless and much of it unclimbable. To the west the land drops down slowly to the arid Kalahari basin. The great plain is drained by a succession of languid rivers meandering in a westerly direction between banks lined by willow trees; they are most easily fordable near their sources in the Drakensberg. With their facility for naming the characteristics that had initially struck them of every geographical feature, the Boers were later to call these rivers the Riet (reeds), Modder (muddy), Wilge (willow trees), Valsch (false or deceptive holes), Rhenoster (rhinocerus), Olifants (elephan), Buffels (buffalo) and Vaal (dark river).

Beyond the Vaal the great plateau continues to rise to the Witwatersrand and Magaliesberg, but from there the ground slopes gently down towards the Limpopo, interrupted at first by the Waterberg Mountains and then by the long line of the Zoutpansberg range. This vast interior tableland extends for 850 miles at its greatest length and is roughly 300 miles broad. Geologically it is made up of a series of horizontal rock formations from which the rain over aeons of time has washed away successive layers, leaving occasional areas of harder rock which have resisted erosion. In consequence the green-gold steppe is broken by scattered heights, blue in the African light, and ranging from extensive table-topped mountains girdled with sheer precipices, to isolated koppies whose slopes are strewn with boulders as though marked by the glaciers of an alpine moraine. Only these eminences break the stretched sweep of the high veld and there is a curious sameness about its reiterated detail. Yet it possesses a beauty of its own: this is utterly different from the artless variations of Europe so that its charm is not at first revealed to northern eyes. But the long white-blue sky, the sense of an empty land stretching away into infinity, the wistful silences, and the faintly bitter scents rising from the earth, somehow add tenderness and nostalgia to the scene and bid every traveller who lingers there to return.

The climate of the high veld is one of the best in the world. It is always fresh and buoyant. Winter is marked by a series of bracing incandescent days and cold nights filled with the smoky smell of frost. In summer the heat is mollified by frequent thunderstorms which add a marvellous clarity to the air. The veld is thus remarkably healthy, both for men and beasts. Its pasturage is all that graziers can dream of, and the amount of game seen by the early explorers and the Voortrekkers exceeded even that of the old Colony. Huge herds of blesbok, springbok, wildebeest, bontebok, quagga and hartebeest were to be seen everywhere, interspersed with Burchell's zebra and ostriches.

Beyond the Witwatersrand the ground descends slowly to 2,500 feet, the fine pastureland fading near the tropic of Capricorn into bush veld and then low veld. The low veld is a wilderness of shimmering thorn bushes and iron-stemmed mopani trees, its sea-like horizons broken by rocky koppies, and gnome-like baobabs, and an occasional fig-tree gesticulating against the sky. It was criss-crossed in those days by the paths of pedlars who carried trumperies from Portuguese Sofala, Inhambane, and Lourenço Marques to barter for ivory and slaves in the interior. This is a hot country filled with tentative apologetic shadows, tainted by mosquitoes and tsetse flies, and shrilling after rain with the noise of countless cicadas. It spreads away at last to reach the even more unwholesome Limpopo valley which today forms the northern boundary of the Republic of South Africa.

The Drakensberg is a mighty extension to the Stormberg and Sneeuberg ranges, and the Boers were to refer to it with simple awe as 'The Berg'. The range rises several thousand feet above the eastern edge of the high veld up to a series of peaks, and then drops down sharply to the idyllic land of Natal which had been given its name as long ago as 1497 by Vasco de Gama. The Drakensberg runs like a backbone through much of South Africa; it is a smaller Andes whose great eastern scarp is broken by precipices, gorges, canyons and ravines, and it forms a natural barrier between the elevated grasslands of the interior and the sub-tropical littoral of the Indian Ocean. Natal is for the most part comparatively low-lying, a series of foothills below the Berg giving way to fertile, rolling country, reaching to the golden beaches of the Indian Ocean. The country is cut nearly in half by the Tugela river. Most of Natal is watered by innumerable streams, some of which, like the Bloukrans and the Bushman's rivers, were to become ominous names to the Voortrekkers.

All this vast territory of the high veld and of Natal had been populated centuries before by Bantu tribes which had pushed southwards from the Congo rain forests, mingling their genes on the way with Hamitic people and Bushmen. They were a pastoral, war-like people, for ever quarrelling among themselves over grazing rights. The land between the Drakensberg and the sea was occupied by Nguni tribes, while the interior high veld became inhabited by Sotho-speaking people. But during the ten years following 1818, Natal south of the Tugela and most of the great plateau had been emptied of people by a cataclysmic disaster which black Africans still speak of with awe as the *Mfecane* – the crushing.

What had happened was this: as land-pressure increased after the Bantu expansion had been checked on the Fish river, there had been a sudden collapse of the long-established equilibrium among the Nguni tribes north of the Tugela. It had led Dingiswayo, chief of the Mthethwa tribe, into breaking with immemorial usage at the beginning of the nineteenth century and adopting a new and tough form of warfare. He trained warriors to fight in close formations which resembled the European regimental system and with new tactics. Such was their success that very soon they brought their neighbouring tribes into a loose confederacy under Dingiswayo's control.

Tradition has long insisted that Dingiswayo learned his military methods from a Dr Cowan, a Scottish explorer who is known to have perished on the banks of the Limpopo in 1808. But tradition in this case errs, since Dingiswayo instituted his reforms well before that date. Indeed, it is far more likely that he copied the Portuguese of

Mocambique in his new approach to war. On Dingiswayo's death in 1818, power passed to Shaka, chief of the related and previously insignificant Zulu tribe. The new king adopted and then improved on Dingiswayo's tactics, arming his soldiers with a short stabbing assegai to be used like a bayonet, protecting them with cow-hide shields six feet long, and training them to attack in a spear-crescent formation whose two flanking 'horns' at a given signal closed in to envelop and destroy an enemy. So effective were his methods that within a few years Shaka's invincible army had extended his rule all over the country east of the Drakensberg between the Pongola and Tugela rivers. At the same time the Zulu nation had grown rapidly in numbers by carrying off the maidens of the tribes which had crumbled before its onslaught, and in wealth by amassing vast herds of cattle booty. The need to provide pasture for these herds now led Shaka to embark on a further series of wars of conquest and annihilation. It has been estimated that until his death in 1824 this single man was responsible for the deaths of a million and a half human beings. That part of Natal lying south of the Tugela was almost completely cleared of inhabitants and the remnants of its shattered peoples fled over the Drakensberg to the great plateau beyond. One tribe – the Ngwaneni, led by its chief, Matiwane – on being driven from its homeland had fallen on the Hlubi and when Shaka's attacks continued, followed them in flight on to the high veld, bringing terror to its Sotho peoples. This was only one instance among many of the forced Bantu migrations. Wave after wave of famished men, with their women and children trailing like scavengers behind them, began to mill about the veld. Two and a half million human beings were involved in the chain-reaction of chaos. The succession of massacres which now took place was as futile and as meaningless as any of those which swept central Europe during the Thirty Years War. In some ways it was worse: many starving warriors, having acquired the taste for human flesh, formed themselves into cannibal bands whose sole purpose was to hunt down more human victims for food. Like animals driven by beaters no horde dared linger in a favoured locality for fear of another stronger wave of refugees advancing over the crest of the Drakensberg, and would move on across the high veld between the Vaal and Orange rivers, leaving behind another swath of scorched earth, empty of stock, the pasturage littered with hapless heaps of human bones, and with only a few stunned men and women left behind in hiding and living on wild plants until they, too, perhaps were obliged to turn to cannibalism.

Colonial forces expelled the refugees who attempted to cross the Orange but some tribes discovered a haven in the inhospitable Kalahari. A rabble of Batlokwa or 'Wild Cat People', led by 'a woman of great intelligence' named Manthatisi found safety in the mountains of present-day Lesotho which they came to share with the tribes of Matiwane and Moshweshwe. It was typical of the terror which had overwhelmed the high veld of Southern Africa that by this time Manthatisi should have been credited with all kinds of fearsome powers: it was said that she had a single great luminous eye in the middle of her forehead, while the level-headed Dr Moffat, in the comparative safety of Kuruman, learnt that 'a mighty woman, of the name of Mantatee, was at the head of an invincible army, numerous as locusts, carrying devastation and ruin wherever she went; that she nourished the army with her own milk, sent out hornets before it, and, in one word, was laying the world desolate'.

The land north of the Vaal was also affected by the Nguni holocaust in its turn. The Matabele, kinsmen of the Zulus, aroused Shaka's hostility in 1822 and retreated slowly across the breadth of modern Transvaal, destroying or driving away the Sotho and Tswana residents. They settled down ultimately in the fertile valley of the Marico river at what seemed a safe distance from Zululand. Under their leader, Mzilikazi,[2] the Matabele became as great a menace to the peace-loving Sotho as Shaka's impis.

Thus, much of the land to which the Boers were contemplating migration had been virtually swept clear of its people by the 1830s. But beyond lay formidable warrior nations. Groups of refugees were rallying around Moshweshwe and Manthatisi's successor, Sekonyela, in the tangled Lesotho mountains; the Matabele were firmly established in the Marico valley; and, most redoubtable of all, the Zulus ruled an empire comprising most of modern Natal. Their army was well disciplined, organised in regiments a thousand strong, each unit wearing its own uniform, including a feathered head-dress, and each had its distinctively coloured shield. Their king, Dingaan, who had succeeded the great Shaka in 1828, could put an army into the field of 50,000 men as compared with Mzilikazi's mere 6,000 warriors. Nathaniel Isaacs, who came to know the Zulus very well during Shaka's reign, has left some vivid and engaging descriptions of these most interesting of the Bantu peoples: the men, he says, were 'tall, athletic, well-proportioned and good featured', but he deplored their main vice which was a passion for war; the women, he found, were 'rather prepossessing than otherwise, their figures inclining to be somewhat graceful and their features pleasing and regular', but, he adds coyly 'We could not mistake the expression by which they manifested to us their sensual depravity'. They impressed Isaacs, too, with their toughness: one woman, he tells us, in a single day walked twenty-five miles 'with a child on her back in the fashion of gypsies, carrying on her head a two-gallon pot filled with water', and was effortlessly delivered of a baby next morning.

We must now return to consider the *Commissie Treks* which in 1834 had been organised by the Boer farmers living in the eastern province of Cape Colony. Like Joshua's spies, they were to reconnoitre the land beyond the Orange river. Three separate expeditions were mounted. The first one as we have seen came back from the present-day South West Africa with reports only of barren land quite unsuitable for settlement. The second exploratory trek led by a burgher named Scholtz rode due northwards as far as a range of mountains which they named Zoutpansberg – the salt-pan mountains. By good fortune they did not encounter any Matabele patrols but near the mountains they fell in with the Buys folk. Presently they returned to the colony with reports of seemingly endless high plains filled with fine sweet grass, that were practically empty of human beings.

The third *Commissie Trek* had an even more arresting story to tell. This was the largest of the expeditions, comprising twenty-one men, one woman, many coloured servants and fourteen wagons. It was led by Pieter Uys from Uitenhage, and followed in the tracks of Dr Andrew Smith who two years earlier had blazed a trail up the eastern coast to Natal. Smith had already painted a glowing picture of the country: Natal, he said, was abounding in 'rivers and rivulets, the waters of which could be led over thousands of acres at comparatively little expense'. A Boer named Willem Berg, who had accompanied Dr Smith, was even more enthusiastic about Natal. 'Almighty,' he said to his friends repeatedly, 'I have never in my life seen such a fine place.' Now Natal similarly astonished and enchanted Uys' exploring party. Below the clean upthrusting line of the

Drakensberg lay a country with the feeling of a shaded garden, newly watered, and it was every bit as fertile as Smith had promised. 'Only Heaven,' exulted Pieter Uys, 'could be more beautiful.' Natalland, as Uys called it, derived an added advantage by possessing a fine natural harbour at Port Natal. For the past ten years thirty Europeans, English for the most part, had set up here as traders and ivory hunters. They enjoyed good relations with Dingaan, and gradually gathered over two thousand Africans around them as followers. So secure did they feel that on 23 June 1835, they were to promote their straggling settlement into a township which they named Durban in honour of the Governor of the Cape. These people warmly welcomed the members of the Natalland *Commissie Trek*. Uys then proceeded to try to make contact with Dingaan and he gained the impression that the king had no objection to the Boers occupying the empty land south of the Tugela. With this encouraging information (which turned out to be the product of self-delusion)[3] the party returned home.

The *Commissie Treks* had done their work well; if they had shown any failing it had been their inadequate assessment of the strength and possible opposition to be expected from the Matabele and the Zulus.

But, the expeditions' reports held the seeds of a controversy which would be the cause of bitter dissension among the trekkers during the years ahead. For which was the Afrikaners' promised land? The high veld so thoroughly recommended by Scholtz, or Natal with which Uys had so clearly fallen in love?

There were, of course, advantages and disadvantages to both. The great plateau beyond the Vaal was further removed from British control but there was no near-by port which would achieve the only real independence for the emigrants; Natal on the other hand was served by a splendid harbour (so splendid, in fact, that there was always the danger that the British might become interested in it), and the ground was apparently more fertile. But the Drakensberg range which a large migration would have to descend was said to be impassable for ox-wagons; and, finally, however friendly Dingaan seemed, the Boers had a clear insight into African unpredictability, so that, brooding over the country like a dark cloud, lay always the menace of Dingaan's 50,000 trained warriors.

The debate about quitting the colony continued to occupy the trekboers' minds for months during this curiously fluid time of the early 1830s in South African history, but once it was resolved in favour of trekking they turned to arguing about the migrants' destination. The Zoutpansberg or Natal? Everyone talked but no one moved. It was as though the competitors in a long-distance race were all lined up but no starter had appeared to set them off. In the end the signal came from Andries Hendrik Potgieter, who was the first to risk everything in what became a national attempt to preserve a past that was now threatened by destruction. He mustered his own numerous relatives, together with the Steyn, Liebenberg, Kruger, Botha and Robberts families and prepared to trek north.

There was much to do before the march could begin: farms had to be sold, even at a loss, and the money used to buy stores and ammunition, food supplies were accumulated, wagons were repaired and packed with all possible movable property, and countless letters dispatched to friends formulating plans or arranging a future rendezvous. The trek was to move off in family groups, and only in the potentially dangerous country beyond the Orange were these to join together for mutual security. So theirs was to be not a sudden massive break away from the life they had known before; it was to be a gradual process as each family in turn uprooted itself, a sort of leeching away of less than two hundred people as though the knife of Boer antagonism was still so blunt it could make but a small and jagged wound in the body of Cape Colony; only afterwards, when the news of the revocation of Queen Adelaide festered like an angry wound and began to hurt, would the emigration become large enough to prove almost lethal to the Colony.

And while his preparations were being made, Potgieter dispatched two separate family groups to blaze a trail to the Zoutpansberg. There they were to seek out suitable land to settle, and while waiting for the main body of Potgieter's trek, attempt to open communications with the Portuguese at either Lourenço Marques lying on Delagoa Bay, Inhambane or Sofala. As leaders of the *voorste mense* – the 'people in front' of the Great Trek – Potgieter chose his cousin, Johannes Van Rensburg, and a prosperous farmer named Louis Tregardt.

NOTES

1 The aptly-named Dragon Mountains.
2 The missionaries and Boers used a variety of spellings for these Bantu potentates. Mzilikazi, for instance, often appears as Moselekatse.
3 The Tugela was in flood and only shouted communications with the Zulus on the far side were possible.

3

The Voorste Mense

During the anxious weeks while the envoys of Great Britain and the Thirteen Colonies were hammering out the terms of a treaty which would bring the American War of Independence to an end, at the small village of Oudtshorn in the Karoo a Mrs Johannes Tregard was safely delivered of a son. The date was 10 August 1783 and the little boy was soon afterwards christened Louis Johannes Tregard. The father was the grandson of a Swedish employee of the Dutch East India Company. His famous son Louis was later to write his name as Tregardt, but we should note here in passing that there has always been a great deal of confusion about the spelling of the family name: for Louis' descendants have used all sorts of variants like Trigardt, Triegaardt, and most commonly of all, Trichart; this latter form has been employed for the several towns and villages named in honour of the Great Trek's pathfinder.

We know very little about the upbringing of young Louis Tregardt, but the diary he was to keep during his years of greatest endeavour, show him to have been a reasonably well educated man with wide and cultivated interests. When he was old enough Louis Tregardt set up as a farmer, first at Boschberg and then later at Somerset East. In 1834 he moved across the Fish river and rented land near the Kei from the Xhosa chief Hintsa. Here in Xhosa country he found himself the acknowledged leader of an exiled Boer community which numbered thirty families.

Afrikaner mythology has typed Tregardt as one of the farmers who like so many of his countrymen were driven out of Cape Colony by despair at the hesitant British frontier policy. But there exists a good deal of evidence to suggest instead that Tregardt was a ne'er-do-well who quit the colony because he ran into trouble with the British authorities: he is said to have been a receiver of stolen cattle and to have shown overt hostility to the regime. The British even accused Tregardt of having incited the Xhosa to begin the frontier war of 1834–5; certainly during its course Colonel Harry Smith offered a reward of 500 cattle for the apprehension of this 'villain of a Boer'.

Whatever may have been the truth of these allegations, there is no doubt that when he heard that the authorities had issued a warrant for his arrest Tregardt slipped away from his farm in Hintsa's country ahead of the British troops and crossed the Orange river. Feeling more secure now, the exile passed 1835 grazing his cattle in the triangle of land formed by the confluence of the Orange and Caledon rivers. He received support and assistance during this time from his friend Hendrik Potgieter of Tarka, and there too he found himself the neighbour of another party of dissident Boers under the leadership of Johannes Van Rensburg. For some time now Van Rensburg had been living at Zevenfontein where the Paris Evangelical Society was later to set up its mission station of Beersheba.

Early in 1836, at the instance of his patron Potgieter, Tregardt uprooted his family once more and stepped into history. He trekked into the far north.

There are a number of unusual aspects about the expedition upon which Tregardt now embarked. To begin with his party formed a task force undertaking a sort of dress rehearsal for the massive emigration known as the Great Trek. It was, though these people formed the tentacles of the greater movement. Then again we must realise that Tregardt was setting out on a journey into a void, into a no-man's-land filled with unpredictable dangers: at first sight this might not seem particularly remarkable – after all the annals of discovery are filled with expeditions into totally unknown country; but in Tregardt's case his party was not composed of professional explorers seeking riches or prestige, it was made up of men, women and children who had no intention whatsoever of returning to their homes. For when they discovered suitable ground these people wanted to settle down for good. It was as though they were a group of astronauts without the means to return to earth who intended to make a new life for themselves in new surroundings. These earthly spacemen had encased themselves in a little capsule of veld lore and Western civilisation, whose essential trappings they carried, so that when at last they came to rest they could survive on foreign soil and send down strong roots for nourishment.

We must understand too that Tregardt's trek had also something of the nature of a reconnaissance for he carried instructions from Potgieter to report back all the information he could accumulate about the country he traversed. Finally, once arrived at the Zout-pansberg, Tregardt was to wait for the main body of the Tarka emigrant farmers to join him, but at the same time attempt by send-ing out patrols to survey wagon trails to one of the Portuguese ports – Lourenço Marques on Delagoa Bay or Inhambane or even Sofala – which it was hoped might eventually serve the emigrants as a free harbour.

It was understood that the journey would become more hazardous as it proceeded. The Boers in the Eastern Province had a fairly clear picture of Transorangia, but they knew very little indeed about the country across the Vaal except that it was dominated by the Mat-abele war machine. And Tregardt knew nothing at all of Lourenço Marques or the other coastal settlements save that they lay some-where to the east or north-east of the Zoutpansberg, and that they were all used as ports of call by Portuguese slave traders.

Tregardt's expedition was composed of seven Boer farmers, together with their wives and thirty-four children; in addition it in-cluded an aged schoolmaster named Daniel Peffer who was to teach the children during the journey. The Boers also brought along several Bushmen slaves, some of whose names we know – Keyser, Winter-vogel and the woman Rachel – as well as a handful of Bantu servants who in the end turned out to be far less faithful than the Bushmen and deserted when a convenient opportunity presented itself.

For mutual security Johannes Van Rensburg with a second party of farmers travelled in company with Louis Tregardt's expedition. Van Rensburg's ultimate destination like Tregardt's was Delagoa Bay, but his reasons for trying to get there were different. Van Rensburg was a foot-loose elephant hunter: he wanted to break into new territory and then sell his ivory in Lourenço Marques where it would fetch a good price. He was accompanied by several hunting companions together with their families, since they could scarcely be left unpro-tected in Transorangia.

It is unfortunate that very few of the Voortrekkers kept journals, but an exception was Louis Tregardt the leader of the *Voorste Mense* or the Great Trek's 'people in front', and his day-book enables us to obtain a very clear idea of his European companions. Of them the most interesting by far is Karel, Tregardt's eldest son, partly because he too in later life was to gain great fame as an explorer. But during the long journey to the Zoutpansberg and Delagoa Bay, Karel (or Carolus as his father preferred to call him) was so undeveloped that he strikes us as an erratic and conceited young man whose poor powers of observation, incidentally, several times landed the entire company in trouble. Admittedly Carolus even then possessed some skill as a blacksmith and handyman, but the picture we carry away of him and his wife is that of a sulky couple who were a burden to the older man. Carolus was later to describe the relationship between his father and himself as that of counsellor and executive, but in fact Louis Tregardt's day-book shows that they were very often at cross purposes and on the brink of an irrevocable quarrel.

Petrus Frederick Tregardt, the younger son (usually referred to by his father as Pieta) is a much more likeable person, and it is easy to understand why he was so obviously his father's favourite. Pieta was only seventeen when he began the trek, but he remains always bright, reliable and observant during its course. The sub-leader of the expedition was a man named Jan Pretorius and he was even more troublesome than Carolus. His attitude, as Doctor Punt has explained, was perhaps due to his motive for emigrating: it was different from Tregardt's; because the British authorities had stopped ammunition being traded across the Orange, Pretorius wanted to buy gunpowder from the Portuguese in Lourenço Marques, and he thought that joining Tregardt's caravan was the safest way of getting there. Pretorius was a rather mean-spirited man who repeatedly disputed Tregardt's decisions during their journey; all through it he remained a thoroughly bad influence on his companions; as we shall see he induced several of them to desert the main body at a critical moment.

When considering the other members of the expedition we must remember that in southern Africa at this time a man's position was very much judged by the number of cattle he owned, and on this basis four of the men among Tregardt's party were poor and belonged to the squatter or *bywoner* class. They were respectively named Hendrik Botha, Gert Scheepers, Hans Strydom and Isaac Albach. All had originally been members of the Van Rensburg group. Scheepers fawned on Pretorius and became a thorough sycophant; it was his fate to be the first among the adults on the expedition to die.

His widow afterwards won everyone's respect for the way she controlled her brood of nine unruly children. Albach was of Alsatian origin and claimed to have seen service during the Napoleonic Wars; he caused a good deal of concern to Tregardt by his constant bickering with Hendrik Botha and his (Albach's) coloured wife.

Finally there was Daniel Peffer, and he was just about the most unlikely person one would have expected to find wandering about untamed Africa at this time. Peffer was a dear old man of eighty-seven who acted as teacher or *meester* to the children, so he was probably better educated than his companions; Peffer was also the proud owner of a map showing the Mozambique coastline with a great blank space for its hinterland but on this he had jotted notes gleaned from hunters who had travelled across the Orange. Peffer endured all the hardships of the trek to Delagoa Bay, but he died there with most of the other members of Tregardt's party.

The number of animals which the *voorste mense* took north is staggering: with them they drove 925 head of cattle, 50 horses and more than 6,000 sheep and goats. The majority of this stock belonged to Louis Tregardt,[1] but Jan Pretorius owned 250 cattle and 500 small stock, while each of the *bywoners* possessed a few beasts. The very size of these herds and flocks limited the distance that Tregardt's caravan could move each day. The animals cut such a wide swath of grass through the veld and so pulverised the ground beside every water-hole that their spoor could still be followed several years later. At the end of each day's journey several hours were devoted to rounding up the livestock. Tregardt was always concerned when he lost an ox but he accepted decreases in the sheep with more equanimity, if only because several were slaughtered each day for food.

The sheer vulnerability of the trek must be constantly borne in mind. For defence against possible attack by Africans, Tregardt could only count on nine men capable of handling guns, although in a grave emergency several of the boys in the party could be relied upon to assist in the fighting while the women would act as loaders. Perhaps it is as well that the *voorste mense* were never severely tested by hostile natives since surprisingly enough none of them seems to have been a very good shot; certainly they turned out to be most unsuccessful hunters. In his diary Tregardt repeatedly records their failures in bringing down game, and one day he admits 'that a rhinoceros was only killed after twelve or thirteen shots although one ought to have been enough'. Game meat accordingly was scarce; the trekkers became tired of the ever-lasting mutton and they were always glad to come across an African kraal where they were able to barter trinkets for grain, beer and honey.

The trekkers' safety depended less on their guns than on the character of their leader, and never once during the next perilous three years did Louis Tregardt fail them. He was a very determined and a very patient man, and he needed both of these qualities to keep the peace in what was essentially a cantankerous community. In the pages of his diary he often blows little gusts of scorn at his squabbling companions. One day he writes of admonishing Carolus who had been punching his younger brother: 'I asked,' Tregardt writes, 'if he alone had permission to strike others and do as he wished; and if he desired to lord it over the children who were in my care, he must wait until I was dead; and I would never permit him to ill-treat any of them without reason. I asked him to tell me what Pieta had done, and if I thought he was in the wrong I would give him a thrashing myself; but I would not allow him to vent his rage upon Pieta like a barbarian.'

On another occasion Tregardt tells us that when Pretorius was being more than usually prickly, he chastened him by saying 'I see you are fond of fighting. You should fight Carolus because he likes to fight. I am fifty-five years old and have never yet had a fight.' Another entry simply sighs, 'I sometimes remarked to my children on the murmuring of the Children of Israel and told them we would do better to thank God for his protecting hand.'

Tregardt directed his trek almost due north from his starting point near the Orange. The veld ahead was marked by the spoors of hunting parties and no doubt his wagons followed those which seemed most suitable at the time. Sometimes Tregardt travelled in company with Johannes Van Rensburg's caravan, but when pasture became insufficient to feed the herds and flocks of both treks they would separate for a while.

We do not know quite so much about Van Rensburg's company as we do of Tregardt's partly because no one among them kept a journal but also because later that year the entire party was wiped out in somewhat mysterious circumstances near the Limpopo river.

Johannes Van Rensburg himself came from Stellenbosch and in 1835 he was fifty-six years old. Like Tregardt's, his trek was made up of nine families and numbered altogether forty-nine whites; but there were less wealthy people and their entire property amounted to no more than 450 head of cattle, 3,000 small stock and 30 horses. In consequence Van Rensburg was able to move faster than Tregardt, and when the occasion to separate arose, it was invariably he who drew ahead.

It must have been a wonderful thing to have seen Tregardt's ox-wagons go by; to an observer on one of the mountain tops which flanked the march it would have looked as though a brown cater-pillar was crawling over the slight undulations of the veld, sur-rounded by a swarm of ants, and with one tiny animalicule ranging on ahead as though leading all these creatures in an assault on the next horizon. One would have had the feeling that the caravan was moving across a landscape which was much too large for it, pitting itself against a dangerous immensity, and if the observer had been a classical scholar no doubt the thought must have crossed his mind that presently it would be swallowed up in the vastness of the veld just as, according to Herodotus, the Sinai desert once engulfed a Persian host.

Only rarely did the trekkers come upon signs of human life other than the ruins of old kraals and bones bleaching in the sun, but occasionally they would stop at a group of tumbledown huts whose apprehensive inhabitants stood in silent staring little groups, in-quisitive and then fascinated by these apparitions who for all they knew could have come from another world. The march may have been slow but it was never tedious; there was always plenty of work to be done. The attention of everyone was riveted on seeing that the animals were kept together or watching out for possible danger from hostile tribesmen. Between five and ten miles was the limit of a normal day's travel, but hardly any day was normal: when a calf or lamb was born the trekkers would pause to give thanks for the increase and allow time for the little animal to gain the use of its legs; they would halt again from time to time while a road was laboriously hacked through a difficult stream bed; wagons broke down frequently and there would be more delays while repairs were effected; the animals too often fell sick and had to be tended. Yet with all these difficulties it must have been an exhilarating experience to traverse the virgin veld, this land designed as though to suit their heart's dearest wish for it was filled with lush sweet grass which

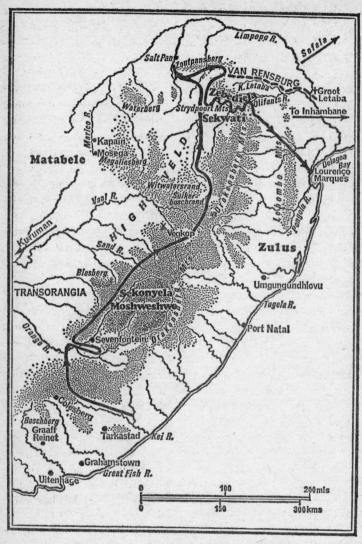

The treks of Louis Tregardt and J. Van Rensburg

swayed in the breeze as far as the eye could see, like an unending field of tawny-green corn.

To begin with the *voorste mense* moved across country which was not entirely strange to them thanks to reports from Boer hunting parties. It is known that they passed close to the mountain of Thaba Nchu or Blesberg which later was to become an accepted rendezvous for subsequent bodies of emigrants.[2] But beyond the Vaal everything was obscurity and rumour: the only certainty was that this country was known to be regularly patrolled by the Matabele, and as they approached the Vaal (which was crossed at Robert's Drift in January 1836) the two caravans drew close together for mutual protection and veered away towards the east. So far Tregardt's journey had been fantastically easy, so easy in fact that it carries with it a vague impression of unreality; now when they were approaching a real hazard, fortune continued to favour them and allowed them to slip through a gap left by the rival impis of Mzilikazi and Dingaan, which had both withdrawn to their bases after a bloody clash on the Suiker-boschrand only a short time before. Then the wagons went down the fertile valley of the Olifants river, with piquets of mounted men still keeping watch on the left flank for signs of the Matabele. (It is said that when they came to a river flowing northwards they named it the Nyl, believing they had reached the headwaters of the Egyptian Nile.) They found their way through a low mountain range by a pass which they called Sekwati's Poort after the name of the Bapedi chief living to the east. Here during the April of 1836 differences arose between the two trek leaders. Van Rensburg's men had been firing off a good deal of ammunition and he was anxious to replenish his store quickly at Lourenço Marques: Tregardt counselled him to stop wasting bullets but rather to repair his wagons for the last stage of their journey to the Zoutpansberg mountains, now only seventy miles away. It seems that Van Rensburg took exception to this advice, told Tregardt he was perfectly capable of looking after himself and resumed his march alone. The two parties never saw each other again. Because of this unpleasantness between the two men the place where they said good-bye has since become known as the Strydpoort — the Pass of the Quarrel — and the name was subsequently applied to the whole of the mountain range it penetrated. But perhaps more has been read into the trek leaders' difference of opinion at Strydpoort than is justified: plenty of other reasons existed now for separating:

there was less need to travel in convoy since the patrol area of the Matabele had been passed; the pasture stretching away to the north was poor because of drought and would hardly sustain the stock of both parties; and finally we must remember that the two men's objectives differed; whereas Tregardt intended to stay at the Zoutpansberg and examine its possibilities until Potgieter caught up with him, Van Rensburg's immediate goal was Lourenço Marques. At all events Van Rensburg's people drew ahead across the sun-punished plain, and now in front of them they could see the great mass of the Zoutpansberg range, fully eighty miles long and placed across their path like an invincible barrier. As he came up the mountains, Van Rensburg turned towards the east and camped for a few weeks at the present farm of Gewonden near where Elim Hospital stands some twenty miles east of the present town of Louis Trichart. From here he sent out patrols to seek a way to Delagoa Bay. In June his *trekkie* rolled off again before Tregardt caught up with him, taking a pedlar's path towards Lourenço Marques, where it was hoped that his immense hoard of ivory could be bartered for powder, lead and food. Van Rensburg's cattle by now were sickening and dying, probably from heart-water.[3] Tregardt was to find their carcasses a little later lying beside the wagon spoor.

But at the time of course Van Rensburg's movements were unknown to Tregardt who lingered at Strydpoort for several weeks. It was nearly the end of May before he trekked northwards again. Now in his turn he watched the mountain mass of the Zoutpansberg growing larger in front of him every day, towering over the tilted plain, the grass on its slopes burnt by the winter drought so that if the range had the outline of grossly magnified Sussex downs, its verdure standing up against the sky was the colour of burnt sienna rather than that of English green.

In June Tregardt passed close to Van Rensburg's recently vacated camp, and, turning away to the left, during the remainder of the month trekked along the southern flank of the Zoutpansberg until he called a halt at the salt pan lying near the western end of the mountain range. For here Tregardt encountered 'the fly that stung the cattle to death', and he now learned from the local natives and from the Buys folk he had met that the veld both north and east of the mountains was badly infested with tsetse fly. Gradually a clearer picture was beginning to form in his mind of the problems which beset his task of finding a way to the coast: it appeared that a route to Inhambane would traverse fly country for three-quarters of its way, the route to Lourenço Marques on the other hand would not only be shorter but exposed to fly for only a third of its course, and there seemed every chance that a way could be found round the northern edge of the Drakensberg. Even as he was pondering over this new geographical comprehension, Hendrik Potgieter rode into Tregardt's camp with eleven companions.

By this time the first wave of the Great Trek was already rippling forward; Potgieter's caravan of 200 people had crossed the Orange river four months earlier in the February of 1836. Leaving them camped on the Sand river near modern Winburg Potgieter himself had hurried ahead to discover what had become of his *voorste mense*.

We can imagine the conversation which followed at the Zoutpansberg camp. The overriding concern was the finding of a place for permanent settlement close to an outlet on the coast, but the situation was complicated now by a growing anxiety over the fate of Van Rensburg. It was finally decided that while Tregardt remained below the mountain to guard his camp, Potgieter and five of his companions would investigate the African pedlars' paths leading to the north which were said to go all the way to Inhambane and Sofala, and along which he might pick up some news of Van Rensburg.

Potgieter was back at Tregardt's camp on 24 July, having ridden far into present-day Rhodesia. He had seen no sign of Van Rensburg, but at least he had proved that the trade route he had ridden along was for all practical purposes closed to ox-wagons by tsetse fly. It remained to reconnoitre the tracks leading from the Zoutpansberg which Van Rensburg had taken to the east and which led eventually, according to local Africans, to Inhambane.

By now rumours of the massacre of the Van Rensburg party were filtering through to Louis Tregardt, and so while Potgieter rested his horses, he followed Van Rensburg's spoor with five mounted companions. At the end of a long journey he learned that the whole party had perished. This loss of forty-nine persons to a generation which has known the horrors of two world wars may not seem very significant, but in the context of the time the fact that nearly half the *voorste mense* had been wiped out in a single blow was of the utmost consequence and ominous for the future.

A good deal of mystery has grown up around the end of Van Rensburg's *trekkie*, but thanks to the research of A. H. Tromp and Dr W. H. J. Punt we can now obtain a much clearer picture of what took place. It seems that Van Rensburg started off from the Zoutpansberg intending to reach Delagoa Bay. He trekked through the difficult Spelonken country (so called because of its numerous caves) and then down the Klein Letaba river. At this point he realised that it would be easier to make for Inhambane rather than Lourenço Marques and he struck off nearly due east through the present Kruger game reserve, crossed the Lebombo range and so reached the Limpopo river in Mozambique. It was here in the last week of June 1836 that he came to a ford over the great river close to where the Djindi stream runs into it; and it was here too that he fell in with the *bloot kaffirs* (naked warriors) of Soshangane.[4] At this place all the party was murdered during a single night of horror.

Probably their journey in any case was now doomed to end in tragedy, and the *bloot kaffirs* merely gave it the *coup de grace*. For Van Rensburg's cattle were already going down with another mysterious disease – nagana, which is contracted from the bite of the tsetse fly – and towards the end the wagons had to be drawn by relays of the surviving beasts.

Soshangane was a fighting man who had fled some years before from Zululand and with a numerous following was making his way by bloody stages to his final dwelling place in the highlands of Rhodesia. He coveted the iron work in Van Rensburg's wagon and when they were strung along the banks of the Djindi river at night he loosed an impi on them led by the *induna* Malitel with instructions to destroy the white people. It is said that the Boers fought off the attack all through the night but at dawn when their already scanty ammunition was running out the *bloot kaffirs* added to their troubles by driving a herd of cattle into the makeshift laager and killed its defenders in the confusion which followed. Tradition insists that two white children were spared and brought up in Sagana's kraal and there died some years later from malaria. It seems that Tregardt believed the story of their survival and long afterwards in 1867 it received apparent authentication when two white adults and their children were brought in to the magistrate at Lydenburg. They were almost naked and spoke no European language. Many people at the time assumed that the two adults were the survivors of the Van Rensburg massacre, but it is almost certain now that they were in fact African albinos.

While searching along Van Rensburg's spoor during the last days of July 1836 Tregardt very nearly stumbled on to the place of the massacre and on to his own death too. He came to Sagana's kraal and was disturbed by hearing a weeping child whom he believed to be one of the Van Rensburgs; there may well have been some justification for his suspicions since the wailing of an African baby is very different from that of a white child. Nor were Tregardt's fears lessened by the hostility with which Sagana welcomed him. The chief brusquely informed him that Van Rensburg's wagons had passed through the village some weeks before and had not been heard of since. Tregardt guessed that Sagana was not telling the whole truth, and he realised that if he persisted in following the ox-wagon tracks, the chief would preserve his secret by murdering him and his five companions. But Tregardt got out of what was an ugly situation with some subtlety: in effect he said to Sagana 'I have your word for it that my friend passed this way. I cannot catch him up now on my tired horses. But I will go back to the Zoutpansberg and bring my women, wagons and all my cattle and leave them in your care at this kraal while I go off to seek my companions.' Sagana was delighted at the prospect of more loot and he happily agreed to Tregardt's proposal. One can imagine Louis Tregardt's relief as, with a pleasantry about looking forward to their coming meeting, he bade Sagana good-bye and headed back towards the Zoutpansberg.

As soon as Tregardt returned from his unsatisfactory quest for Van Rensburg, Potgieter rode south again to his own camp at Sand river. His intention was to bring his people back to the Zoutpansberg without delay. But as we shall see almost at once he found himself in such peril that all thought but that of his own people's survival was driven from his mind, and Tregardt's situation not unnaturally became for him of secondary consideration. And so for over a year Tregardt remained in the shadow of the mountains waiting in vain for Potgieter's return. And hardly had Potgieter gone than his strength was drastically reduced when the old-standing trouble with Jan Pretorius came to a head and that stormy petrel trekked off to the east with his own family and those of Albach, Botha and Scheepers. It was a curious incident in its way: ostensibly Pretorius explained what amounted to desertion by declaring himself dissatisfied with Tregardt's failure to produce positive proof of Van Rensburg's death. But since he took his women and children along with him it is far more likely that Pretorius now believed he was within striking distance of Delagoa Bay, and that nothing was to be gained by hanging about any longer in the Zoutpansberg district.

If so it turned out to be a disastrous decision. Pretorius ran into grave trouble. In the low veld the members of his party went down one after the other with malaria and Scheepers died; later Pretorius was immobilised when his trek-oxen were fly-struck. Despairing messages brought assistance from the ever-forbearing Tregardt and after six months' absence the party returned sulkily to Tregardt's camp rather like a bunch of naughty children.

And all this time Tregardt remained waiting for news from Potgieter. He repeatedly changed the site of his camp in the hope of avoiding malaria and the mysterious disease, nagana, which was now beginning to affect his own cattle. As early as 21 August 1836 he moved away from the salt pan and until the following May established himself at various sites close to the modern town of Louis Trichardt. In the new year he settled down at one such place which he called De Doorns – the thorns – and it was here that he was rejoined by Jan Pretorius. Wattle and daub living huts were set up at De Doorns, together with a trading store, a smithy, a rough school-room for Peffer's twenty-one pupils, and a work-shop, while an irrigation furrow fed a garden of mealies and sweet potatoes. All these combined to give the place the appearance of a permanent settlement. His stay at De Doorns is important to the historian for another reason: from now on Tregardt began to make the regular entries in his journal which enable us to obtain an extremely vivid picture of the second part of his prodigious saga.

The interminable waiting had been a trying time, yet for the first few weeks of 1837 we can still detect a note of firmness and hope in Tregardt's diary entries. But as February passes into March the mood begins to change. There is still no sign of Potgieter and, what strikes Tregardt as of even more concern, his people at De Doorns are going down far too frequently now with malaria. On 11 March 1837 we learn that Anna Scheepers has died of fever; she is followed to the rough graveyard beside the settlement by Alida Strydom and then by two of Louis Tregardt's younger children. Life for the trekkers was further complicated by their becoming involved in a tribal war which had flared up in the Zoutpansberg district. They were running short of food, clothing and gunpowder, and their cattle continued to go down with nagana. All these tribulations combined to make Tregardt long to get his people away from the Zoutpansberg and from now on his chief concern lies in preserving their lives and leading them to safety. But where to go? Alarming rumours of Potgieter's encounters with the Matabele had seeped up to De Doorns and ruled out journeying towards the Vaal; the massacre of the Van Rensburgs excluded trekking through the Spelonken; only a route to Lourenço Marques which would avoid Sagana's country remained practical. Three times Tregardt wrote to 'The Honourable gentlemen and friends at Delagoa Bay' asking for assistance: in his letters he offered to exchange slaughter oxen, ivory, wool and skins for merchandise and arms. The second letter was carried by Gabriel Buys, one of old Coenraad's coloured sons, and in this one at least it is clear that Mrs Tregardt had a hand in its composition for besides a request for '3 lbs of tea, 5 lbs of coffee, and 5 lbs of sugar' there is a rather pathetic entreaty for 'linen, cotton thread, needles, some thimbles, and sewing rings'.

Unfortunately the Portuguese at Lourenço Marques could not read Tregardt's letters, but Buys was able to describe the trekkers' predicament and the Governor responded to it by sending two armed Lascars back to the Zoutpansberg with instructions to guide the Boers to Lourenço Marques. Their names were Antonie and Lourins, and the authority they carried made Tregardt lose whatever colour prejudice he may have had, for he always refers to them with great respect as 'the Portuguese soldiers'. But he declined to take the route down the Great Letaba river which they recommended as avoiding the Drakensberg since it meant traversing fly country and would pass uncomfortably close to Sagana's *bloot kaffirs*.

Buys and the 'Portuguese soldiers' arrived at De Doorns on 7 August 1837 and the decision to leave was quickly made. The wagons were loaded for the last time, stock was rounded up, extra trek-oxen were bought (or seized according to some accounts) and on 23 August Tregardt's people turned their faces away from the Zoutpansberg where they had spent the last year; they simply abandoned the forlorn group of shanties, graves and huts, to stand there for a little time longer, left like a line of surf where the first wavelet of Christian civilisation had spent itself.

To begin with, the party trekked south for about a hundred miles.

Then it turned east and headed straight for the legendary Dragon mountains. Tregardt was quite unaware that at this very time, far away to the south, the main mass of the *Voortrekkers* who had followed his spoor beyond the Orange river, were approaching another portion of the long and formidable Drakensberg range.

Although Tregardt had already accomplished some notable exploits of authentic exploration, it is only now that his trek becomes one of the great journeys in history. As his expedition approaches the mighty Drakensberg whose mountain peaks stand dizzily suspended in the sky it becomes an epic of endurance and pioneering effort, and fortunately from now on his prodigious efforts are faithfully recorded in the day-book. Ostensibly the journal was written to amuse Mrs Tregardt, but it is much more than a pot-pourri of trifling incidents: beside being a most important and accurate source of information about the virgin country through which the company passed and the different tribes it encountered, it is a monument to human resolution. Modern travellers who pass the same way will have no difficulty in recognising the geographical features which impressed Tregardt in the Drakensberg, and indeed, although there were of course far more game animals to be seen at the time and a wide tarmac road now threads its way through the mountains, the scene of his endeavours otherwise still remains marvellously unchanged. Tregardt's diary is quite unlike those of the Victorian explorers; there is for instance none of their acclamation at being the first white man to have seen a previously undiscovered place. In it too, over and over again, one notices odd gaps in the writer's total awareness; he has no eye for the wonderfully beautiful scenery which he is the first European to look upon and one can find no single instance of the descriptive writing which twenty years later was to give such euphony to Livingstone's journals. The entries suggest that Tregardt's main source of literature has been the Old Testament; for the most part its tone is sombre, yet his pen waxes positively eloquent when discussing practical problems such as water supplies and the value of different pastures for his stock. Occasionally a note of weariness creeps into the day-book, as though some entries have been made dutifully and with some sacrifice at the end of an arduous day, and somehow the effect is enhanced by their being written with the poor substitutes which the pioneers of South Africa had to use for pens and ink. Sometimes blanks occur, presumably because Tregardt had gone down with fever. It is singular too to find that this man expresses far more feeling when writing about his cattle (which are counted regularly every few days) than he does when referring to his human companions. Another curiosity is the careful records made about weather conditions which would allow a modern meteorologist to write a monograph on the climate of the eastern Transvaal prevailing in 1837. Other pages remind us of the Boer deftness for providing quaintly apt names for all the rivers and other features they came to.

In stilted, almost biblical terms, Tregardt writes of encounters with hostile tribesmen, lions and crocodiles, and with the harassment of the expedition by tsetse flies and malaria. Almost at the very beginning of the march, like an omen suggestive of the hazards ahead, personal tragedy strikes at the Tregardts: their youngest child dies of malaria and is hastily buried in a shallow grave on the open veld, because as the trek leader sadly notes 'we have no home'. From now on disease among the expedition's members and its animals is a constantly recurring theme in his account, but nothing ever seems to daunt or frighten this extraordinary man: he is concerned only with getting his people through to Delagoa Bay, and he allows no difficulty to stand in his way of accomplishing this.

The route Tregardt took to the Bay has been the subject of considerable debate. To begin we know that he moved south down the tracks his wagon wheels had made the year before, no doubt in order to mislead the Zoutpansberg natives about his ultimate destination. This part of the trek led the party southwards a little to the east of the present national road, past modern Pietersburg and then to a second pass through the Strydpoort range close to Zebediela's kraal. Afterwards the trekkers followed the Gumpies river to the Olifants whose valley took them towards the most complex mountain mass in southern Africa. The going was already incredibly difficult: as they approached the wild mountain grandeur of the Drakensberg the wagons had to ford the Olifants river no less than thirteen times in finding a practical route along one or the other of its banks. All around them now the Berg rose up in a series of immense precipices and scarps strewn with boulders; it was a wilderness of gorges and canyons, of forested slopes seamed with deep ravines. Nothing could be imagined more hopeless of accomplishment than the finding of a way over these mountains with primitive ox-wagons and immense herds of stock. Even now an expedition equipped with Land-Rovers would balk at facing such obstacles. Yet somehow or other Tregardt got his wagons through, and in a queer sort of way the mountains north of Ohrigstad seem endowed like a memorial to him. For standing today on those tumbled heights the mind's eye persistently discerns the figure of the pathfinder peering ahead, and then pointing to some ravine climbing into the mountains' heart and urging his oxen towards it; then the vision fades and one turns away with a feeling of dull awe at the temper of this man.

As they climbed the trekkers hacked out a rough track to traverse the steep slopes. They used their own straining muscles to supplement the endeavours of the oxen, yoked relays of teams together to surmount particularly steep gradients, yet sometimes they would make only a few hundred feet during a whole day of desperate exertion. One might have supposed that in the face of their ordeal the European members of the trek would have clung together but this was far from being the case. Constant animosities disturbed them; there was continual quarrelling about the best routes to take. Only Tregardt's willpower drove them on. But finally on 30 November 1837, more than three months after leaving De Doorns, his wagons stood at last on the grassy summit of the Drakensberg. It was altogether a legendary moment, and the Sikororo tribesmen, who because of the trekker's white skins believed them to be men risen from the grave, still speak of the feat with wonder. Even now they call the spring at which Louis Tregardt quenched his thirst at the top Lebese's well, the nearest they can get to pronouncing his first name.

The trekkers' problems were by no means over: the 3,000-feet descent of the Berg's escarpment was hardly less difficult than the ascent, even worse in some ways since there was more chance now of disastrously damaging the wagons. Back wheels were taken off and replaced by tree trunks to act as brakes; then the wagons were tobogganned rather than driven down the slopes with the men hanging on to stout *riems* to steady them. And while all these strenuous exertions were being made it is clear from Tregardt's day-book that his already strained relations with Jan Pretorius were becoming impossible. Months of close contact had made all the old dissensions and irritations fester, while Pretorius, hating the whole idea of coming over this near-impossible mountain route, was at his most truculent. He was for ever trying to show how clever he was by taking his own route up and down the mountains and he was always getting stuck for his pains. Tregardt, who could hardly abandon him, was in consequence often delayed by having to detach his own oxen to get Pretorius out of his difficulties. This was the most maddening time of all, but one day when the task of dropping down the mountains seemed impossible the *trekkie* was blessed by a stroke of good fortune: the womenfolk decided to make a reconnaissance of their own and it disclosed a relatively easy place of descent. The worst was over two days before Christmas 1837. 'It was for us,' rejoices Tregardt in his diary that evening, 'the gladdest day in all our adversity.' Blazing a trail afterwards through the foothills of the Berg presented its own difficulties, but these ended on 22 February 1838 when the trekkers reached the site of modern Acornhoek. Abruptly they passed then into an entirely different landscape; trees and scrub took over from grasslands, but from now on the going would be easier: before them lay the low veld, level to the coast except for the insignificant barrier of the Lebombo mountains. The trekkers continued to be still very much on their own, however, in the low veld which today is roamed by the wild animals of the Kruger National Park. They passed an occasional African kraal, but for days on end they were in country where even a modern archaeologist would have to search very assiduously for signs of men ever having lived there, or of having created something which could be described as temporary let alone semi-permanent – a few hut circles perhaps or a grove of euphorbias marking the burial place of a chieftain long since dead, but for mile after mile with never a sign of cultivation. Here lay a land of oppressive stillness and indifference, a sea of spaced indigenous trees and flowering shrubs with an occasional rocky koppie rising island-like above them. Yet the mountains behind them now, as though sad to see the trekkers go, gave them the gift of some magical moments in the evening when the brazen ball of the sun flattened itself along their crenellated summit and turned the scarp of the Berg into a symphony of purest lavender, indigo and violet. Slowly these evening visions faded behind and the mountains were reduced to pale insubstantiality by distance and the heat as the wagons approached the sluggish streams and swamps and the torrential rains of the coast.

The fifty-two survivors of the Tregardt trek knew but one hour of glorious triumph when the last lap was accomplished and their weary oxen plodded up to the square stone fort at Lourenço Marques, to be welcomed with generous hospitality by the Governor. The impossible of accomplishment had been truly accomplished. Yet almost at once the party was overwhelmed by lethargy. It seemed as though a reaction had set in. For two whole years its members had been out of touch with the world as they struggled over tremendous landscapes and endured incredible hardships, but now having achieved what they had set out to do the inspiration and impetus which had kept them alive seemed to disappear. The heart had gone out of them; their hoarded resistance to an alien environment was evaporated. And for two years now they had been heartened by the prospect of seeing a European settlement again, a port which might become an outlet to freedom for their people. But Lourenço Marques was no port of freedom: it was a pestilential anchorage for slave ships, standing in a swamp stinking of putrescence and swarming with mosquitoes. One after another the trekkers went down with malaria and perished.

Within a week of his arrival poor old Daniel Peffer sickened and died. In quick succession nineteen of the trekkers followed him to the lonely little graveyard standing outside the settlement. It is as though an Elizabethan tragedy is concluding and just before the final curtain descends many of the characters have to be disposed of in a cursory sort of fashion to round off the story.

Mrs Tregardt died on 1 May 1838.

Louis Tregardt's diary entry on this day still has the power to touch us. He writes that early in the morning he visited his wife's room in the fort and learned that she was very weak. The day-book goes on 'I went to her at once and wished her good morning. She spoke so softly that I could not understand her words.' I asked: 'Doesn't my good wife know me?' She answered: 'As if I would not know you' – but so faintly that I could barely understand what she said.

'Then I saw that my foreboding was all too true – that I would never see her well again. From that moment such sorrow took possession of me that I did not know what to do or say. The children wept with me and this made me all the more grief-stricken. I bade farewell to her in this life, but thought to see her again in the home of the Heavenly Father, and I did not reproach Him, but prayed to

Him to come to my aid. The will of the Lord must be done. All our trouble and care was in vain.

'About eleven o'clock, Almighty God took her away. I place my firm trust in him, and I know that my dear love has entered into salvation. Nevertheless I am not comforted. Sorrow so overpowered me, that I hardly knew what I did. The Governor and his wife did their best to console me, but for me there is no solace on this earth.

'I told Carolus to make a coffin before her death, when I saw that there was little hope for her. That night it was ready. Jan Pretorius had asked the servants to help him. My dearest and precious pledge was taken from me for ever.'

Louis Tregardt made only one more entry in his diary: on 10 August 1838 he wrote 'I had a quiet birthday and must think things over.' Ten weeks later he too was dead of malaria.

Nearly a year afterwards twenty-five of the *voorste mense* who preceded the Great Trek were evacuated by ship from Lourenço Marques to Port Natal. We read that they were very pale, their eyes dark and sunken, and the children's bellies so swollen they could not stoop. Carolus did not sail with them. Before his father died he had charged him with the task of finding a more suitable home for his people since the hinterland of Delagoa Bay was clearly a death trap. In the third week of June 1838 the younger Tregardt accordingly embarked on a journey which in its own way was just as remarkable as the one accomplished under his father's direction. He sailed on a Portuguese coaster first to Inhambane and from there penetrated 350 miles inland. From his next port of call, Sofala, he entered the healthy uplands of Rhodesia and decided that they might well be the most suitable country for the Voortrekkers to settle. But the wanderlust was still upon him. Carolus now ascended the Zambesi as far as the Caborobasa rapids (and possibly the Victoria Falls) before deciding the land here was unhealthy. But even now his journey was not completed: Carolus next sailed northwards to investigate the possibilities of Abyssinia and reached Harar before deciding against its suitability. On his way south again by boat, Tregardt did not omit to visit Madagascar which he described as the 'Crown of the World'. When, towards the end of July 1839, the younger Tregardt came back at last to Lourenço Marques his surviving companions had already been evacuated to Natal. He then made an epic journey on foot to rejoin them; on the way he passed the site of the Van Rensburg massacre and buried the bones of his countrymen there. Whatever may have been his short-coming during the long trek from the Zout-pansberg to Delagoa Bay it must be granted that Carolus had splendidly discharged his father's last instructions. Carolus Tregardt settled down at last in the Transvaal which he clearly considered to be superior to everything he had seen during his travels, and there died at an advanced age in 1901. He is honoured today for his demonstration to the emigrant Boers that they could find no better place to settle than the high veld of South Africa.

These journeys of exploration of Carolus Tregardt have never received the attention which is their due. And in the same sort of way his father's trek from the Orange river to Lourenço Marques was for many years looked on as nothing so much as a tragic failure; he was regarded as the leader of an unfortunate expedition which lost itself in the blue. But succeeding generations of South Africans have realised that this is quite a wrong interpretation of the Tregardt saga: they have appreciated that the central fact which gives structure to the whole adventure is that Louis Tregardt conquered all the obstacles which stood in his way during his journey by ox-wagon across more than 1,000 miles of untamed Africa, and that he pushed the boundary of Afrikanerdom right up the Limpopo and nearly to Delagoa Bay. And as the years fall away the story of the Tregardt trek has glowed more and more under the gentle haze of romance; it has cast a potent and ever-increasing spell over Afrikaner imagination. For however often the tale of the trek has been told, its climax at the crossing of the Berg remains an incredible thing, a miracle of a sort accomplished by human will-power rather than muscle.

And today when the Afrikaners ponder upon the tense unconquerable spirit of their trekker forbears, it is of Louis Tregardt that they most often think. In kindly retrospect and with loving detail they recreate his sturdy figure standing on the summit of the Drakensberg, surveying the country over which he has passed, and then turning to look at the way which will take now to the sea.

1 A few of those in his care, however, appear to have been the property of Hendrik Potgieter.
2 For those who would like to follow the march today it is believed that the Tregardt and Van Rensburg parties joined up at Beersheba (Sevenfontein), passed through present-day Dewetsdorp, and a little to the east of Thaba Nchu. From there they proceeded north-east with the threatening mass of the Drakensberg on the right hand, and near to the sites of modern Standerton and Middelburg.
3 Cattle die more quickly from heart-water (conveyed by ticks) than nagana. If they are fit, horses and cattle will not succumb to the bite of a tsetse fly for several months.
4 We must note at this point that Soshangane (whose praise name was Manukosi) was often spoken of as Sagana while Tregardt in his journal always refers to him as Sekana.

4
Potgieter

Occasionally when surveying the broad sweep of a nation's past one is struck by an incident evocative of such drama and significance that it can be picked out unhesitatingly as one of the important hinge-points in that nation's history. To my mind such an episode was the crossing of the Orange river during the February of 1836 by the first wave of Voortrekkers to have followed Louis Tregardt into the northern wilderness.

To these people, some two hundred in number, the great river represented both a Rubicon and a Jordan; it was a frontier between the life they had known in Cape Colony and the new existence they were about to begin in a land promised to them by the Lord Himself.

The Orange river was always a welcome and marvellous sight to travellers of last century when they came up to it after weeks of weary travelling through the harsh landscapes of the northern Cape. Thus, only the year before, this river had set the English explorer Cornwallis Harris rhapsodising: 'emerging from desolation and sterility the first glimpse that we obtained of it realised those ideas of elegant and classic scenery [sic] which exists in the mind of poets. The alluring fancies of a fairy fiction, or the fascinating imagery of a romance, were brought here into actual existence. The waters of this majestic river, three hundred yards in breadth, flowing in one unbroken expanse, resembled a smooth translucent lake; and as gentle waves glided past on their way to join the restless ocean, bearing on their limpid bosom, as in a polished mirror, the image of their wood-clothed borders, they seemed to kiss the shore before bidding it farewell.'

Now a year later when Potgieter's trek reached the Orange, the river was in dangerous spate. An anxious council was held on the bank: then, while some of the men swam their horses and cattle over the great stream of yellowish water, others hacked away at the Babylonian willows growing beside it and constructed a stout raft. On to it they loaded the wagons and a mountain of stores, next the sheep and goats, and finally the women and children.

It was a scene of high theatre as the last raft-load took the current and drifted slowly across the water. The children were gay and playful, but presently above their laughter and the sound made by water rippling against the pont, there rose the clear notes of a psalm sung in thanksgiving by the women. The very air and sunlight seemed keener and brighter as the raft approached the farther bank: and when the women stepped ashore there were joyful shouts of 'Now we are free'.

They were free from the English it was true, but they were entering a wilderness where there was no legal writ or authority to support them in case of trouble. And troubles they could expect in plenty. Already the more nervous of the party were peering anxiously into the far distance as though expecting to see an impi of warriors descending upon them. Fortunately no such catastrophe occurred. When their wagons had been reloaded and the trekkers moved forward again from the Orange they admittedly suffered from stock thefts by unseen Bushmen at night, but the few people they saw were friendly – an occasional white pastoralist, and groups of Griquas who were under missionary influence and happy to sell grain to these new emigrants from the Colony.

Potgieter's leadership was accepted without question by his party, wagon and it numbered about two hundred people. Most of them were related to their leader. Potgieter during his lifetime married four times; his wives not only bore him seventeen children but through them he was connected to many of the families in the Eastern Province. Some of them – the Krugers, Steyns, Liebenbergs, Robbertses and Bothas – had joined Potgieter as he trekked towards the Orange; others were to attach themselves to his party beyond the river. Besides the Europeans the trekkers had brought along a handful of coloured drivers and servants, but in spite of them the young girls often had to act as the *voorlopers* who led the spans of oxen drawing the heavily-laden wagons.

Potgieter's trek was made up of sixty families each with its own but on the far side of the Orange his position was regularised when a meeting officially appointed him Trek-Commandant. It was wholly fitting that he should have led the first full wave of Voortrekkers into the Promised Land for his place in the story of the Great Trek is a special one. From its inception to the end it is he who dominates the drama, and as he rides in his moleskin jacket, abbreviated Dopper trousers,[1] and wide-brimmed straw hat across the vast stage of the high veld, he seems to be the very embodiment of the Afrikaner nation which the emigration brought into being.

At the time of the crossing of the Orange, Potgieter was forty-two years old and his character was already formed. He was one of those men who have been born with an *idée fixe*, in his case with a consuming hunger to break new ground and with it to enlarge his authority. It was a hunger which could only be appeased by establishing himself as the unrivalled patriarch of a settled community in the wilds, and the thought of doing so inspired his career. Of all the Voortrekkers he is the nearest in spirit to the Conquistadors. It was not gold he was seeking to be sure, but he was possessed by the same anxiety to hack out a fief for himself which he could rule as undisputed governor, and one feels that he would have got on very well with Cortes and Pizarro. He was splendidly adapted for his self-imposed task: behind him lay all the molten experience of frontier life – the roving boyhood as a trekboer's son, service on commando against the Xhosa, the mortification that came with British rule, the agony of Slagters Nek whose executions took place close to his home, and the final crowning prosperity as a farmer of the Tarka district.

Potgieter waged life rather than lived it. He was naturally pugnacious and endowed with remarkable staying power. He was also quick to take offence; there was no room for compromise in his nature, no slack to be taken up and very little patience with those who disagreed with him.

Potgieter was also a ferocious fighting man, who lived by instinct with a quick eye and a faster hand. He was not much given to words, but he drove himself and his men as though all the devils in hell were chasing him. He was to put the touch of fire on all sorts of quaintly named places like Vegkop, Mosega and Kapain, yet although he could be remarkably bold at times, there was always a point of risk beyond which he would not venture, and this was to cause accusations of faintheartedness and great trouble in the future.

Potgieter never strikes us as being hypocritical in his outlook: all through the Great Trek we see him as a man who is simply doing what is best for himself and for his people; never for a moment does he make any pretence of being an outrider of Christian ethics or of bringing the benefits of civilisation to the Africans among whom he settles. But at the same time he treats them very fairly, dispenses to them friendship but never condescension, and in the end he wins the respect and confidence of them all, even of Mzilikazi, the king of the Matabele, who for so many years had been his greatest enemy.

No authentic portrait of Potgieter survives but his contemporaries have often described him: he is tall and thin; his chin is fringed by a grizzled brown beard, the blue eyes are fierce but they have an uncanny way of lighting up when he is in the presence of children. He favours blue clothes and behind his back is referred to by his followers as 'Ou Blouberg' – the old Blue mountain – a tribute to his physical and personal eminence. All accounts of him speak too of the Dopper clothes he dresses in and especially of the floppy straw hat with the green lining which is worn throughout all the prodigious journeys he accomplishes on horseback.

It was inevitable that this man who had been born with nearly all the gifts except patience and tact, should have fallen out with other leaders of treks which followed him out of Cape Colony, and in consequence his character has been blackened by spiteful propaganda. For this egocentric man, who combined the high virtue of loyalty towards his immediate followers with a high disregard on occasion for the fortunes of his other countrymen, without doubt attracted much prejudice to himself, just as Piet Retief attracted affection and Andries Pretorius collected admiration and honour. Any number of accusations have been made about Potgieter's behaviour: thus he was believed to have shown both cowardice and treachery at the Battle of Italeni, and towards the end of his life many of his countrymen believed him to have been concerned with slave trading. What was never in dispute was a strong personality conditioned by a restless and sometimes almost illogical independence which led him not only to trek away from British control but to withdraw too from the community of the other Voortrekkers.

But all this lay far away in the future when, after dispatching his cousin Johannes Van Rensburg and Louis Tregardt ahead to spy out the land, Potgieter gathered his kinsmen together and started out for the unknown north.

He and his followers belonged to the Dopper sect which seceded from the Dutch Reformed Church. They were noted for the strictness of their Calvinistic austerity. It dominated all their actions. Like the Puritans of another age they could be recognised by the curious clothes they wore: the men favoured short jackets of brown nankeen and moleskin, and trousers flapping high above the ankle. Among the most prominent of the Doppers was Sarel Cilliers who joined the trek with a considerable party from Colesberg as Potgieter journeyed through the 'bald veld' some twenty miles west of modern Smithfield. One imagines that Potgieter welcomed Cilliers without very much enthusiasm for in him he must have recognised a potential rival. Cilliers' character has been likened to that of a Scottish Covenanter, but when considering it, the modern historian is irresistibly reminded instead of one of those Welsh divines who fifty years ago drummed so effectively on the British nonconformist conscience. Certainly no one could have been less like Potgieter: Cilliers was short and stout, a little vain and excitable, and much given to public prayer and preaching. Such was his austerity that one always tends to think of this sub-leader of the Potgieter party as a venerable old man, but in fact when he joined the trek he was only thirty-five years old. Cilliers had another claim to fame besides his powerful preaching. He was eloquent too on paper and much of our knowledge of the Great Trek is derived from his reminiscences. Admittedly some of them were penned many years later when details must have faded from his memory but they remain beset by old prejudices. He holds forth at great length for instance about his reasons for emigrating, and one can see that nothing has been forgotten. 'I was dissatisfied,' he writes, 'with the Bastardland which we had bartered with the Boesjesmans [Bushmen], and after that the Bastards came and killed the Boesjesmans and took possession of our property, and we lost it. Secondly we had sent a commission of 100 men to the Vet, Sand and Valsch rivers who found that tract of country waste and uninhabited. We memorialised the Governor of the Cape. Seventy-two persons signed the memorial, all family men who had no land and it was refused to us. Thirdly the freedom of the slaves. Government promised us that two agents would be sent, and after being valued the money would be paid out. I possessed slaves valued at Rds. 2,888[2] and I only received about Rds. 500 worth of goods in return.'

Potgieter's augmented trek now included sixty-five good fighting men, and it was with more confidence that it moved northwards towards the Blesberg mountain which stands out abruptly from the surrounding veld. The Blesberg was known to Moroka's Barolong tribesmen who lived in its shadow as Thaba Nchu. During all the discussions which had gone on during the past few years among the Afrikaners of the Colony who were contemplating trekking, this landmark had been accepted as a convenient rendezvous where they would meet. The mountain can be seen from afar. On its summit is set a rocky pinnacle stained white with the droppings of vultures and dassies, and the Boers gave it the name of Blesberg – the white mountain – for this reason. Moroka, the chief in the country below the mountain, lived in mortal fear of the Matabele who raided the area from time to time; accordingly he was quite prepared to co-operate with Potgieter's trekkers in return for their protection, and here under Blesberg the emigrants rested for some weeks. Then the wagons pressed on again through a fine pastoral country of far-distant vistas which rolled away ever northwards like an ocean of grass flanked on the right by an horizon of blue mountains whose peaks stabbed the sky with the cutting edge of a diamond. The trekkers came first to the Vet river where Potgieter was able to establish good relations with another friendly chief, Makwana. Beyond they reached splendid grazing ground along the Sand river. Unaware of any danger the Boers spread out from here in small family groups seeking suitable farms; and on 25 May 1836, after warning them to remain south of the Vaal which the Matabele were understood to regard as their boundary, Potgieter set off with eleven companions to make contact with Louis Tregardt. The little party was well-mounted and it travelled light.

The story of Potgieter's ride from Sand river to the Zoutpansberg and then far into modern Rhodesia is a saga in itself. He followed first along the spoor left by Van Rensburg and Tregardt. There was no difficulty in doing this; the passage of 10,000 head of stock and eighteen loaded wagons a few weeks earlier had cut what looked like a gigantic fire-break through the grasslands, and the camping grounds where a hundred persons had passed a night were easily recognisable. Fortunately one of the Boers – J. G. S. Bronkhorst – wrote an account of the journey. In it he tells us that during its first eighteen days the horsemen rode without seeing any sign of human inhabitants but only the ruins of kraals which had been destroyed during the *Mfecane*. He goes on to write of finding 'real sugar cane' near modern Heidelberg on a ridge which appropriately was named the Suikerboschrand, and of the good pastures on both sides of the Olifants river. Beyond the Olifants the horsemen quickened their pace since they were now in country which was regularly patrolled by the Matabele, and before the end of June 1836 rode into Tregardt's camp at the western end of the Zoutpansberg. Here there were considerable numbers of natives to be seen, and the trekkers noted with interest that some of them were wearing gold ornaments. Bronkhorst was delighted with the area and thought that a large town might well be founded in it. 'We were there in the month of July,' he writes, 'and saw all kinds of fruit in full growth and blossom and got from the gardens all kinds of vegetables, sweet potatoes, millets and many other varieties. There is an abundance of water to irrigate the ground. . . .'

Potgieter did not linger in camp: almost at once as we have seen he set off across the Limpopo river, seeking a way to a Portuguese port, and hoping no doubt to pick up information too about the missing Van Rensburg party. It is uncertain how far north he went: he may have reached the Sabi river a little down-stream from where it is crossed today by the Birchenough Bridge. Bronkhorst tells us that at their farthest point they were only six days' journey from a 'town' where Portuguese was spoken and where 'there were ships waiting for elephants' teeth'. Presumably reference was being made to Sofala. At least it was clear that the road they had been following did not lead to Delago Bay which lay much farther to the south. From this point Potgieter had to turn back: for several weeks now he had been riding through fly country and his horses were sickening with disease. Before the end of July his little party was back in Tregardt's camp.

He remained to guard it while Louis Tregardt in his turn rode off to look for Van Rensburg along the Limpopo. As soon as Tregardt returned with the reasonably certain knowledge that the whole party had perished, Potgieter set off on 17 August 1836 to rejoin his own people on the Sand river. At the time he intended to bring them up to the fine Zoutpansberg country where Tregardt had established himself. Towards the end of the month he reached the Vaal. News was waiting for him there, and it was appalling. The Matabele had attacked isolated groups of the trekkers in his party, and now events had clearly passed out of the emigrants' control.

To obtain an idea of the calamity which had burst like a bombshell over the people he had left fanning out from the Sand river we can do no better than follow the account written by Bronkhorst. He writes that as soon as they left the peaceful Zoutpansberg a few men pressed on ahead to get fresh horses. Approaching the most advanced trekker camp – that of the Liebenberg family – they saw a wagon standing in the river and with uneasy presentiment a single man cantered on to investigate. 'He returned,' Bronkhorst writes, 'with the tidings that our camp presented a bloody scene; they all then rode thither, and found Mr Liebenberg, Sen., and the wife of H. Liebenberg, lying dead; there were also several corpses who they could not identify. They returned to us the same afternoon with this sad account; five of them then rode thither, and found the killed to be B. Liebenberg, Sen., Johannes du Toit and wife, H. L. Liebenberg, Jun. and wife, S. Liebenberg and a male child, MacDonald a schoolmaster and a son of C. Liebenberg.' Within three days by hard riding, Potgieter was back on the Sand river, and there learned more bad news. Not only had the Liebenbergs who had crossed the Vaal against his advice been massacred, but a hunting party led by Stephanus Erasmus had also lost heavily after a surprise attack by another Matabele patrol. The veld was on fire.

We must now turn to consider the reaction of Mzilikazi, King of the Matabele, to the first news of the incursion of white men into his territory. From his capital of Kapain in the Marico valley and the military kraal of Mosega sixty miles away to the south near modern Zeerust Mzilikazi exercised control over 30,000 square miles of country between the rivers Limpopo, Crocodile, Vaal and Molopo. He ruled this enormous area by fear, but although he may have been ruthless to the Bantu tribes he attacked, Mzilikazi was by no means always the blood-thirsty tyrant that he has been represented by Boer propaganda. The Matabele king liked white men and welcomed them to his country if they came peacefully in small groups, acknowledged his personal authority, and refrained from shooting game without his permission. At the same time he stipulated that they must enter his kingdom from Kuruman where his good friend Robert Moffat could be relied upon to screen all strangers. The king even allowed a group of American missionaries to set up a station at Mosega, but he remained morbidly sensitive about the security of his southern boundary on the Vaal, for from this direction in the past had come Zulu impis and Griqua *bandetiiri* to seize his women and cattle. Accordingly Matabele patrols were sent out periodically to the river with instructions to destroy any trespassers in the king's domain.

First Van Rensburg, then Tregardt and finally Hendrik Potgieter had slipped across the Vaal without detection. Those that followed them were not so fortunate. In the June or July of 1836 a Matabele patrol brought news back to Kapain that parties of strangers with horses and wagons had crossed the river and, to compound their guilt, were shooting game. From their description they did not seem to be Griquas, and Mzilikazi came to the correct conclusion that these were white invaders.

He accordingly sent off an impi under the most renowned of the Matabele *indunas*, Mkalipi, to deal with them. Mkalipi's orders were to kill all the white males and to bring back their women and girls to form part of the royal seraglio at Kapain.

After an eight-day march Mkalipi's scouts warned him that he was approaching several groups of white people. Dividing his impi into separate task forces the warriors then fell upon two separate camps. One was that of a group of elephant hunters led by Stephanus Erasmus; the other was the camp of the Liebenbergs who despite Potgieter's instructions had ventured across the Vaal in the vicinity of modern Parys.

When the blow fell the members of the hunting party were scattered in search of elephants and by good fortune some of them were able to escape. Stephaus Erasmus himself galloped with one of his sons to safety. He came to the Liebenberg camp and hurriedly warned them of the approaching impi. Unfortunately the Liebenbergs did not take his news seriously and merely shouted after him, 'All you want is to entice us back over the Vaal.' They were overwhelmed a little later by the Matabele assault, but miraculously a few members of the family escaped death: four children lay unnoticed in the wagon during the massacre, while one of the Liebenberg girls survived after being left for dead from several assegai wounds.

A few hours later Erasmus whipped his lathered horse up to the next Voortrekker camp and this time his warning was effective. The Boers had time to drag their wagons together at a place where the river Vaal makes a sharp bend and gave them protection on two sides. Even so the issue was touch and go; thirty-five white men were pitted against a force of 500 disciplined warriors, and only after six hours of fighting did the Matabele withdraw.

That evening Mkalipi reconcentrated his regiments and set out to report to the king. With him he had five looted wagons, seventy-four head of cattle and twenty-three horses taken from the trekkers, together with three of their Hottentot drivers and two little white girls, trophies of war to be presented to the king at Kapain. These children were never seen again and despite all attempts to discover their fate, no one knows what befell them.

The Americans in Mosega remained in no doubt as to whether the king had in fact been driven into ordering the attacks on the white trespassers by fear alone. One of them wrote that 'We believe, however, that he [Mzilikazi] was moved by avarice', and Dr Wilson, another of the brethren firmly reports that 'these attacks by Mzilikazi were unprovoked on the part of the farmers'. But whatever the reason may have been the Matabele impi that August had been responsible for the deaths of fifty-three white men, women and children. The Voortrekkers only four weeks after the Van Rensburgs perished at Soshangane's hands had suffered a second and even more grievous check. From now on there would be no peace on the high veld until either Mzilikazi's power was broken or the trekkers utterly destroyed, and as August turned into September and Potgieter studied the odds against him he must have feared that the Great Trek was doomed almost at its outset.

NOTES

1 Members of the Dopper sect of the Dutch Reformed Church wore distinguishing clothes as will be explained later.
2 Rix dollars, each worth about 7½p.

5

Vegkop

Riding south towards his headquarters at Sand river Potgieter passed scores of trekkers who had already heard that the Matabele were on the war-path and were withdrawing hastily from their exposed positions along the Vaal. The veld was filled with their hurrying wagons and herds of cattle, bellowing as they were urged forward by mounted men. At Sand river which he reached on 2 September 1836 Potgieter discovered that the most prudent of his people had already retired towards Blesberg where the second wave of the Great Trek was now arriving. Had Potgieter decided to go back with them everything afterwards in course of the Voortrekker story would have been different, worse probably, but certainly different.

But Potgieter had no intention of retreating any farther. He ordered his remaining followers to go into laager. One party did so on the banks of the Vet river while Potgieter himself took his wagons to an easily defensible site he had noted some seventeen miles south of modern Heilbron. Here he would pit his forty available fighting men against the whole strength of the Matabele army.

In meeting the Matabele challenge head on, Potgieter was of course staking his life and those of his kinsfolk on the superiority of a few men's muskets fired from a wagon laager over the assegais of several thousands of warriors. Looking at it dispassionately he was betting on an extremely thin chance, for we must remember that in 1836 the tactical advantages of fighting from a laager had only rarely been demonstrated, and he would be outnumbered by a fantastic margin.

The site he chose on which to fight stood immediately below one of the few elevations that stand out of the plain separating the Vaal and Sand rivers. It is a low koppie about a thousand yards long and with two strata of reddish rock running round its mimosa-studded slopes. It is so shaped that it reminds the modern visitor of a slag heap. This strangely unimpressive hill which Potgieter was to clothe so splendidly with immense renown was always afterwards to be known as Vegkop – the fight hill. An active man can climb Vegkop within five minutes and from the top he will see the undulating veld stretching for many miles into the distance, and a scout stationed there would be able to give long warning of the approach of a Matabele impi. From its base on the south the ground falls gently away to a shallow spruit and is so devoid of cover as to provide a perfect killing ground to marksmen like the Boers. Here Potgieter placed his laager.

The laager wall was made up of some forty wagons[1] which were drawn up in a rough square 'with the tongue of one wagon running under the wagon which stood next to it.' With their fixed back axle the wagons were difficult to manoeuvre and it required all the men's efforts to wrestle them into line. The wagons were all chained together and the spaces underneath packed tightly with the thorn bushes which still grow abundantly on the slopes of Vegkop. Seven wagons were drawn up in the middle of the laager and covered with thick hides. Here wounded could be tended and they gave cover to the younger children. At two opposite corners of the laager the Boers constructed wooden loop-holed structures which they called *schiet-hokken*: these enabled the Boers manning them to enfilade all four sides of the laager.

Two openings were left in the laager wall to act as gates, each one the width of a wagon: they could be quickly closed by man-handling wagons kept in readiness beside them whose axles had been carefully greased. Once the wagons had been placed to his satisfaction Potgieter had the wiry grass surrounding them cleared by dragging trees through it and by trampling it down with driven cattle.

The wagon laager was not Potgieter's invention: it had been used during the Kafir wars on the eastern frontier of the Cape and as we have seen only a short time before had saved a group of trekkers on the Vaal. The concept may even have dated back from the days of Catholic persecution in Holland when the trekkers' Dutch forebears had been in the habit of holding their church services within a circle of carriages, which in an emergency could be defended. But never before had the Boers placed a wagon laager in the path of an enemy, deliberately inviting an attack on what looked like a frail and vulnerable refuge but which in fact was an extremely effective defensive work. The wagons, being chained together, could not be pulled out of line; assegais would not penetrate the tough wagon tilts after they had been stengthened with hides, and the defenders could take up commanding positions in the *schiet-hokken* and the wagon boxes, or keep under cover below the wagons in positions which allowed them a free field of fire.

The laager at Vegkop was in fact a strong fortress, but its garrison was grievously small, and now at this late stage two men who had no eye for glory slipped away to safety.[2] When the attack did come Potgieter had only thirty-three men and seven boys (one of whom was eleven years old and named Paul Kruger) to meet it. In addition there were upwards of sixty women and children in the laager. But the women were no liability: the assault which followed could hardly have been beaten off without their help in loading guns and replenishing ammunition.

Once the laager had been formed the trekkers at Vegkop seemed to find comfort in their common acceptance of peril and they could await developments with some confidence. The guns were effective at about 100 yards, while the strongest Matabele warrior could not hurl his assegai with any accuracy beyond half that range. But the Boers did not relax; scores of tasks remained to be completed. Spare muskets, the smooth-bore flintlocks of the time, each one as tall as the man who served it and nearly as heavy, were piled up conveniently to hand behind the wagons; gunpowder was poured out into tidy little heaps close to the firing positions and powder-horns were carefully filled; tin plates were melted down and used to temper leaden bullets; little buckskin bags were sewn together by the women and filled with a dozen or more solid slugs (these missiles were deadly at close range; they burst like miniature shrapnel shells and each slug was nicked to make it more lethal). A good man, and each Boer at Vegkop might be so described, could be relied upon to fire his *snaphaan* six times in every minute provided that his wife who stood beside him did not fumble when she reloaded his gun, and passed it back quickly to where he stood in his firing position. And these men very rarely missed their target.

Yet despite these undoubted advantages the trekkers must have waited on developments with great anxiety, making resolutions of their own or secret pacts with friends to kill their wives and children if the Matabelle breached the wagon line. And they still had to tend their stock.

Five thousand head of cattle and ten times that number of sheep grazed round the laager as far as the eye could see. It was galling to think that when the Matabele put in their attack, all these animals would have to be abandoned; there was hardly enough room within the laager for the saddle horses.

Although they can have given little thought to it these trekkers waiting in the veld were very important people; only they stood between the survival and destruction of the Great Trek; on their resolution and prowess depended the issue between white men and black men in a vast area of southern Africa. But this we must presume was hidden from them; all they could have recognised was their own dangerous situation as they waited for the inevitable Matabele attack. As it turned out they had several weeks to wait. Then, one October day, some terrified Bataung tribesmen ran into the laager shouting that an immense impi commanded by Mkalipi himself was only a few hours' march away. It was getting on for sunset, and Potgieter (no doubt a little impatiently) waited until Cilliers had conducted a short religious service, before riding out with him to size up the Matabele host. They came back saying that they put the number at over five thousand.

Next day, 16 October 1836,[3] Potgieter again rode out of the laager, this time with most of the fighting men, on a manœuvre which a military man would describe as a reconnaissance in force, but on this occasion it had the additional task of seeking to parley with Mkalipi. After riding north for an hour and a half the little commando came upon the Matabele host drawn up for battle, and at once the impi began pushing out its horns as though to envelop the Boers. An urgent and curious dialogue then proceeded. To shouts asking for a truce the Matabele spokesman answered 'Mzilikazi alone issues commands, we are his servants, we do his behests, we are not here to discuss or argue, we are here to kill you.' The ubiquitous Bronkhorst was present and he gives a slightly different version of the encounter: 'We sued for peace through an interpreter,' he writes, 'shewing them our hair, as a sign that we did not wish to war with them, and that they should retire: they cried no, and attacked us immediately, while we retreated to the camp.' It was during this withdrawal that the Boers displayed the tactics they had devised of galloping up repeatedly to within range of the enemy, loosing off a volley from their horses and then swerving away to reload before the range closed to within spear-throwing distance. It was extremely effective, and it proved for the first time that the secret of Boer invincibility was not the horse, nor yet the gun, but the proper use of them in com-bination. Cilliers tells us that he fired sixteen shots into the impi's dense ranks during the withdrawal to the laager, killing three men with each shot, and he gloated over the high Matabele losses.

At the laager there was only time, as Cilliers assures us, for the trekkers to clean their guns before the Matabele came round the corner of Vegkop and spread out in a great circle around the wagons, whetting their spears with stones, feasting on two of the Boer cattle which they devoured raw, and happily discussing what they would do when they had stormed the laager. The trekkers were reminded un-easily of cats watching and playing with their prey before making the final pounce.

The Boers were separated from death now by the width of a single wagon, but each wagon was marvellously broad in the sense that it divided two separate peoples and two separate civilisations. One doubts again whether the trekkers looked at their situation in this way. They were calm enough; there were no dramatics in the laager; everyone knew exactly what had to be done when battle was joined; but the waiting was nerve-racking. The Matabele sat on in their circle and for hours everything seemed to hang in suspense, as if the old and the new Africa were determined to pose a dramatic tableau. The waiting proved too much for an impetuous man like Potgieter. He tied a red rag to a wagon whip and waved it high in the air. The gesture seemed to infuriate the Matabele: they scrambled to their feet and came at the wagons in a great rush screaming out their battle cry of 'bulala, bulala' – 'kill, kill' – as they ran.

There was a certain ferocious chivalry about a Nguni charge; it had no half measures about it; once it was set in motion the warriors either conquered or died. And of course it was a most impressive sight to watch but for those at its receiving end, the charge at Vegkop was enough to make the stoutest heart quail. The warriors' 'uni-forms' were especially designed to enhance the effect of their war-like bearing. Cornwallis Harris who watched these men a little later when they returned from Vegkop to their kraals said their costume 'consisted of a thick fur kilt called an *umcooloobooloo* composed of treble rows of cats' or monkeys' tails descending nearly to the knee. A tippit formed of white cow's tails encircled the shoulders, and covered the upper part of the body, the knees, wrists, elbows and ancles [*sic*] being ornamented with a single ox tail fastened above the joint. . . . Nothing could be more savage, wild or martial than the appearance presented by the barbarian army returning to their despotic sovereign, wreathed with the laurels and laden with the spoils of victory.'

For what must have been agonising moments the Boers held their fire and only when the range had closed to a distance where every shot would tell did the murderous shooting begin. Cilliers tells us that he then fired slugs until the range had shortened to thirty yards after which he changed to ball; he notes too in his account that 'all the children that were able to use a gun, helped in the firing'. Yet the Matabele attack was pressed home with fury: the warriors ran through a curtain of black powder-smoke to tear at the wagons in the laager; they attempted to scramble over them, and wrenched at the thorn entanglements. The thirty-three men and seven boys fought back against the 5,000, shooting until their guns were too hot to hold, holding their bullets in their mouths and spitting them one by one down the barrels, setting the charge by thumping the musket's butt on the ground (fearful that the scorching barrels would ignite the powder), using their clubbed muskets in flurries of hand-to-hand fighting, each one's shoulder aching where it had been kicked brutally by the fouled pieces through which they had fired a hundred rounds, each one only aware of the struggle immediately in front of him, quite oblivious about what was happening on either side.

The first attack at Vegkop failed, though only by a narrow margin. The warriors withdrew sullenly out of range of the terrible muskets: for the first time they had not conquered after a charge and they had not died, but they had been temporarily whipped. It was a life-giving respite for the white men: guns were cleaned and reloaded, spare powder and bullets were distributed, and the wounded were succoured. Then the laager's fighting men turned their attention to the circle of warriors lying around them. The sun was beating down on the veld by now, and some of the bodies were already covered by a ghastly fur of flies, but here and there the trekkers could see little runnels of perspiration running across the black skins of the fallen men. Dead men don't sweat', Potgieter cried, and a bullet was pumped into each prostrate figure which it was considered might live to join in another attack.

For one was being prepared. It was ushered in by a flight of assegais whipping through the air, the Matabele pitching them so high that they fell almost vertically inside the laager. Then a second charge came in and it too was beaten off.

That was the end. Five thousand warriors had failed to defeat thirty-three white men and seven boys. Mkalipi had been wounded by a bullet in the leg and had already retired from the fight; it was left to his successor to appreciate that the Matabele had been fought out and the only thing to do was to withdraw. The wounded impi drifted slowly away from the battlefield, leaving the best part of five hundred dead behind. But as they went the Matabele gathered up the Boers' herds and flocks, driving them to the north. Soon only a cloud of dust on the veld's horizon marked their passing. The laager was left like a little island of victory in a sea of grass. Two Boers had been killed: one of them was Nicholas Potgieter, brother of the trek leader; their bodies were buried in the vlei a few hundred yards away. The women tended the wounded; fourteen men had been hurt, mostly by the assegais thrown over the wagons; Cilliers himself was stabbed in the thigh but he writes almost gaily that he plucked out the assegai and killed his assailant with it. The assegais within the laager were gathered up and everyone stood amazed as 1,137 were counted out. Then led by Cilliers the trekkers united in thanking God for their deliverance, repeating after him, if legend speaks truly, the verses of the 118th Psalm. And how stirring it must have sounded to the victors of Vegkop as they intoned the great words 'I called upon the Lord in distress: the Lord answered me and set me in a large place. . . . The Lord is on my side; I will not fear: what can man do unto me? . . . All nations compassed me about. . . . They compassed me about like bees; they are quenched as the fire of thorns. . . . Thou hast thrust sore at me that I might fall: but the Lord helped me. . . . The Lord has chastened me sore: but he hath not given me over unto death. . . . This is the Lord's doing; it is marvellous in our eyes. . . .'

That evening the trekkers lighted their mutton-fat candles, hung crude lamps on the wagon tilts and mounted guard lest the Matabele returned for a fresh assault.

No attack materialised. The Matabele had learned a salutary

lesson and from now on the trekkers' gun would be the rulers of the high veld. But the danger for those at Vegkop was not yet over: food was short and they had lost their trek-oxen besides their beeves, so that they were marooned, hungry, in the hostile veld.

The laager seemed a fearful place next day, surrounded by a hideous circle of bodies turning black and swollen under the sun; they encircled the trekkers like grisly captors. Each day now some of the men would ride out through the thick cloud of flies to make sure the Matabele had gone and if possible try to retake some of the cattle, but 'all we found' sighs Bronkhorst 'were killed and skinned (about 1,000)' Eventually the wagons were dragged by the horses for about four miles to a healthier site and Potgieter's brother Hermanus galloped off to Thaba Nchu for help.

The two weeks that followed were in some ways the worst part of the trekkers' ordeal. There was no milk; what little corn they had was soon exhausted and no one dare venture far out of sight of the laager so that hunting was impossible. 'It was a bitter trial to me,' wrote Cilliers, 'to see my children cry from hunger, and I as well, and nothing to give them.' But what a marvellous victory these people had won. Even allowing for exaggeration of the numbers they had killed one cannot but be filled with admiration for the success of the thirty-three against 5,000 highly disciplined warriors; even the missionaries who were by no means always enamoured of the trekkers activities wrote admiringly 'How gallant was their determination' at Vegkop.

During the long wait the thirty men (for two of the original number lay now near by in shallow graves and Hermanus Potgieter was seeking aid) and their womenfolk grew to hate the silent hill of Vegkop which watched them all the time like a malevolent spirit. But succour came at last. The missionary at Thaba Nchu, James Archbell, and chief Moroka joined in sending food and milch cows for the near-starving pioneers, and trek-oxen to draw their wagons back to the safety of the main camp under Blesberg.

Meanwhile the Matabele had made their way back to their kraals at Mosega and along the Marico river. One imagines that their feelings were a mixture of grief at the losses they had sustained tempered by unbounded satisfaction at the loot that had been taken. Dr Wilson, one of the missionaries at Mosega, wrote that 'There was nothing but lamentation in the land for weeks on end on account of

83

those slain in battle,' but Harris tells us in his book that 'The king appeared in high glee' at the soldiers' success and he goes on to explain that 'Plunder is the principal object of all savage warfare and ... Mkalipi had yet succeeded in the more lucrative object of his expedition.'

Potgieter emerged from the ordeal of Vegkop more purposeful than ever, more formidable and more ruthless, and he conveys a growing impression now of real weight and power. He could think of little else but of revenging himself on the Matabele and recovering his stolen cattle. And at Thaba Nchu he found the weapon he was seeking – fighting men in plenty. For by now the stream of the Great Trek was beginning to run more strongly and an imposing array of wagons was drawn up under Blesberg. On 19 November further re-inforcements rolled up when Gert Maritz led in a hundred wagons. It was a well set-up party; his people made a great impression on the other trekkers, one of whom described the new-comers as being 'numerous, prominent and influential'. Maritz himself travelled in a wagon that was tastefully painted in light blue and topped by an elegant canopy.

Maritz, after suffering financially from the emancipation of the slaves, had left Graaff Reinet two months earlier. He heard of the Vaal massacres as he came up to the Orange river. With some anxiety he pressed on northwards and at Blesberg was relieved to learn that the immediate threat from the Matabele had been thwarted by Pot-gieter's success at Vegkop. Maritz was a man of some administrative experience, and he pointed out that with so many trekkers now gath-ered together they had a need to organise some form of government. Accordingly a public meeting took place on 2 December 1836 in Potgieter's camp. No one had a very clear idea of how to conduct an affair of this sort, but in the end seven men were elected by secret ballot to exercise executive, legislative and judicial powers over the united trekkers. Potgieter who had recently shown such an uncom-mon capacity for fighting was chosen as 'laager commandant', but the forty-year-old Maritz wearing all the prestige of a man who knew the law received the rather more important post of President and Judge. It was apparent that Hendrik Potgieter, the first of the Voor-trekkers, had now to contend with a formidable rival.

Since Gert Maritz was to become another of the heroes of the Great Trek we must pause here to consider his rather enigmatic figure. Maritz, unlike the other Voortrekker leaders, was essentially a townsman. As a young man he had set up as a wagon-maker at Graaff Reinet and soon became one of the town's most prosperous burghers. He was a handsome man who dressed fashionably, preferred negotiation to fighting and even included law books in the extensive library he had carried off with him on trek. His good-humoured sophistication and telling felicity of phrase contrasted very strongly with the stiffness and withdrawn silences of Potgieter, and it was inevitable that the two elected constitutional leaders would soon clash. But for the time being all was concord and unanimity in the camp. Maritz agreed that the trekkers' foremost task was to chastise Mzilikazi, recover all the stock that had been stolen, and once and for all remove the Matabele threat to the future of the emigrant farmers in the interior.

Between them Potgieter and Maritz were able to muster a little army of 107 white burghers supported by forty mounted Griquas under David Davids who had a personal score to settle with Mzilikazi, and forty Barolong on foot who were of dubious fighting value but were intended to herd the cattle it was hoped to capture. Potgieter's own followers set out from Thaba Nchu on 2 January 1837; Maritz's men who had no intention of serving directly under Potgieter (and wore red distinguishing bands around their hats to make this clear) followed the next day. The combined force crossed the Vaal at Commando drift, and, instead of making directly for Mosega, veered off to the right in the hope of misleading any Matabele scouts that may have seen them. Only near the present site of Pretoria did the commando turn sharply westwards. They were guided now by two men: one was Matlaba, a Barolong chief who had served under Mzilikazi and hated him; the other was a Matabele renegade who, having been taken prisoner at Vegkop, 'durst never present himself again before his royal master'. At the end of a 325-mile ride the commando was within striking distance of Mosega.

The Matabele settlement at Mosega was made up of fifteen different kraals. These were situated in a rich alluvial depression which is surrounded by a circle of high hills, penetrated in several places by narrow passes. Harris describes the place as 'a lovely and fertile valley bounded on the north and north-east by the Kurrichane mountains and in form resembling a basin of ten or twelve miles in circumference'.

85

The commando reached the rim of hills without being seen, on the night of 16 January 1837, and while Maritz's sharpshooters occupied the southern passes, Potgieter's force concentrated under cover of the most southerly hill. At first light next day his horsemen galloped for the nearest kraal.

The surprise was complete. As they came out of their huts rubbing the sleep from their eyes the Matabele were shot down in their scores. The Boers raced their horses from one kraal to another to continue the killing; they burned the huts as they passed and drove the survivors headlong towards the north. The missionaries at Mosega counted themselves lucky to escape the slaughter. 'Early in the morning,' wrote Dr Wilson, 'I was awakened by the firing of guns; I arose and looked and saw the farmers on horse-back, pursuing and shooting the natives, who were flying in every direction.' The Rev. Daniel Lindley, who was awakened by an anxious Stephanus Erasmus seeking news of his son, tells us that 'Thirteen, some say fifteen kraals were attacked and destroyed. Few of the men belonging to them escaped and many of the women were either shot down or killed with the assegai. We have no means of knowing how many lives were lost in this affair; we think two hundred. . . . On the part of the assailants only two were killed. These were Bechwana[4] one of whom creeping into a house in search of booty received his death wound from the man within; the other was carelessly shot down by a Boer mistaking him for one of Mzilikazi's men. They took away with them about six thousand head of cattle and made our field of labour a desolation.'

The massacre may have been cruel and brutally indiscriminate, but in all fairness one must place the Boers against their own time and situation. No one could survive here on the high veld unless they made themselves just as violent and just as ruthless as the Matabele. Nor must one ever lose sight of the fact that it had been Mzilikazi who had first made unprovoked attacks on the trekkers. At all events now that the fighting was over it was vital for the Boers to give the Matabele no chance to rally or their small force would risk annihilation. Before the morning was out all the Bantu survivors hiding in their huts had been mercilessly winkled out, and not a single warrior was left alive at the great basin of Mosega.

But although Mosega had been destroyed and the Matabele humbled, not much really had been settled. Admittedly more cattle had been taken than had been lost at Vegkop but the defeat was not decisive: the main Matabele army was still in being and neither Mzilikazi nor Mkalipi had been involved in the action; a real victory could only be won by the destruction of Kapain, and the Boers' horses, it was decided, were too worn out to attempt an additional sixty-mile ride with the whole country now thoroughly aroused.

In fact the commando as it retired from Mosega did so with undignified haste for the Boers were anxious to get their cattle booty across the Vaal before the Matabele recovered from their panic. The American missionaries, realising that they might very well be killed to expiate the Matabele defeat, elected to accompany the commando south, and they tell us that they had to drive their wagons that first night for twenty miles without stopping. 'The horror of the flight,' sighs Lindley, 'was increased by constant alarms. Herds of wild game moving along the plain were taken for regiments of pursuing Matabele, the dust raised by them and the sound of their hoofs not being distinguished from the tread of an army.'

The success of the attack of Mosega was further marred by the unseemly wrangling that followed between the two leaders of the commando. Maritz and Potgieter could not agree over the division of the plunder: Potgieter insisted on the lion's share to compensate his people for their losses at Vegkop and one cannot help feeling sympathy for his attitude; Maritz on the other hand demanded that the loot be equally divided between the two sections of the commando. In his learned way Maritz quoted so many parallel cases and talked so fast that he could hardly be understood, but in the end, by exercising the intractability which was the very essence of his nature, Potgieter got his own way. But this first quarrel represented the opening bars of fifteen years of discord and it was an angry dissatisfied crowd of men who rode into Thaba Nchu on 28 January 1837.

Now that they were economically independent again, and furious that the other trekkers would not join them at once in a second onslaught against the Matabele at Kapain before they regained their balance, Potgieter's people moved away from Blesberg. The enchanting vision of the rolling plains they had begun to farm before the Matabele assault was still dancing before their eyes, and they settled down happily along the upper reaches of the Vet river. Potgieter himself continued north, hoping to re-establish contact with Louis

Tregardt. But near the Zebediela river he learned that Tregardt had already left the Zoutpansberg and was on his way to Delagoa Bay. A little sadly, Potgieter returned to the Vet. He was worried about the fate of the *voorste mense* and still anxious to crowd the defeated Matabele. But he would have to wait a little longer before he met Mzilikazi in a final round.

NOTES

1 Various authorities give different numbers of wagons and one says only twenty-seven were used.
2 Again there is no agreement among contemporary sources about the number of deserters; one gives it as seven, but two is the most likely figure.
3 This is the most generally accepted date for the battle of Vegkop but we must remember that the Voortrekkers had no almanacs (although they possessed crude wooden peg calendars), and it may have taken place a few days later.
4 Lindley like many others described the Barolong as Bechuanas.

6

Pillar of Smoke by Day

During 1836 things moved rather slowly for the discontented Boer farmers remaining in Cape Colony. It was as though fate wished to give them a chance for second thoughts about the emigration they were contemplating. Then suddenly the situation changed: the two victories of Vegkop and Mosega may have been small things as battles go, but they had tremendous local importance: they injected new resolve and energy into those who were wavering, so that in 1837 what had been a spiritual restlessness became a mass migration, and a trickle of emigrants grew into a flood. During the next two years more than 6,000 Afrikaners went rumbling northwards in their wagons through the Colony and crossed over the Orange river.[1] There they followed the tracks in the veld worn by Potgieter's oxen and scored by the wheels of Maritz's wagons. The world seemed full of golden opportunity that New Year; yet of that 6,000 more than 500 were to die very shortly, for the most part from massacre and battle.

The trek was no longer a migration in the normal sense, it had become something larger, and resembled one of the great military movements which marked the decline of the Roman empire. For these Voortrekkers were not continuing their forebears' centuries-old quest for new farm land: they intended to subjugate the indigenous people living beyond the Orange and turn their country into a state where their own social and political ideas might be practised and perpetuated without outside interference.

The trekkers were uncertain about the way the British authorities would react to their departure. Naturally they hoped that official opinion would accede to it willingly. After all no other state was proposing to colonise or pacify the region beyond the Orange, or even to bring Christianity to it; and being so close at hand the trekboers seemed the logical people to undertake these tasks. In any case this was a peaceful secession and not an armed rebellion.

And in fact, obedient to Whitehall's constant cries for retrenchment the Cape government at the time was setting its face against extending British responsibilities in South Africa. The official reaction to the emigration was thus confused and ineffective; admittedly the Cape of Good Hope Punishment Act which was passed in the August of 1836 made the trekkers liable to punishment for crimes committed south of latitude 25° south, but this was no more than an empty gesture since there existed no means of enforcing it. No attempt was made to declare the emigration illegal. The Lieutenant-Governor of the eastern province went so far as to announce that 'He was not aware of any law which prevented His Majesty's subjects from leaving his dominions and settling in another country, and such a law, if it did exist, would be tyrannical and oppressive.' Only later when the realisation grew of the extent to which the Trek was bleeding life out of the Colony, was an attempt made to control it by redressing the trekboers' grievances and compensating war losses more liberally; thus we find Sir Benjamin D'Urban, the Governor of the Cape, admitting that 'He could see no means of stopping the emigration except by persuasion and attention to the necessities of the farmers'. Eventually the British Government was to oppose the trekkers' intent and claims by force of arms, but at the beginning of the Great Trek nothing much was done to impede it.

The attitude of the British settlers in Cape Colony was even more favourable to the trekkers: they sympathised and understood their aims, and they wished them well. On one famous occasion at Grahamstown on his way north the British community gave the redoubtable Pieter Uys a splendid send off and presented him with 'a folio copy of the Sacred Scriptures ... in massy Russia binding'. A small number of Britishers accompanied the emigrant farmers into the wilds and one feels that more would have done so had they possessed the veld lore of the Boers or known the mechanics of trekking.

The Predikants of the Dutch Reformed Church on the other hand dismayed the emigrant farmers by their discouraging attitude to the trek. No minister was prepared to accompany the Voortrekkers across the Orange; nearly every one of them denounced the migration from the pulpit. They said it would mean that the trekboers would never hear the true word of God again, and were even jeopardising the souls of their children since they must remain un-baptised. And so the emigrant farmers for years to come were to be denied the ministrations of one of their own consecrated pastors, a circumstance which was to be responsible for a good deal of the discord which marred their early fortunes.

The dislocation from their farms was a comparatively painless one for most of the emigrants: their homes were makeshift, their flocks and herds were movable and they had been brought up to trek. There were sad moments to be sure when the Boers bade farewell to the family graves they would be leaving untended but this grief was com-pensated by the thought of the new and exciting life which lay ahead of them.

Generally the trekkers marched north from their farms in separate small parties (which they referred to as *trekkies*) since this facili-tated pasturing their stock. But often they would amalgamate sooner or later into larger groups under an accepted leader. On the other hand the caravans were occasionally large affairs and well-organised: the wagon-convoy led by Pieter Jacobs out of Beaufort was a par-ticularly impressive one, while a hundred families followed Pieter Uys from Uitenhage. But whether the groups were large or small, the emigrants all clung to the notion that they would eventually be as-sociated in a single *Maatschappij* or community.

The trekkers found numerous crossing places over the Orange along the 100-mile stretch which separates Aliwal North from Phil-ippolis, but the ford they most favoured was Alleman's Drift. Beyond the river the hostile reception of the Hottentots and Bushmen un-happily encouraged the trekkers' African servants to desert in large numbers: nearly always the task of getting the heavily-laden wagons along thus fell on the white men and women; even the girls were often pressed into service when the naked black children, who usually led the trek-oxen, ran away. Beyond the Griqua country, however, the convoys moved through a sparsely inhabited land, and here the emigrants could relax and find happiness in their shared adventure and the tremendous psychological sense of liberation. One trek leader reported back to the Colony that although some of his people were suffering from fever they were finding no difficulty in traversing the great interior plain; water and grazing were both plen-tiful; they were feeding well on game, fish and honey, and they were even able to obtain grain from the occasional kraals they passed.

91

It is of course increasingly difficult for us in these days of South Africa's arterial roads and teeming motor cars to appreciate what it was really like to trek across the country 135 years ago. In a way the journey then resembled a voyage at sea since for weeks on end each day was like the one which had preceded it, and filled only with the minutiae of routine tasks. These Pilgrim Fathers of the veld moved north at the unhurried pace of an ox but they felt themselves to be the special wards of God.[2] Every occurrence was interpreted in biblical terms: thus a grass fire seen burning on the veld ahead was accepted gratefully as the pillar of smoke by day and the pillar of fire by night, which the Lord himself had placed there to guide them to a new Canaan.

The wagons in which they travelled lay across the undulating plains of Transorangia like ships of the line ploughing their way through a khaki-coloured sea with flat-topped hills for its islands. But the tracks they left scored in the veld might be spread for several miles across the countryside, since, to avoid the dust, the wagons often travelled several abreast; but these tracks drew together again as they approached the drifts where shallow water and low banks

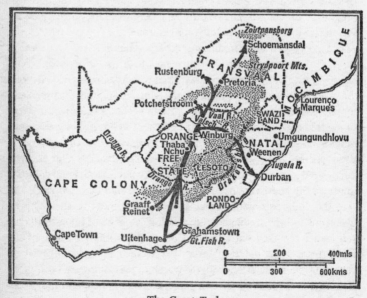

The Great Trek

92

permitted a crossing over the rivers along their route. Lighter and narrower than the 'prairie schooners' of the contemporary American pioneers, the wagons measured eighteen feet in length and were six feet broad. Each one could carry a load of more than a ton. Their wheels were shaped like saucers with the concavity looking outwards: the larger wheels at the back standing as high as a man's shoulders were fixed to a solid axle and had fourteen spokes of assegai wood; those in front, turning on a pivoted axle, possessed only ten spokes. The felloes of the wheels were made from white and red pear trees and projected far enough out from the spokes for them to be slanting and they provided some springiness to the nerve-jangling discomfort of the wagons. The trek-oxen were led by a *voorloper* and urged on by a driver with a long whip who spoke to each animal by its individual name.

Taking up much of the space inside the wagons were the latticed beds on which the trekker women slept, gave birth and died. Wedged in below them were a hundred household articles, including brass-bound churns and chests crammed with old clothes. Massive pieces of furniture that were heirlooms passed on from generation to generation were set up beside rough tables and stools which would presently provide part of the beginnings of a home in the interior. Single-furrow ploughs, spades and picks were lashed to the sides of the wagons, and beside them hung little basket-cages filled with squawking hens. Places were found in the wagons too for barrels of gunpowder, and ropes of tobacco, and into odd niches were packed bags of seeds – mealies, sorghum, oats, wheat and vegetables as well as fertile stones of citrus, plums, apricot and peach trees, all ready to be planted out when the Great Trek came to its appointed destination.

Each wagon was drawn by a span of sixteen wide-horned Afrikander oxen, and they moved at a little under four miles an hour. The oxen were inspanned before dawn every day, rested during the midday heat, and then usually covered a few more miles during the cool of the evening. The women and young children travelled in the wagons. Ahead or beside them rode the menfolk on their small shaggy horses of Basuto stock crossed with Arab, ungroomed and unshod, bridled with clumsy strips of leather, and all veld-reared.

The days drifted away as the emigrants moved slowly northwards. The men's eyes constantly swept the country ahead as they rode loosely in their saddles. No movement or feature on the veld was without significance to them. They would shout instructions occasionally to the *voorlopers* leading the oxen, and warnings of rocks and antbear holes and tree stumps which must all be avoided.

The Voortrekkers would strike us now as being very simply dressed. Those men who could afford it wore clothes of tanned leather, but the majority were content with linen jackets and flap-trousers; sockless feet were thrust into home-made *velskoens,* their heads were covered with wide-brimmed hats of straw or felt. The women favoured print and linen dresses together with an embroidered shawl spread across the shoulders and a *kappie* on the head to protect it from the sun. Sunday clothes were packed into a *kis* within the wagon and they would only rarely be taken out until their journey came to its end.

The morale of the trekkers was good. Looking back on it afterwards one of them wrote that 'Every individual I looked at appeared in high spirits and wore a pleasant countenance'. For they knew that they were removed at last from a society that to them was dominated by pernicious racial doctrines, which, as one woman among them had written, were 'intolerable for any decent Christians'.

They were very conscious of their Lord's ever-watchful eye over their progress. Although they had no Predikant to minister to them, the trekkers each evening always sang their psalms and heard their portion, and they never let a Sunday pass without having one of their number bend across his brass-clamped Bible and lead them in some form of religious service.

Through these services they clung to the life they had known before, and they prepared for them carefully. 'The following morning was the Sabbath,' wrote one emigrant during his long journey, 'and the spot where divine service was held was made by wagons drawn up on each side, covered over at the top; at the upper end a large tent was placed, the front pulled up, and looking into the space thus covered in; this served us all for a church; the service being performed twice in the day.'

When they reached a particular favoured site with good pasture and water the convoys halted for days on end to rest the trek-oxen. But now there were more tasks than ever to be done. The stock which every night had been kraalled in rough *zarebas* made of thorn trees, when these were available, was now given free range and spread across the veld for five miles and more to fatten. Injured or sick animals received attention, their wounds being treated with a mixture of grease and tar. The women settled down to domestic tasks which had of necessity been neglected; clothes were mended and butter made to provide a welcome change from the substitute used on trek which was derived from the fat of sheep's tails. Fat was in demand too to combine with woodash and soda in making soap, as well as for greasing the *riems* used to harness the oxen. The best-quality fat for this purpose came from the zebras hunted with other game by the men. There was never any shortage of antelope meat: 'The encampment is surrounded by all sorts of wild animals,' exulted one trekker, 'such as lions, wolves, gnus, blesbok, bonteboks, spring bucks, &c.' The lions often caused trouble and had to be shot to protect the stock, and no less than 200 are said to have been killed by the trekkers between the Orange and the Vaal. But the emphasis of the hunt lay on the provision of meat to vary the monotonous mutton dishes, the dead animals being dragged for miles to the encampment on rough sledges made from forked trees.

The men had other tasks since the wagons were always in need of attention; they were for ever mending broken *disselbooms*[3] or fitting new spokes to damaged wheels or replacing their iron tyres. But the trekkers knew lighter moments too: the young men played games together like their favourite *jukskei*,[4] while the children fashioned simple toys for themselves; a popular one consisted of the jaw bone from an ox together with two rows of animal knuckles which did duty as a wagon and its span of oxen. Sometimes two or three men would mount a wagon in the evening with their simple musical instruments and play the old-fashioned folk tunes which everyone knew. Often too they would unite in singing hymns and psalms or in listening to Bible readings. But most of their spare time was passed in conversation; there were endless discussions about past grievances and future hopes, of the day's happenings, or a simple revelling in convoy gossip; nothing was too insignificant to be mentioned, explained, debated.

Cornwallis Harris on his way south towards the Orange at the end of his adventurous journey to Mzilikazi's country came across a group of trekkers, halted and looking like a scene from a travelling circus: 'Forty Dutch colonists with their kith and kin,' he writes, 'were encamped on the banks of the Calf River. ... The assemblage of snow-white wagon tilts, around which herds of oxen and droves of horses were grazing, imparting to the animating scene the appearance of a country fair.' It is not difficult when reading descriptions of this sort for the inward eye to conjure up a vision of idyllic content and peace during the stops along the pioneer road.

And thus slowly, having marched for anything up to 200 miles and skirted the Basuto country, the trekkers came up to the agreed rendezvous, to the camp of the United Laagers under the Mount of Blesberg with its blunt basalt pinnacle stained white with birds' droppings and standing close to the Barolong town of Thaba Nchu. The Barolong play a surprisingly important and on the whole an honourable part in the story of the Great Trek. They were ruled as we have seen by a chieftain named Moroka and in the past had suffered severely at the hands of the Matabele. In 1836 Moroka had allowed Potgieter's people to outspan their oxen at Thabu Nchu and had shown them the best grazing and water; soon afterwards he had provided food and teams of oxen, to bring the stranded people back to safety after the action at Vegkop. And now when the main body of trekkers came into his country the chief received them with equal hospitality. This is all the more creditable since the Barolong were comparative new-comers to the district and had hardly had time to settle down themselves. Only a few years before this branch of their tribe had been led by the missionary James Archbell to Thaba Nchu to get farther away from the warlike Matabele. Archbell had built himself a substantial house with thick stone walls on the outskirts of their native town; beside it stood an open-air church entered from the house by a side door, in which he preached his Sunday sermons to the uncomprehending Africans. His comfortable house standing in the wilds must often have reminded the trekkers of the homes they had left in the Colony and it provided a touch of civilisation to these people who had no dwelling places now but their wagons. The trekkers camped four or five miles from the town, most of them below the southern flank of Blesberg where there was an open spruit. They always favoured such sites, for the southern slopes of mountains and hills provided at least psychological protection from the hostile north, and they were often better wooded than the other sides so that fuel and building materials were more easily obtained. On this flank of the Blesberg there are a series of re-entrant valleys which led to basins covered with thick sweet grass; the trekkers' stock could thrive there and after only a few weeks' grazing the humps on the Africaner cattle trembled with stored fat as they walked.

The number of trekkers at the rendezvous was constantly augmented as new convoys rolled in. By mid-1837 someone counted 1,000 wagons standing in the main camp, and marvelled at the vast spread of canvas tilts above which the smoke rose in the still evening air and gave the settlement a look of cosy security and permanence. So concentrated were the wagons that the farmers sometimes built fences round them to ensure a little privacy for themselves, and at Blesberg today one can still see where the fence truncheons have taken root to provide a homely memorial to the great days of the past. The trekkers lived better here than on their journey north. 'Provisions of all descriptions are abundant' rejoiced one emigrant after reaching Blesberg, and he added that the local tribesmen 'bring daily to the camp large quantities of produce on their backs and laden upon pack-oxen – such as mealies, kaffir corn, pumpkins, potatoes, beans, &c., &c.'.

To begin with Maritz was by far the most important personage in the enormous camp: his duties as President and Judge were varied in the extreme, and included such an onerous one as vetting the suitability of prospective brides and grooms for each other: we find an emigrant named Barnard Roedolf noting one day in his diary that 'Three young couples passed the matrimonial court held by Maritz, previous to the celebration of marriage'. But such celebrations bristled with vexatious difficulties since no ordained pastor had accompanied the trekkers. This did not admittedly unduly worry Potgieter who was happy to accept the services proffered by Mr Archbell and regularly attended his church rigged out in the glory of a smart nankeen coat and velvet trousers, all topped by a tall bell-shaped hat. But Maritz's people preferred to have as little as possible to do with an American parson whom they deemed only one niche better than an English minister. Instead they turned for spiritual guidance to Erasmus Smit, their leader's brother-in-law.

Erasmus Smit was a droll-eyed and unassuming man, fat, just turning sixty, and possessed of a glorious weakness for drink as well as a melancholy inability to forget his injuries, failings which were going to cause him a great deal of trouble in the future.[5]

Smit had received rudimentary training as a missionary in Holland and this permitted him to officiate at some church services, but unhappily he had never been properly ordained. Moreover many of the trekkers distrusted him on account of an earlier connection with the London Missionary Society which they associated with the detestable John Philip. Others refused to accept his ministrations for the odd reason that he had a cast in one eye, since they held that a priestly personage must be without physical blemish. But despite his short-comings one cannot help feeling a good deal of sympathy for Erasmus Smit, partly because his wife dominated the sickly man and made his life a misery, but more particularly because we owe him a deep debt of gratitude for recording in his journal many episodes during the course of the Great Trek which otherwise would have been forgotten.

And so although the unfortunate Mr Smit was reluctantly allowed to conduct wedding ceremonies, many of the trekkers led by Hendrik Potgieter resolutely refused to sanction his administering the impor-tant sacraments of Baptism and Holy Communion, on whose regular celebration the Voortrekkers placed such store. And the arguments about the extent of Smit's pastoral field very soon caused a deep rift in the camp.

But far worse dissension arose over the destination of the trek-kers.

Potgieter was for ever riding into the main camp to assert that the high veld beyond the Vaal was the land intended for the trekkers by the Lord. He would then go on a shade more mundanely to point out that this country lay beyond the limits of the Cape of Good Hope Punishment Act and so would be completely free from British con-trol. Natal on the other hand he believed would be annexed eventu-ally by the Cape Government, for already British traders were settled at Durban. Potgieter would then go on to say that he heartily dis-trusted the Zulus but as events had shown he had the measure of Mzilikazi's warriors, and any way it was far safer to farm open land in the high veld than to live in the broken country of Natal which lent itself to ambush and surprise.

But an increasing faction of the trekkers was inclining to the belief that the advantages of the high veld were more than offset by the good soil, good water and good grazing of the country beyond the Berg. They pooh-poohed the danger of British annexation and were sure that the mere hanndful of English settlers at Durban could easily be swept aside and allow them to use the port as the outlet to the sea which would make them independent of the harbours of Cape Colony. There is no doubt too that they were influenced by all the hazards which Potgieter had demonstrated lay between the high veld and its natural outlet on Delagoa Bay.

J. N. Boshof when he chronicled the trekkers' history as early as 1838 draws attention to this shift in the general view-point, and writes: 'It was the intention at first to proceed far into the interior, with the view to settle in the vicinity of Delagoa Bay, for the purpose of carrying on a trade with the inhabitants of that settlement; but as many of the party never calculated the distance to be so great, and learning moreover that the climate was rather unhealthy, they prevailed upon Retief to explore the country towards Natal.'

And so the argument droned on with no firm decision taken and no direction from the trek leader. For Maritz was of two minds about their goal: he favoured Natal but at the same time believed that the Matabele threat to the north ought first to be removed and the high veld more thoroughly explored before becoming definitely committed.

The controversy about the trekkers' destination was by no means all that disturbed the unity of the so-called United Laagers. There was increasing argument too about the constitution which had been agreed upon after Mosega, and the polemics on this subject became more bitter every week. Maritz quarrelled with Potgieter and Potgieter quarrelled with Smit. A contemporary chronicler records that 'From this time onwards for some years jealousies were so rife and party feeling ran so high that it is not safe to take the statement of any individual among the immigrants as an accurate version of occurrences'. All in all the Voortrekker camp under Blesberg was a remarkably contentious place.

There is something absurd and even puerile about the trekkers' endless disputes, and it is only by making a genuine mental effort that it is possible to convince oneself that these men who were embarked on so hazardous an exercise should yet have wasted their time and energies on arguments about objectives which should have been agreed upon at its inception. One can only surmise that these Boers of the open veld, now that they were herded together like townsmen in the close confines of the wagon camp and with any amount of time on their hands, could only find excitement in bickering and contradiction. At all events it seemed impossible for the Voortrekkers at this stage to live together without taking sides, either with Potgieter or with Maritz.

It came then as a relief when in the April of 1837 news arrived that a man from the Winterberg district, possessing more prestige than any of their present leaders, was approaching Blesberg with 400 followers and a convoy of 100 wagons. Here must be the Moses sent by the Lord to lead them – Piet Retief.

And indeed Piet Retief was a man of luminous integrity and faith. Born in 1780 the realities of his earlier career have been somewhat obscured by the mythology which surrounds its ending. But this does not greatly matter: all we need know about it is that, as he himself explained, unwise speculations as a business contractor during the 1820s caused him to be 'reduced from opulence to great pecuniary embarrassment'. Retief however, succeeded in struggling back to comparative prosperity and in becoming a figure of importance in the eastern province; this was recognised by the British authorities when they appointed him to the post of Commandant which carried with it magisterial powers.

Like so many of his compatriots Retief became highly concerned over the inadequate measures taken to secure the eastern frontier. Unfortunately a letter to Cape Town voicing his criticism was answered with a threat to deprive Retief of his official position. Retief conceived this to be an insult; soon afterwards the revocation of Queen Adelaide Province finally decided him to quit the Colony. From now on, so insistent was his determination to found an Afrikaner State beyond Cape Colony's boundaries that it gives what remained of his life a curious intensity, and one is always conscious of his urgent feeling that there is no time to waste in proving that what he was doing was in the best interests of his countrymen.

It was in January that Retief made his final plans to emigrate and on 2 February 1837 he published a manifesto in the *Grahamstown Journal* which explained his reasons for doing so.

To his credit Retief wrote down his views where hundreds before had only muttered and grumbled about their situation. His pronouncements were well reasoned and dispassionate, elegantly phrased and dignified. In them we first read the familiar litany of the trekboers' grievances, and then Retief goes on to sum up the feelings of the frontiersmen better than anyone else had ever done before. 'We despair of saving the Colony,' he wrote, 'from those evils which threaten it by the turbulent and dishonest conduct of vagrants who are allowed to infest the country in every part; nor do we see any prospect of peace and happiness for our children in a country thus

100

distracted by internal emotions.' There was a good deal more about 'the unjustifiable odium which has been cast upon us', and the losses from emancipation. Finally after setting forth a policy for an independent trekker State, the manifesto closes with a 'firm reliance on an all-seeing, just, and merciful Being, whom it will be our endeavour to fear and humbly obey'.

For a century or more since 1837, Retief's protest has rung through South Africa with far more telling effect than all the clumsier efforts at self-justification of the other Voortrekker leaders. During this time the manifesto has come to provide the Afrikaner nation with a sort of charter for itself. It has been analysed and taken apart sentence by sentence with devout care by generations of South African historians. But what in 1837 was of prime importance was the added prestige the manifesto gave to its author as he travelled slowly towards the camp at Blesberg.

On 8 April 1837 when Retief drew near, Gert Maritz and hundreds of the trekkers rode out of camp to meet him. A fever took them. They were enchanted beyond all reason by the new-comer's personality. Never before had they come across a man with such quiet authority and presence or with that urbane polish which often goes with French blood (for Retief was of Huguenot descent). Here stood the very model of everything that their captain should be, and within a few days, moved by his quality (and soothed too by the fact he was still unidentified with the party squabbles which threatened to destroy the trek), Retief was elected Governor and Commander-in-Chief of the *Maatschappij* at Blesberg.

With their election of a Governor the Afrikaners in effect had severed their relations with the British Crown and transferred their allegiance to a new head of State. But they were quite unable to do so without causing immense offence to some of their own countrymen. In the arrangements that were made Maritz retained his position of Judge and became chairman of a Council of Policy. Hendrik Potgieter on the other hand (and to his towering rage) was deprived of office. But whatever we may think of the rights and wrongs of what they had done, it must be admitted that the majority of the trekkers had at least found some sort of unity among themselves, even if it had been at the expense of the man who had led their vanguard across the Orange.

Piet Retief was considerably older than the general run of the trekkers; already his brown hair was greying at the temples. But even he with the magnetic personality and all his unlimited capacity for enthusiasm could not please everybody. And in fact one of his first acts as Governor further infuriated Potgieter's Dopper followers. He took the side of Erasmus Smit in the dispute over the Trek's spiritual leader. 'We have, thank God, a truly good Divine among us,' wrote Retief at this time, 'whom we acknowledge as a faithful shepherd to his flock', and the grateful Smit was duly installed as Predikant to the United Laagers at a salary of 600 rix-dollars a year.

But Retief was careful to conciliate Potgieter in another matter by falling in with his demand to make a further assault on the Matabele, although in the event the threat of a Griqua raid on Blesberg led to its postponement.

As regards the destination of the Trek, Retief was not prepared yet to commit himself; instead he compromised by leading the majority of the emigrants northwards to an area between the Sand and Vet rivers from which they could move equally easily across the Vaal or eastwards over the Drakensberg. Finally, in the early days of June 1837, while scouts were sent out to seek passes through the Berg, the Governor called another mass meeting to discuss the *Maatschappij*'s constitution again. The meeting approved a basic code of legislation set forth in Nine Articles which established the authority of the leaders who had been elected, but a series of by-laws gave offence to some trekkers who grumbled that they had crossed the Orange to get away from troublesome regulations of this sort. It was a relief to come to the less controversial subject of choosing a name for the State they were going to found: after much discussion 'New Eden' and 'East Africa' were both discarded in favour of 'The Free Province of New Holland in South Eastern Africa'.

Soon after this Piet Uys, a thick-set shaggy man with a hundred adherents, arrived at the United Laagers and proceeded to make them still less united with a blank refusal to accept the Nine Articles. He made it clear too that he disliked Retief's growing interest in 'Natal-land' which after his successful Commission Trek he had come to regard as something in the nature of a family preserve. In the end Uys rode back from the main Voortrekker laager to establish his own camp on the banks of the river Caledon and there he angrily awaited events.

Retief next found the time to demonstrate his diplomatic talents by making formal treaties with the chiefs Moroka, Moshweshwe[6] and Sekonyela, which secured his lines of communications to the south. Only a little later the scouts returned from the Drakensberg with the news that they had discovered five practical passes down the mountain scarp. 'Had we known sooner that we would have found a pass over the Draakberg [sic],' wrote Retief, 'we should long ago have been at the end of our journey. From all accounts we had been led to believe that we should be compelled to travel round the point of the mountain.' For their report had decided the Governor: he came down heavily on the side of those who considered Natal to be the proper destination for the Voortrekkers. The high veld, he announced, must be abandoned.

Retief called yet another meeting at Tafeltop in mid-September to discuss the project of Natal, fondly hoping that he would be persuasive enough to compose the trekkers' differences. Predictably Potgieter reaffirmed his intention of settling on the high veld, while Piet Uys confused the issue with the announcement that although he was done with the United Laagers, he was quite prepared to assist in another punitive expedition against the Matabele. The unity of the *Maatschappij* was now irrevocably broken, the grand dream was fragmented into two even more intense sub-dreams, and the Great Trek was great no longer. And so while Retief set off with a few wagons for the Drakensberg passes, trusting that the main mass of emigrants would follow him, Uys and Potgieter made their preparations for the final settling of the account with Mzilikazi.

The commando numbered 330 and it was composed of just about as tough a lot of men as could have been found in southern Africa at the time, a heavy-handed irrepressible lot. This time there were to be no inconclusive engagements. Hendrik Potgieter by now had learned the hall-mark of a successful commander – he planned on complete victory, on a victory which would give him dominance over the high veld. He was seeking a finish-fight; there were to be no loose ends left as there had been after Mosega. Kapain itself must be destroyed and the Matabele expelled.

Towards the end of October the commando came up to Mosega and found it to be deserted. Pressing through the wild forested Marico valley the Boers then approached the Matabele nuclear area round Kapain.[7] Beyond it the Marico river runs through three successive *poorts*[8] in the mountain ranges lying to the north. The Boers' strategy was to threaten each *poort* in turn and drive the Matabele ever northwards. The country was occasionally rough enough to compel the trekkers to fight on foot, but whether mounted or not their tactics were always the same: they provoked the Matabele to make an attack and it always came according to the traditional manner in a 'chest' and two 'horns'; the white men would then concentrate their fire on the points of the two enveloping flanks; invariably the 'horns' withered away and the whole assault bogged down. Applying these tactics for nine successive days the trekkers proved again that on the high veld the assegai would never match up to the musket, or naked savages, however brave, compete in battle with mounted men. They drove the Matabele towards modern Gaborone in Botswana, and on to the Tswapong mountains. On 12 November 1837 Mzilikazi's impis finally broke. The Boers called off the pursuit at Deerdepoort, and there offered up prayers of thanksgiving. Then Kapain and the other kraals were put to the torch as Mzilikazi led the remnants of his tribe away to the north. He was to cross the Limpopo and to found an empire in Rhodesia that lasted a further fifty years.

The Boers estimated that the Matabele lost 3,000 men during the nine-day running fight along the Marico. They themselves did not suffer a single casualty. This was the sort of victory the high veld Voortrekkers had been looking for, and Cilliers added to his account the quaintly engaging aside that 'What was theirs was now ours.' Potgieter at once gave substance to the remark: before the dust had settled over Kapain he issued a proclamation annexing all Mzilikazi's former territory by right of conquest. It comprised a huge area embracing much of modern Botswana, three-quarters of the Transvaal, and half the Orange Free State. The cattle loot was enormous too: the conquerors gathered in 7,000 head for themselves and gave many more to the Barolong herders who had accompanied the expedition.

But as at Mosega earlier in the year, now that the danger was over, a reaction set in among the victors. The booty proved the usual bone of contention. Potgieter again demanded the major portion of the cattle and he was supported in this claim by Uys. Maritz (who had missed the fight because of illness), however, protested that the losses of Vegkop had already been made good after Mosega, and this time it was he who got his way.

So once again it was an angry, quarrelling commando which came riding south towards the main trekker encampments near the Sand river. They were found to be empty now. The emigrants there had heard good news from Natal and already their wagons were streaming towards the Drakensberg passes.[9]

For Retief a little time before had found his way down the mountains and had ridden off with a handful of men to seek an interview with Dingaan in Zululand. Presently he had sent a message that all the land between the Tugela and the Umzimkulu was open for settlement by the trekkers.

Uys and Maritz at once set out for Natal, and very half-heartedly Potgieter followed them with his wagons. He was filled with forebodings: Potgieter had always predicted trouble for the trekkers in Natal and he exuded the impression that he was acting now against his better judgment. But not even in his most pessimistic moments could he have imagined the doom which even now was building up and would presently threaten to overwhelm the emigrants.

NOTES

1 This was not the final total. In the end the Great Trek leeched 12,000 Boers out of Cape Colony.

2 One observer noted that the trekkers 'fancy they are under divine inspiration'.

3 The central pole of a wagon to which the two rear trek oxen were yoked.

4 Originally the name was applied to a wooden yoke for draught animals. The Boers developed a skittle-like game in which the jukskei was thrown at a butt on the ground. The game has been elaborated and is now played throughout South Africa.

5 For all his flabbiness Erasmus Smit had an uncommon instinct for survival. The ship in which he travelled from Amsterdam to the Cape in 1802 was wrecked, and Smit was the only one among its 250 passangers to be saved. His rescuers took him first to West Africa and finally to New York before he was able to find another ship sailing to the Cape. There he experienced all the dangers and tribulations of the Voortrekkers in Natal, and died at the age of eighty-five from, it was whispered rather unfairly, the ravages of drink.

6 Pronounced Mo-shoe-shoe, and often abbreviated to Moshesh.

7 Close to Silkaats Kop (a derivation from Mzilikazi) on the modern map.

8 Passes; see map p. 182.

9 They had no idea that 200 miles away to the north Louis Tregardt's party was also making its way to the Berg. See chronological table in appendix.

7

Serpent in Eden

Only fifty-four wagons had followed Retief towards the Berg during the September of 1837. The going was slow: pasture was hard to find because of grass fires and, since it was the lambing season, the sheep were only able to cover a mile or two a day. By the time these trekkers had come to the site of modern Bethlehem on 2 October the more faint-hearted among them were already talking of retreat and drifting back to the laagers on the Vet and Sand rivers. Sorely aware that his numbers were rapidly dwindling Retief waited several days for Maritz to join him, and then impulsively, when his wagons failed to appear, on 5 October decided to ride on with fourteen horsemen and four wagons to seek interviews first with the English settlers at Port Natal and then with the Zulu king. He left his stepson, Abraham Greyling, to bring along the nineteen wagons that still remained with his party.

Retief was on the threshold of the finest adventure of the Great Trek and of its direst tragedy. He was in an exalted mood and the season seemed to fit his feelings. For by the time his horsemen were breasting the raised rim of the high veld which leads to the Drakensberg, spring had come to South Africa. It was the transitory *bloemtyd* – the flower time. In this season the first rains fall; the earth softens with the push of new grass; and trees burst into leaf and blossom. And during this delectable time, on 7 October, Piet Retief came to the last jagged rampart of the Berg and looked down into Natal.

It was like seeing a new world, an Elysium made up of wandering streams and fertile pastures all falling terrace by terrace to the distant sea but intermingled with dome-topped hills and wooded valleys. 'From the height of these mountains,' exulted Piet Retief after resting his eyes on this Pisgah-vision, 'I saw this beautiful land, the most beautiful in Africa.' He was not exaggerating. The prospect of Natal from the Drakensberg's Mont-aux-Sources is one for the connoisseur of landscapes. Africa here has subdued itself and become peaceful. To Retief a century ago it must have looked fresh from the hand of God, a special creation empty of all signs of human habitation, alive only with immense and unhurried herds of game. It was a land to delight the heart of a farmer as well as that of an artist: to carry such game the grass must surely be good; to grow such trees the soil must certainly be deep; and here, unlike so much of Africa, there was no scarcity of water. This was surely the Canaan which had been promised to the trekkers by the Lord.

Only one sombre note was struck as the enraptured Retief gazed down on Natal: one of his companions who had noted the way the shadow of the Berg was marching across the paradise below mumbled something about a land so marked must lie under a curse. But if Retief heard him he paid no heed.

Next day the little party climbed down the Berg by the so-called Steps Pass which had been worn by game moving over a succession of terraces to their winter grazing. It was a difficult descent: a little later Retief wrote about it to his family whom he had left behind on the high veld: 'From Drakensberg to Port Natal,' he wrote, 'I have passed five nearly perpendicular acclivities – the first took us six hours with the wagons, the others less; in some places we greatly fatigued our horses in riding right and left to find a path to descend – as also in crossing large rivers and valleys, through which we could not find a passage for a considerable distance; and as during the whole of that time we did not fall in with a single soul, we were obliged to find our way in the best manner we could.'

Far behind him Greyling's wagons were toiling up towards the land's sudden drop. Not until 19 October did they reach the escarpment, and, since storms were lashing the Berg, camped in the lee of a weathered sand-stone cliff which led up to a lofty pinnacle. It was a delightful place to camp: sweet grass grew around in profusion, and the gentle slope was divided by huge boulders into separate apartments as though to ensure privacy for each wagon. Erasmus Smit in his journal noted 'Here we saw another of Nature's wonders, namely one or two loose rocks on or close to the high mountain, one of which was like a dark cave'; this cave, he goes on, consisted of 'three adjoining spaces . . . which could with little difficulty be made into a church, or a place for religious gatherings'. Smit soon afterwards did in fact hold a service in the cave and christened the eminence above it, the Kerkenberg or a church mountain.

Meanwhile Retief was urging his wagons on towards Durban.[1] From now on until the day of his death four months later his actions seem to be kindled by the fatal urgency of one about to die. It is as though he knows that there is much to accomplish in little time. Of course too this precipitancy was due to some extent to the realisation that until he could make a *fait accompli* of his settlement in Natal, unity would never return to the *Maatschappij*, whereas its successful accomplishment would at once bring the dissentient factions to heel. One suspects as well that Retief was anxious to stake out his own people's claim to the best land in Natal before Piet Uys turned up with his turbulent followers. And there is no doubt, too, that during the first days of October Retief was more than ever concerned to come to terms quickly with Dingaan since his trekkers' cause had been jeopardised by an unexpected event; a band of horsemen carrying guns and dressed in European fashion had that very week raided a Zulu cattle station below the Berg and carried off 300 beasts. Retief felt that it was important to reassure Dingaan immediately that the raiders were not white men, and this might well be difficult since the leader of the cattle-raiders had been at pains to incriminate the emigrants as culprits: 'While taking the cattle,' a missionary explained in a letter to his directors, 'he called to some of Dingaan's people who were at a distance, saying the party were Boers, and that others had gone to Natal; and that Dingaan might expect to be treated by them as Moselekatse had been.'

At all events Retief hurried over the 220 miles which separated him from Port Natal continually amazed as he went by the succession of ruined kraals he passed whose inhabitants had been killed or driven away: it has been estimated that at this time only 3,000 refugees were living (hiding would perhaps be the better term) in the whole of Natal south of the Tugela. Once arrived at the Port, Retief was relieved to discover that it had not been annexed by the British Government as he had feared, and on the whole the welcome he received from the settlers was satisfactory enough. The English traders and hunters living there were divided, like the trekkers, into two factions: while all of them were now on bad terms with Dingaan and only remained at the settlement on sufferance, one party was anxious to proclaim British authority over it; the other faction led by Alexander Biggar and John Cane looked forward to obtaining security through an Afrikaner occupation of the country. Thirteen settlers out of the thirty-eight at Port Natal went so far as to sign an address of welcome to Retief, and Biggar wrote thankfully to the *Grahamstown Journal* that 'The arrival of Mr Retief...was hailed by us as a matter of no small moment. The conviction that we shall for the future be permitted to live in peace has infused a lively spirit among us. We can now proceed with confidence, and an assurance that our future exertions will no longer be cramped by doubts of our stability; but be rewarded by the fruits of our industry.'

There was much for Retief to do at Port Natal and he remained there until 27 October obtaining information about the surrounding country and the Zulu kingdom. But he found time to write to his people at Kerkenberg that the English settlers at the Port would place no obstacle in the way of the Boer emigrants accupying Natal and that no difficulty was to be expected from Dingaan who had already on four separate occasions alienated the country south of the Tugela to Europeans. One piece of information came to Retief as a surprise: that very month a missionary, the Reverend Francis Owen, had arrived at the Zulu capital and appeared to have been well received by Dingaan. This at least meant that there was a European at the king's court who could speak to him through an interpreter, and Retief took the opportunity of writing a letter for Owen to translate to the king. Owen read the letter to Dingaan on 26 October and noted afterwards in his diary that it had expressed the emigrant Boers' 'desire for peace and good understanding with the Zoolu [*sic*] nation: to effect which it was their wish to have, by means of their chief head, a personal interview with Dingaan; who would at the same time also arrange with Dingaan the place of their future residence which is to be in some part of the uninhabited country adjoining the Zoolu territories.'

Without waiting for an answer to his letter Retief set off for Umgungundhlovu the following day; with him rode four of his own men and two settlers from the Port who would act as interpreters. On the road he received a conciliatory letter dictated by Dingaan; it said that his soldiers had captured some sheep from the Matabele which he believed to be trekker property looted at Vegkop, and these he intended to return. This sounded promising enough and Retief rode into the Zulu capital certain that an easy success to his mission was not far away.

The Boers had never seen anything like Umgungundhlovu[2] before; the king's 'Great Palace' was quite different from any other African kraal they had known. The town was set on a gentle slope above a stream named the Umkumbane and was surrounded by a palisade of mimosa poles fully two miles in circumference. Inside stood nearly two thousand huts, six rows deep, and according to Retief 'each capable of accommodating twenty warriors'. They surrounded an empty space of two or three acres where military exercises and ritual

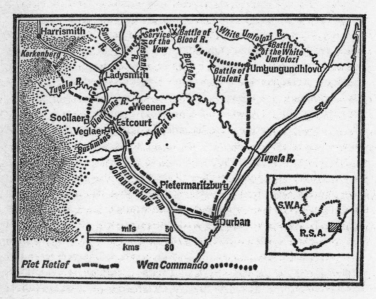

Routes of Piet Retief and Wen Commando

dances took place. At one end of this parade ground stood the king's private quarters which went under the name of the *isigodhlo*. Here too were the huts of his mother, those of some of his ninety wives, and a small enclosure especially reserved for the king's ablutions (it was much used since Dingaan bathed himself several times a day). Near by there was an artificial mound from which he could overlook the entire capital, and above all towered the king's hut which the Boers referred to as a palace. A more barbaric building could scarcely be imagined, and its rude magnificence certainly impressed Retief. 'The king occupies a beautiful habitation,' he reported. 'The form is spherical and its diameter is 20 feet. It is supported by 22 pillars, which are entirely covered with beads. The floor is perfectly smooth, and shines like a mirror.'

The extensive African town below literally hummed with the activity of its people so that the Boers were reminded of a giant colony of black ants. Above all the noise rose the shouts of Dingaan's *mbongos* who continually called out the praises of their master in brazen voices which could be heard miles away.

There were large numbers of cattle in the kraal too that November: Dingaan had concentrated the pickings of the royal herd there to impress the Boers and set Owen scribbling in his journal that the king 'has lately been collecting an immense herd of oxen from distant parts of the country, for no other conceivable motive than to display his wealth to the Dutch'.

Wooded undulating country lay outside the royal kraal on the far side of the Umkumbane stream; about half a mile to the east of the town on its eminence rose a parallel ridge called Hlomo Amabuto, the soldiers' hill, for here it was customary for the Zulu impis to mobilise for war. Towards the north its crest led on to a spur known as Kwa Matiwane. This was Dingaan's execution place.

On Kwa Matiwane, between the black rocks which littered its slopes, grew a tangled mass of coarse grass, aloes, mimosa trees and strangely Byzantine euphorbias which lifted up their branches to the sky as though they held sockets in which the candles of day might burn. The air of this Golgotha of Umgungundhlovu was foul with the sickly-sweet smell of putrescence. For Dingaan forbade the shedding of blood within his kraal and those he sentenced to execution were always dragged to Kwa Matiwane to be battered to death with sticks or to have their skulls shattered with the rocks that are strewn around on the hill. Some of the king's unfortunate victims, however, were made to suffer the more extreme form of Zulu torture here when a pointed stake two inches in diameter was rammed through the anus and up into the body and, thus skewered, they were left to die on these appalling slopes. The hill took its name from a chieftain named Matiwane who incurred Dingaan's wrath and was put to death by having wooden pegs forced up his nostrils into the brain. The event took Dingaan's fancy: he would often jokingly remark to his courtiers that while he ruled over the living in the town, Matiwane reigned over the dead on the hill across the stream; and gradually it became to be known as Kwa Matiwane – the place of Matiwane.

The corpses on this hill were never buried but lay left to scavenging beasts and birds, and this added to its horror. Even from a distance, vultures could be seen swinging incessantly in lazy circles over Kwa Matiwane, waiting for the next meal; indeed the vultures were so familiar with the procedure that they attended all the trials in the town as interested spectators and fluttered joyfully ahead of the prisoner when they saw him pinioned and led away to execution. The king called the repulsive birds his children and took pains to keep them well fed; after a particularly bloodthirsty exhibition of temper he would watch them happily on the hill as they squatted there, filled to repletion, their heads and scraggy necks sunk beneath wings clotted with gore, too sated when disturbed to do more than to run clumsily along the bloodstained ground flapping their great wings in an effort to rise.

Dingaan had come to the throne in 1828 after murdering his half-brother Shaka. He continued his predecessor's work of turning the Zulu nation into a military machine, but he lacked Shaka's warlike genius, and he did not personally lead his impis into battle. During the September of 1837 Dingaan learned that white trekkers were moving across the high veld; soon afterwards rumours reached him of their victory over the Matabele at Mosega. Only a little later scouts told him that the white men's wagons were approaching the Drakensberg passes and preparing to descend into what he considered to be his own domain.

It is not difficult to understand his reaction to the approach of the trekkers: no doubt had they been fewer he would have been pleased at the prospect of the windfall of trinkets and gadgets which they would be sure to shower on him,[3] but now he must have been consumed with suspicion about their intentions and fearful of their military prowess. The king's mind was filled with a host of private demons: he saw shadows and treachery everywhere, and was convinced that he was haunted by Shaka's ghost which dwelt, he believed, in a hut near his own especially set aside for it; nor could he ever forget the epileptic African convict from Cape Colony who after seeking refuge with him prophesied that white men would bring an army into Zululand and take the country away from him. Accordingly after he received Retief's letter from Durban, Dingaan awaited his

112

arrival with anxiety. He considered whether there was some peaceful way of preventing Retief settling in Natal, but in his heart of hearts Dingaan must have known all along that he would have to use guile and duplicity and even wholesale murder to avoid having these terrible fighting men as his close neighbours. He had no illusions about what this would mean. Dingaan once confided to one of the settlers at the Port, 'I see that every white man is an enemy of the black, and every black man an enemy of the white; they do not love each other and never will.' This remark sums up as well as anything else his basic attitude to the trekkers. So now as he awaited Retief's arrival at Umgungundhlovu the king became obsessed with the idea of obtaining some of the horses and guns that 'spat out fiery pebbles' to which the Boers owed their power, and if he could not get them to destroy the emigrants by an unprovoked and treacherous attack.

One cannot help feeling a certain sympathy with his point of view about his danger from a trekker state beyond the Tugela, but only abhorrence at the way he intended to deal with the situation. For he had no scruples about using perfidy and massacre to gain his ends.

The Zulu king was a past-master of deceit as well as cruelty. He made deliberate use of terror to increase his stature in the eyes of his subjects. He was a monster who killed for the sake of killing. Even by the savage standards of contemporary Zululand his actions appalled his people. He seemed less concerned with governing them than with decimating his subjects. Dr Alexander Smith who visited Umgungundhlovu shortly before the arrival of the *Commissie Treks* was horrified by the reign of terror the king had imposed on Zululand. 'As a characteristic of his system of proceeding,' writes Smith, 'I may only mention that when I was in his kraal I saw portions of the bodies of eleven of his wives, whom he had only a few days previously put to death for merely having uttered words which happened to annoy him.' But it is from the Reverend Francis Owen, who had the opportunity to observe Dingaan closely for four gruesome months, that we get the clearest impression of his behaviour. 'The King's cruelties,' he writes, 'do not proceed from rage but are perpetrated in cold blood when he is under no excitement; they are natural to him, common every-day occurrences.' In the hut perched on top of the third hill a mile and a half from the Zulu town where Owen lodged uncomfortably with his family, the missionary was continually recording the savage scenes on Kwa Matiwane which it was impossible for him to

113

ignore, and their very frequency is an indication of the inflationary tempo of horror which ruled Umgungundhlovu. 'Two persons were put to death yesterday,' he wrote on 22 November 1837 and adds bleakly that 'The day before yesterday one of the king's women was put to death.' 'Just as we were commencing our English service,' he jots down a little later, 'another execution took place on the hill opposite our hut.' Towards the end of December the missionary sadly records that a woman had suffered death for being 'somewhat saucy to an *induna*'; three days later he notes that an *induna* had been executed and that now 'the ravens were devouring his carcase,' while that same week he was an unwilling witness when 'Two women were executed today for the alleged crime of witchcraft'. And so the killings on Kwa Matiwane continued.

There were other quirks in Dingaan's character beside his excessive cruelty and duplicity. In him the ordinary Bantu pride in cattle had been carried to preposterous lengths: according to Nathaniel Isaacs the king would amuse himself for hours at a time in watching the gorgeous royal herd of snow-white cattle dancing on the parade ground of Umgungundhlovu and performing military manœuvres with a discipline which resembled that of trained soldiers. The king's other delight lay in his extensive harem: 'His sexual desires and natural propensity for corporeal desires,' observed the scandalised Isaacs, 'are unlimited; and a large proportion of his time is occupied with his females, either in dancing or singing, or in decorating their persons.' His white visitors found this predilection all the more curious because the members of his seraglio were unprepossessing in the extreme. The Rev. George Champion who visited the king's 'Great Place' a little earlier than Retief, recorded that the queens were 'corpulent beyond description, their hips and necks loaded with beads of various sorts, and with no clothing on most, except a short coat round the loins' and he goes on to say 'They present *in toto* as they drag their load over the ground, and in this weather, an appearance which excites in a stranger both ridicule and disgust'.

At the time of Retief's visit Dingaan was in his forties, and although running to fat he was well proportioned and still light enough on his feet to join in all the warriors' dances. Many of his white visitors found him an impressive figure, and would have been able to detect a certain dignity about his expression had it not been for the fact that he had three decayed black front teeth; Dingaan was very conscious of this defect and when speaking was for ever sliding his hand over his mouth to hide it.

When reading about Dingaan's rule the reader is constantly affronted and disgusted by the behaviour of this black reincarnation of Nero and one naturally begins to hunt about for reasons why a human being should behave so abominably. One must of course never forget the pressures to which he was exposed, nor that he had been brought up in a world of treachery and quick revenge. And it must be realised too that this untutored savage had nothing to guide his actions but his everlasting suspicions, a crude instinct for survival, and the sure knowledge that in the barbarous world in which he lived the slightest act of kindness would be interpreted as weakness and lead inevitably to his own destruction.

But even so Dingaan's penchant for cruelty bothers us, and when all has been said and done, we still come to the conclusion that there was something fundamentally wrong with the king's mind. He lived in a private world of egomania, and in it he attempted to rationalise his passion for killing by persuading himself that only by its gratification would his personal security be safeguarded. It is this facet of his psyche which has given to his reign its particular halo of terror. One wonders of course whether closer contact with the Europeans would have greatly altered Dingaan's conduct, but no white man who might have stilled the meaningless welter of brutality and bloodshed stayed permanently at his 'Great Place' until the Rev. Francis Owen turned up in Umgungundhlovu during the October of 1837. In any case the king regarded him not as a teacher but as an agent sent by Providence to supply his soldiers with the white men's arms: although the missionary had of course a certain value as an oddity it was only on this account that Dingaan was prepared to welcome the eager cleric.

Owen had bravely exchanged the comfort of a Yorkshire curacy for the Natal mission field, but very soon after disembarking from his comfortable boat he must have realised that he was hopelessly unfitted for the rough and tumble of African travel. He experienced a very bad time merely in getting to the king's kraal. Indeed that he ever succeeded in completing his overland journey from Algoa Bay to Umgungundhlovu was in itself something of a marvel. It had even begun badly: his Hottentot driver absconded on the second day out with the month's wages which the trusting missionary had paid him in advance, but somehow Owen got his wagons and his womenfolk along to Port Natal. There he engaged Richard King as a driver and a Zulu-speaking European boy named Hulley for his interpreter.

At his 'Great Place' Dingaan greeted this strange little party with clumsy politeness and assigned a near-by hill-top to it as a camping place. It was not a particularly happy choice: according to one of the traders from the Port, Owen's huts and wagons stood 'on top of a high hill where there is not a tree or twig, exposed to every blast of wind and as dreary a place as can be imagined'. And what was worse the camp as we have seen faced directly on to the grisly hill of Kwa Matiwane.

As soon as he was installed Owen addressed himself to the task of Dingaan's conversion. Every day he would walk across to the royal kraal on the other side of the valley, and explain the mysteries of the Scriptures to the uncomprehending king. It was not rewarding work and we find the remorseful missionary becoming as he puts it 'occasionally but sinfully' subject to fits of depression. Sometimes in desperation Owen turned to other subjects than theology in his conversations with the king: several laborious hours were devoted to teaching him the art of painting and one day the missionary unaccountably took it upon himself to explain the mysteries of the diving bell to the puzzled monarch.

Dingaan submitted with surprisingly good grace to Owen's brave attempts at giving him religious instruction (although he took every opportunity to interrupt them with urgent requests for lessons in musketry, and supplies of guns and powder). And indeed a very strange atmosphere hangs over the harangues of the curate from Normanton and the counter-arguments of the Zulu despot, all of which Owen faithfully recorded in his journal. Reading this now one can hardly blame Dingaan for obtaining a very confused idea of the Christian ethic, but at the same time must confess that during the bizarre theological discussion which ensued he gave every bit as good as he received. After he had recounted the story of the Crucifixion, for instance, Owen tells us that 'Dingarn [sic] then asked if it was God that died. I said the son of God. Did not God die he asked. I said God cannot die. If God does not die, he replied, why had he said that people must die? I told him it was because all peoples were sinners and death was the punishment of sin, but he would raise us all from

116

the grave. This,' concludes the missionary sadly, 'gave rise to in-numerable cavils.'

It was hardly surprising considering the number of people Dingaan had put to death: nothing for him could have been more horrifying than the prospect of their resurrection. Not unnaturally then the king returned a little later to this thorny subject. 'Dingarn asked me how many days Jesus Christ had been dead', we read in another of Owen's journal entries and he adds the king's sage comment after being told: 'If only three days, said he, it is very likely he was not dead in reality but only supposed to be. . . .'

Dingaan could be very touchy on the subject of death. When the tactless Owen one day 'reminded him that the great must die as well as the small', the king 'immediately told me the sun was down and I might go', and so drew this particular audience to a swift conclusion.

But the king's apparent interest in theology was of course no more than a cover for his intention of procuring fire-arms through Owen. On one occasion he persuaded the missionary to obtain a supply of gunpowder for him from Port Natal. This however caused much soul-searching on Owen's part, and he brusquely refused the next request. Dingaan in return then so forgot his manners that he sent up some warriors to search the missionary's quarters in case he was con-cealing arms there.

And now into this unhappy place of treachery and blood, rode Piet Retief and a handful of companions. The drawn-out contest between the Boer and Zulu was about to begin. It was 7 November 1837. Four hundred miles away at Kapain, Potgieter at that very moment was completing the final rout of the Matabele. By the curious symmetry of history the two schismatic factions of the Great Trek had simul-taneously reached a climax in their courses.

After Retief's horsemen arrived in Umgungundhlovu, Dingaan kept the Governor waiting two days before he would see him. He was trying to make up his mind about his reply to the inevitable request for land. Whatever course he took he ran the risk either of losing prestige with his own people, or, alternatively, of antagonising his white visitors. Dingaan's chief *indunas* Tambuza and Ndlela were all for murdering Retief at once while he and his men lay within their power.[4] The king in his dilemma could not turn to the white settlers at Port Natal for their advice since now they were openly hostile to him, while Mr Owen seemed only concerned with giving him Bible lessons or instruction in painting. Dingaan therefore decided to play for time and for the present put on a show of friendship and entertainment. For several days he accordingly had four thousand of his warriors amuse the Boers with dances and military exercises, and they marvellously impressed his visitors. We find Retief himself writing enthusiastically to his wife that 'Their sham fights are terrific exhibitions. They make a great noise with their shields and kerries, uttering at the same time the most discordant yells and cries. In one dance the people intermingled with 176 oxen, all without horns and of one colour. They have long strips of skin hanging pendant from the forehead, cheeks, shoulders and under the throat, which are cut from the skin when calves. These oxen are divided into twos and threes among the whole army, which then dances in company, each with its attendant oxen.'

Only on the third day did Dingaan receive Retief. The king was seated on a chair which had been fashioned from a single block of wood and he wore a strange head-dress with a veil and tassels of light cord covering his face as though he hoped to study the Boers without revealing his own thoughts. It seems that the king had expected to meet Piet Uys who had ridden into Natal three years before with the *Commissie Treks* and he was surprised to find a different white man awaiting him. His first discouraging words to the Governor were 'You are too small for a captain'. Then Dingaan listened in silence to Retief's explanation that he had come to purchase land which was lying waste south of the Tugela. It was some time before the king replied, and then only with a half-anticipated accusation. Retief's men, he said, only the month before had rustled a herd of royal cattle and driven them up the Berg, and he silenced the Governor's indignant denials by pointing out that the thieves had been mounted, carried guns, and were dressed in Boer fashion. At last Retief was able to break in to tell Dingaan that he believed the culprits to have been Manthatisi's Tlokwa, the so-called Wild Cat people, led by her son Sekonyela who was known to affect the white men's clothes.

Dingaan's reply is interesting for the light it sheds on his shrewdness; he said that the best way for Retief to prove the Boers' innocence in the affair was to ride in Sekonyela's country with a commando and ten Zulu herders who would be able to recognise any royal cattle there. If they identified the beasts, then Retief must arrest Sekonyela and bring him back with his stolen cattle to Umgungundhlovu. Once this task had been completed Dingaan gave an assurance that he was prepared to cede the land between the Tugela and Umzimvubu to the emigrant Boers; he then went as far as to put his mark on a written declaration to this effect, conveniently ignoring the fact that in the past he had already granted this same country to the British Crown as well as to three other Europeans at Port Natal.

All in all Retief had received a pretty tough assignment in the projected capture of Sekonyela, and it is not difficult for us to realise the way the king's mind was working when he framed it. His suggestion afforded every chance of involving the Boers in a shooting war with the Wild Cat people; on the other hand if Retief succeeded in securing Sekonyela, Dingaan would get his cattle back and the opportunity too of punishing the Batlokwa chief by confiscating his guns and horses which would make his impis a good deal stronger if he had to fight the Boers.[5] Either way he would gain valuable time. But Retief had no hesitation in agreeing to these terms, and a little time later he rode out of Umgungundhlovu and turned his horse towards the Berg, certain that his mission had been successful and that to all intents and purposes Natal was his for the taking.

Meanwhile Retief's followers at Kerkenberg had been living through an anxious time. For three weeks they had heard rumours that English soldiers had occupied Port Natal and then more frightening ones which whispered that Retief and his men had all been slain by Zulus. But they were heartened by the way other trekkers were regaining their confidence in Retief's dream and now were trickling along to join them at Kerkenberg: one day some of Maritz's party in their gaily painted wagons rolled into the camp, and Maritz was said to be close behind them.

Then on 11 November 1837 the two messengers Retief had sent off to Kerkenberg during his journey to Umgungundlovu rode into camp carrying welcome advice from their leader as well as all sorts of luscious tropical fruits. The English settlers at the Port, Retief had written, were friendly and he was optimistic that the Zulu king would cede the country below the Tugela to him for settlement. The letter ended by saying there was no reason now why the trekkers should not descend the Berg.

In a spontaneous outburst of relief and happiness the emigrants gathered together that evening to discuss the future, and then in their exhilaration stepped out their familiar measures to the Afrikaner songs which still delight us. On the next day, 12 November, which happened to be her father's fifty-seventh birthday, Deborah Retief went blithely to the rocky shelter in which Erasmus Smit held his church services and there, where an immense overhanging rock rears itself up as though striving to embrace its smaller fellow from which it has been sundered in some ancient earthquake, she wrote her father's name and the date in green paint on the cave wall. Her writing still survives as one of the more poignant relics of the Great Trek.

At the camp all was now activity. No time was to be wasted in getting down the Berg. While some men sweated to improve the descent roads, hurling boulders down the hill, axing trees and bushes, and levelling the hollow places which would break the back of any vehicle, others worked on the wagons, dismantling some of them completely, changing round the wheels on others so that the larger pair was in front, and tying huge logs to their sterns to act as brakes. Then with only two oxen yoked in front and whole teams of men straining at the back on *riems* to keep them on an even keel, the empty wagons one after the other were skidded down the mountainside. Behind them walked the women and children, while the infirm and invalids were carried along in stretchers. By 14 November twenty wagons were standing safely on the plain below, and Erasmus Smit was rejoicing in his diary that 'only one wagon, that of our friend W. Prinsloo, overturned at the beginning of the descent. A set of chains was broken but nothing else'; Smit here was being a trifle optimistic, for we find someone else lamenting that in his wagon 'a beautiful set of chairs was broken'.

But the impossible was being achieved: six more wagons came down the mountain-side on the following day, and thirteen the next. By the end of the week sixty-six wagons were already below the Berg and rumbling towards the head waters of the Tugela river. The traffic grew even heavier after the good news from Retief reached more of the trekkers waiting on the central plain and soon a hundred wagons a day were being worked down the five practical passes which had been discovered.[6]

Meanwhile Retief was riding back towards them. On the way he called in at Mr Champion's mission station and the missionary warned him that Dingaan might be leading the trekkers into a trap. The sanguine Retief answered that he expected no trouble and added a shade condescendingly that it took a Dutchman rather than an Englishman to understand a Kafir. When the clerical Cassandra gently reminded him that he was an American, and not an Englishman, Retief waved this objection aside with the remark that the difference was far too small to notice.

It was on 27 November that Retief rode into his camp which had been set up at a place called Doornkop close to the site of modern Chieveley. There were a score of other encampments near by: by this time it was estimated that close on a thousand Boer wagons were scattered about in the vicinity.

Retief tarried at Doornkop for a month making arrangements for his foray against Sekonyela. He was concerned about a number of other things. One was Piet Uys who he suspected would resent his arrangement with Dingaan and might try to make a deal of his own with the king. Accordingly he sent a rather hooded message to Umgungundhlovu which read: 'I think it probable that before my return you will be troubled on account of the request I have made of you, and the promise you have given me. I also think it possible that more may be told the king about me and my people than can be shown to be true. ... My wish is that you will not please, before my return, hearken to anyone who may come to trouble you about the land in which I wish to live.'

Only on 28 December, after Retief had been cheered by news of Potgieter's success at Kapain, did he lead a fifty-man commando to Wild Cat country and up to the flat-topped mountains named Imperani overlooking modern Ficksburg. Here Retief by arrangement met Sekonyela in the garden of 'the chief's missionary', Mr Allison.

There is something rather distasteful about the manner in which Retief now proceeded to deal with the unsuspecting Batlokwa chief. His actions at Imperani seem entirely out of character; certainly they infuriated the missionary, and when he later at Retief's request held a service for the Boers, he took as his text the prophetic words 'He who sows wickedness, reaps wickedness.'

The generally accepted account of Retief's encounter with Sekonyela says that the Governor told the chief that he had bought him some costly presents including an amulet especially manufactured for great rulers, and when the grateful Sekonyela obligingly held out his arms, one of the trekkers, Bezuidenhout, snapped a pair of handcuffs on them. Another version of the affair is hardly more edifying: it has Retief explaining to Sekonyela about the way in which Europeans deal with malefactors, at the same time producing the handcuffs with the words 'So that you should well understand the way they are used, allow me to put them on your wrists'.

At all events Sekonyela was secured and then told that he would not be released until he had handed over the cattle he had stolen from Dingaan. And in fact the Boers fined him far more heavily: as Retief informed the king in a letter a little later 'to punish Sekonyela he had made him deliver up 700 head of cattle and also 63 horses and 11 guns, for without these he could not have accomplished his theft'. It was rather a flimsy excuse and it held in it the seed of trouble. For Retief had neither the intention of giving up the extra cattle, the horses and guns to the king, nor of delivering Sekonyela to him for punishment.

Sending on Dingaan's cattle to Umgungundhlovu with the Zulu herders,[7] Retief returned to Doornkop delighted with his successful stratagem. More trekkers had arrived from the high veld during his absence. Gert Maritz himself was now camped below the Berg as well as Andries Pretorius who was paying a visit to the *Maatschappij*, and Piet Uys who had somehow been persuaded to pledge his allegiance to the United Laagers.

Retief had already decided on making a show of force when he paid his second visit to Umgungundhlovu to conclude his business with Dingaan, but there was an uneasy feeling among some people in the camp that things had gone too well, that the Zulu king was quite unpredictable, and that the friendly atmosphere in his capital might have evaporated. One old man called Malan went round telling everyone that he had dreamed of a wholesale massacre, and the ailing Maritz was insisting that since his days were nearly over it would be far better if he and one of two companions interviewed the king rather than risk the person of the Governor. But Retief brushed all suggestions of this sort aside and called for volunteers to accompany him to the Zulu capital. Nearly every man in the camp seemed to want to go on what appeared to be a joy-ride. In the end Retief selected sixty-seven men and three youths (including his own fourteen-year-old son) to ride with him, and in addition he took along

Thomas Holstead from the Port to act as interpreter, as well as thirty coloured servants. On 25 January 1838 this company clattered off along the road to the Tugela and Zululand. It was the warm, green rainy season and how easy it is for us even after all these years to visualise that cavalcade again; the men are laughing and talking together as they ride, and every now and then a handful of the youths will gallop off to course some buck, but for all their gaiety somehow one knows that right from the start the party carried with it sure and certain tragedy. Yet not one among those horsemen had any premonition of what lay before them, and no one remembered Maritz's gloomy words as he saw them off: 'I say to you that not one of you will return.'

NOTES

1 The English settlers knew the port as Durban but the emigrants still preferred to call it Port Natal.
2 The name has been variously interpreted as meaning the place of the elephant and the secret meeting place of the king. The diarist Captain Garden noted that Dingaan gave the place the name of Inkunga-Inhlovu, the slayer of the elephant, to commemorate his murder of his brother Shaka.
3 He had been delighted a little earlier with a trader's gift of a magnifying glass which on a sunny day he employed to burn a hole in a servant's outstretched arm.
4 There is indeed some evidence that Dingaan accepted this advice and arranged to have one of his lesser *indunas* ambush Retief's party on its way back to the Berg. But the *induna* refused the commission and the plan miscarried.
5 Or even better he could put Sekonyela to death on Kwa Matiwane since that chief had recently paid Dingaan the ultimate insult of throwing doubts publicly on his sexual potency.
6 Retief's party descended by the Steps Pass. Others used the De Beer's Pass, Quagga Pad, Middledale Pass and Bezuidenhout's Pass.
7 The remainder of the cattle, several hundred in number, were divided up among Retief's party, an action which as anyone could have foreseen was bound to antagonise Dingaan.

8

The Great Murder

The mood at Umgungundhlovu had indeed changed since Retief paid his first visit. Several events had occurred to increase Dingaan's fear of the emigrant Boers. First the king had learned that the trekkers were descending the Berg in large number. Afterwards news of Potgieter's bloody success at Kapain had filtered into Zululand. Then again Dingaan's fears of these terrible white men had not been assuaged by a new letter from Retief which Owen had read out to him. It was filled with admonitions and buttressed by threats. Admittedly Mr Owen did not see it that way: according to the credulous missionary it merely 'contained some excellent reflections and advice on the conduct of wicked kings' and even assured Dingaan that Mzilikazi's 'punishment had been brought upon him by the righteous providence of God, because he had not kept God's word, but had made war when he ought not'. Pressure on Dingaan to act decisively moreover had grown that December when the tribal ritual of the First Fruits was celebrated at Umgungundhlovu; the warriors as usual had worked themselves up into a warlike fervour during the ceremony and implored Dingaan to 'eat up' the white trekkers in Natal. Finally to compound the king's wrath, on 22 January 1838 he received yet another letter from Retief saying that he intended to retain a proportion of Sekonyela's cattle and had no intention of giving up the horses and guns the Boers had taken from the Batlokwa chief 'as a guarantee of future behaviour'. Worst of all it was apparent that Retief had released Sekonyela.

These affronts aroused more suspicion and a savage hatred, and in the extremity of his rage Dingaan now finally made up his mind to destroy the trekkers in Natal. One can imagine the king's gross figure dilating still further with ferocious anticipation as his plans matured and he turned them over in his mind. He decided to murder Retief when he returned to Umgungundhlovu, and immediately afterwards have his impis wipe out the Boer encampments under the Berg. To be successful Retief's killing at the capital must be initiated by treachery and surprise, and no doubt Dingaan recalled a plan he had made some years before to slaughter John Cane and a group of white companions from Port Natal: for when they came up on a visit to the 'Great Place', Dingaan had asked them to fire a salute in his honour, at the same time instructing his warriors to attack the white men before their guns could be reloaded. But the cautious Cane had, tongue-in-cheek, assured the king that it was customary for a line of men to fire a salute one by one and Dingaan had to forgo his hope of butchering the party in safety.

The king had never got over the disappointment at the failure of this plot. Now he decided that he might as well include Cane as well as a hated missionary named Gardiner in the bloody reception he was arranging for Retief; accordingly he sent out messengers bidding the two men to appear at Umgungundhlovu. Both Cane and Gardiner wisely ignored this command. The king then also decided that he might be able to include the trekkers' women and children in the coming slaughter at Umgungundhlovu: in a hospitable message dictated to Owen on 2 February, he asked Retief to bring the entire *Maatschappij* with him when he came to receive a formal document ceding Natal to him. The letter announced that the king's 'heart was now content, because he had got his cattle again'; and went on 'He requested that the chief of the Boers would send to all his people and order them to come up to the capital with him, but,' in an anxious addition 'without their horses'.

But this part, too, of Dingaan's plan fell away, for on the very next day the sound of shooting was heard in the distance and Retief's cavalcade pranced into view. The Boers had ridden directly from the Drakensberg foothills and not via Port Natal as Dingaan had ordered: it was yet another provocation to gnaw at the king's forebodings.

By believing in Dingaan's continued goodwill Retief was of course making a tragic error of judgment. But the blow which had been arranged for him did not fall at once; the delay was not as has been suggested a case of the cat playing with a mouse; it was probable that the king was waiting for reinforcements to arrive in Umgungundhlovu as well as for Gardiner and Cane to accompany the trekkers into the trap he had set for them. During the first few days of the visit his warriors were again set to entertain the Boers with displays of mock fighting and dancing, while the white men responded by galloping around the parade ground firing off their guns, which of course added to the king's misgivings. When Retief at last showed signs of impatience, Dingaan glibly signed a document which had been drawn up some days before: in it he ceded all the land between the Tugela and the Umzimvubu to the Boers.[1] It seemed to Retief now that his dream had come true. In the short African twilight that evening the Boers wandered happily among the huts of Umgungundhlovu for the last time, gossiping together and making preparations for their departure in the morning. They took little notice of a white boy named William Wood who happened to be visiting the capital at the time and (since he knew Zulu well) had been listening to the warriors' talk. Young Wood suspected Dingaan's real intentions, but when he tried to warn the Boers about his fears he was brushed aside with assurances that Dingaan 'was a man with a large and good heart' and 'We are sure the king's heart is right with us, and there is no cause for fear'.

The day the trekkers were to leave, 6 February 1838, dawned bright and cloudless. After their final preparations had been made and the horses saddled, Retief received a message from the king asking him to assemble his men on the parade ground so that he could bid them all farewell. It seemed ungracious to refuse. Leaving their horses in the care of their grooms under a candelabra tree at the gate of the kraal the white men re-entered the town. Almost at once they were stopped by two *indunas* who explained that it was an offence to come armed into the king's presence and the trekkers obligingly piled their guns in a heap outside the gate.

Then they trooped in to watch a final exhibition of native dancing, refusing boiled meat for they had already breakfasted, but accepting milk for refreshment. One can imagine them sitting there in the blue and gold of the early morning, pulling on their pipes, idly watching the display, cuffing away the mangy dogs which cowered up to them. The air was filled with the smell of dust and sweating bodies and stale cattle dung. Retief had seated himself on the ground beside Dingaan's carved wooden throne; the wallet with the deed of cession of Natal was slung about his shoulders. All around a great circle of warriors were squatting on the ground, apparently unarmed but with

assegais concealed in the dust of the cattle droppings. Occupied in watching the performance the Boers hardly noticed that the circle of dancers was closing in on them. The warriors were chanting an interminable war song and the king himself led the singing. During the last verse, and forgetting for once to put up his hand to hide his rotten teeth, Dingaan suddenly leapt to his feet with a shriek of 'Bulalani abatagati' – kill the wizards. It was the arranged signal. A great mass of Zulus pressed on to the white men. There was a short scuffle against impossible odds. Some of the Boers had time to draw their hunting knives and they are said to have killed twenty Zulus before they were overpowered. Then the white men were bound with rawhide thongs and borne, still struggling, down into the valley and up the slopes of Kwa Matiwane. It must have been a strange and terrifying scene, and it has burned deep into the Afrikaners' national consciousness. Owen on his hill was an unhappy witness of all that was going on. He heard the tremendous uproar in the kraal, the clashing of spears and knobkerries on shields, the hoarse shouts of the warriors and the yells of their victims, and above all the din the sound of Dingaan's voice still shouting out his command to kill the wizards. Unwillingly the missionary lifted his eyes to watch the beginnings of the deed of blood; fortunately he could not see the details of its ending.

There is a quality about the deaths of Retief and his men which does not seem to belong to an incident in history; rather it is like a scene from Grand Guignol or the feverish outpourings of an artist with a macabre mind working on a fresco or painting. On Kwa Matiwane most of the Boers were clubbed to death; for that purpose, the warriors used a wagon-load of sticks which chanced to be standing there. But some died when their skulls were broken with rocks. A few of Dingaan's victims it seems were skewered and left on the hill to a more lingering death. Certainly in another refinement of cruelty Retief was made to witness the agonies of all his companions before he himself was put to death and one can only guess at his thoughts as he watched the killing of his son. After every bit of life had been battered out of him, Retief's chest was ripped open, and his heart and liver wrapped up in a cloth and taken to the king.

In a few words Owen manages in his journal to convey the horror of the scene. His entry begins with 'A dreadful day in the annals of the Mission', and then goes on to describe the struggling groups on

127

Kwa Matiwane; his account ends with 'At present all is as still as death: it is really the stillness of death, for it has palsied every tongue in our little assembly'. For there was no movement now on the execution hill; some of the Boers' corpses had been impaled on tall poles to stand like petrified sentinels on the gruesome slopes. But very soon the scavengers descended on Kwa Matiwane: 'Scarcely had the Zulus left the place of slaughter,' writes Owen's maid, Jane Williams, another eye-witness, 'when the vultures swooped down on the bodies of their victims,' flopping down in scores, waddling among the rocks and triumphantly fighting for the carrion which Dingaan their father had provided that day. The story goes, and it may well be apocryphal, that Retief's heart and liver were buried on the road to Natal in some magic ceremony which was intended to ensure that no white men should again come that way to the king's 'Great Place'.

It must grudgingly be accounted to Dingaan's credit that he sent a warning to Owen just before he killed the Boers, assuring him that neither he nor his family would be harmed. But the missionary was nevertheless made very fearful a little later when he watched a knot of warriors marching up towards his huts. As they drew nearer he turned away to read with a broken voice the 91st Psalm to his wife and sister, and no doubt these poor people's courage was sustained by the deathless words of that triumphant outpouring which sounded over the rocky hill facing on to Kwa Matiwane. 'Thou shalt not be afraid of the terror by night; nor for the arrow that flieth by day. . . . For He shall give His angels charge over you, to keep thee in all His ways.' But Dingaan's soldiers did them no harm, and it is wonderful to relate that after a few days Owen was allowed to leave Umgungundhlova by this violent man whose first instinct had been to kill all Europeans within his reach. The hilltop where Owen had lived was turned into a fold for the captured horses. Today it bears the buildings of a Christian mission.

Soon after the slaughter was completed Owen noticed that Tambuza and Ndlela were deep in conversation with the king. 'I have seen by my glass,' the missionary recorded, 'that Dingaan has been sitting most of the morning since this dreadful affair in the centre of his town, the Army in several divisions collected before him. About noon the whole Army ran in the direction from which the Boers came.' What Owen had been watching was the initiation of the second part of the massacre plot. The captains of several regiments had been

128

Zulu

The mighty rampart of the Drakensbergs

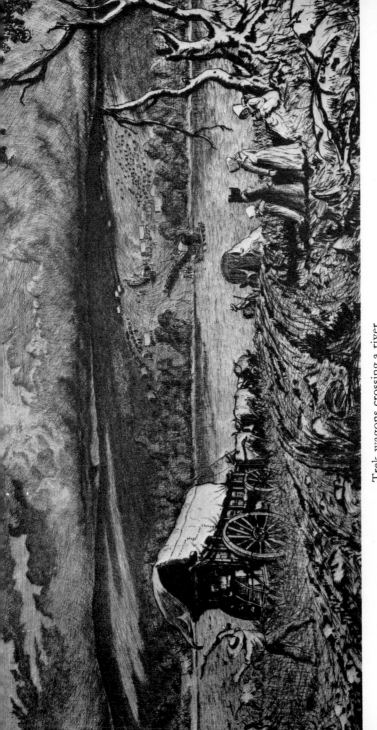

Trek wagons crossing a river

Piet Retief

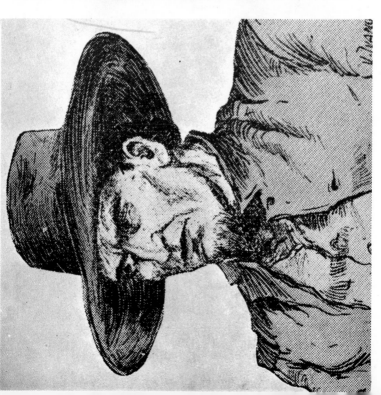

Andries Hendrik Potgieter

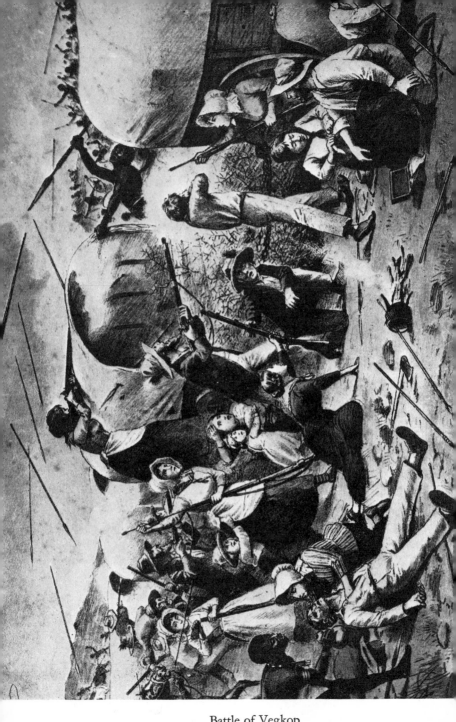

Battle of Vegkop

Trekking through the hills

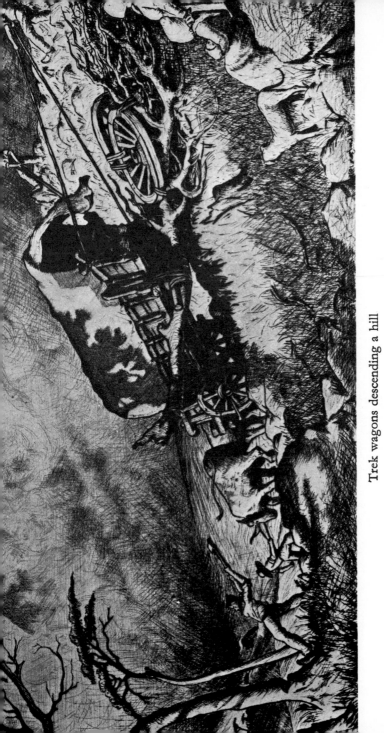

Trek wagons descending a hill

Dingaan

The seizure of Piet Retief and his men

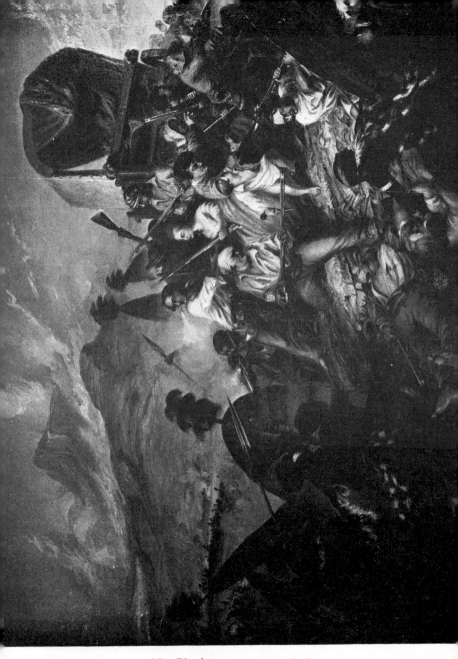

The Bloukrans massacre, 1838

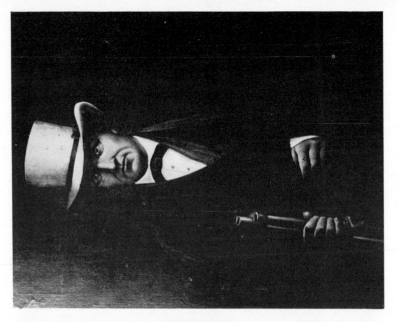

Andries Pretorius

Sir Harry Smith

Attack at Blood River

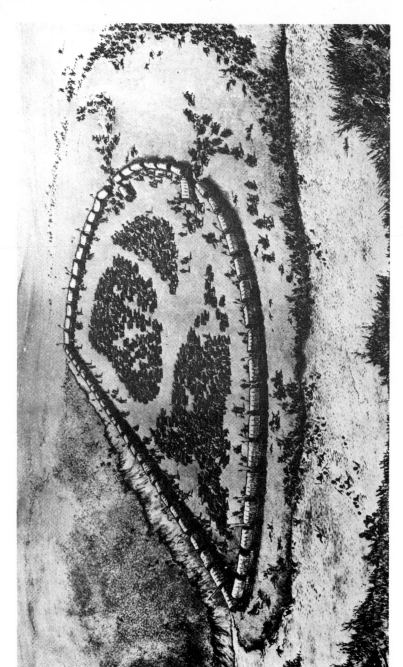

The battle of Blood River

The Retief Stone

Reconciliation of Pretorius and Potgieter, 1852

called up and given instructions to seek out the trekker encampments in Natal and 'eat them up'. They were to approach unseen and fall on them simultaneously during the dark of the moon. When the orders had been explained the regiments made a mock attack on the *isigodhlo* calling out. 'We will go and kill the white dogs'. Then they departed to their task. During the Kafir Wars on the eastern frontier it had been customary for the Xhosa to spare the women and children but Dingaan's orders now were to kill every living thing in the camps.

Yet after launching this fresh butchery Dingaan, like a child who knows he is doing wrong, yearned to find some justification for his actions. He had Owen write to Cape Town to assure the authorities there that the Boers 'wanted before they left to fire a salute with blank cartridge as they did on their arrival, but that their real intention was to kill him, as a proof of which when examined after their death, their guns were found to be loaded with ball'. There is concrete evidence too which suggests that in fact the king had feared that the Boers would attack his *isigodhlo* under cover of darkness during the previous night. Kirkman, the interpreter for one of the American missionaries, was told when he visited Umgungundhlovu soon after the massacre, that 'the Boers had made three attempts to surround the kraal at night, but from their small numbers were unable to do so'. And perhaps Dingaan was still voicing his suspicions of Boer treachery when a little later he expressed to Hulley his regret that Gardiner and Cane had not been present on the fatal day 'as they fully deserved'.

Subsequently the distraught trekkers tried to pin part of the blame for the tragedy of Kwa Matiwane on the British settlers at the Port. Stories went round that Gardiner and a man named Stubbs had visited Umgungundhlovu while Retief was dealing with Sekonyela, and had advised the king to murder the trek leader when he returned to the 'Great Place'. Then again Owen, Cane, Ogle and another settler named Garnett have all been incriminated by Afrikaner tradition for prompting Dingaan to the murders: they are accused of being emissaries of the Cape Government which had no wish to see Natal occupied by the emigrant farmers. None of these rumours contained a single grain of truth: they must be seen merely as a reflection of the trekkers' contemporary anti-British views.

Meanwhile, as eleven days passed and the bodies of Retief and his companions kept watch with the vultures over Kwa Matiwane, tragedy hung over the trekkers Piet Retief had left below the Berg. Ten Zulu regiments lay concealed within striking distance of their encampments. They were waiting only for the moon to wane before annihilating the unsuspecting emigrants.

The advanced Boer camps were spread over a forty-mile front between the Tugela at modern Colenso and the present village of Willow Grange. The more prudent emigrants and groups of late-comers lay scattered right back as far as the foothills of the Drakensberg. The Zulu scouts failed to appreciate that the trekkers were disposed in such depth: accordingly it was the forward Boer encampments which took the full fury of the enemy onslaught, while those behind escaped attack.

The Boers were dangerously dispersed. This to some extent was inevitable since grazing ground had to be found for their enormous numbers of cattle and sheep. But it is difficult to excuse the trekkers for failing to fortify their camps or to throw out vedettes. They were over-confident and had ignored Retief's suggestion that despite Dingaan's good faith they should nevertheless laager their wagons every night once they had descended the Berg. 'It was on account of disobedience and imprudence,' a woman among the emigrants explained afterwards. 'The greater portion of the people were on the mission (to Dingaan) and others engaged in buffalo-hunting; others, moreover, were on the road to the Drakensberg to assist their families in coming down: so that the kaffirs found the women and children quite alone and sleeping peacefully.' A second Boer put the situation rather differently: 'We were in tranquil security, for there was peace; and as Retief had recovered and restored the cattle belonging to Dingaan's people, we could not imagine things would not go alright.'

The improvidence was all the more reprehensible since it seems that rumours about the disaster at Umgungundhlovu were already reaching the trekkers; a Zulu was even reported as having shouted across the Tugela that Retief had been killed. It is true that a patrol was sent out to discover if there was an impi approaching the Tugela, and it was only prevented from running into Dingaan's army by the sharp-witted answers of a Zulu scout it happened to encounter. But only in a few cases was any effort made to pull the wagons round into a laager. Port Natal had learned of the Retief massacre before the middle of February, and some steps were taken there to warn the Boers of coming danger. Alexander Biggar sent one of his sons hastening to the trekkers with the news, but unfortunately he was shot dead by a trigger-happy Boer when he came galloping up to the first camp; Richard King,[2] who had left Owen's service by now, trudged up to the camps on foot with a report of the massacre, but he arrived after the Zulus had put in their attack.

The most advanced trekkers' wagons stood that February along the banks of a spruit running from Willow Grange to the Bushman's

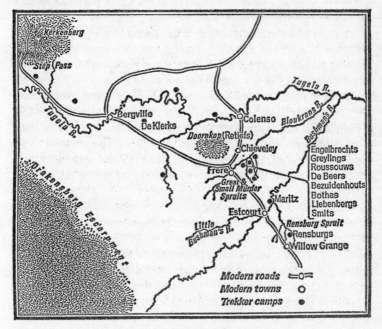

The Great Murder

river below modern Estcourt. Here the Malan, Swart, Breed and Van Rensburg families were encamped. Scarcely less exposed were family groups of Roussouws, De Beers, Bezuidenhouts, Bothas, Liebenbergs and others who were scattered a little farther north along a ridge covered with thorn bushes that rose between two streams running into the Bloukrans river (afterwards they would be named the great and small moord or murder spruits). Maritz's large party was camped between and a little to the rear of these two groups on the banks of the Bushman's river where it makes a horse-shoe bend. Farther still to the west stood the seventy-eight wagons of the Retief and Greyling families on the hill which had been named Doornkop – the thorny koppie.

The Zulus made their assault in sections along the twenty-mile front which they had reconnoitred, and by good staff work the attacks went in almost simultaneously. At one o'clock in the morning of Saturday 17 February 1838 the warriors fell on the sleeping Liebenbergs at Moordspruit and annihilated the whole party. At almost the same moment another division of the impi overwhelmed the Roussouws and Bezuidenhouts near by. Young Daniel Bezuidenhout survived this attack. He says that he was awakened by his dogs barking furiously and got up to investigate. Instead of finding a marauding leopard[3] he was met by a shower of assegais, and found as he notes dryly that 'We had to do with kafirs and not with tigers'. Daniel Bezuidenhout then succeeded in fighting his way through the Zulu ranks and ran to raise the alarm in the neighbouring camps. Thus forewarned the Bothas managed to fight off an attack for some time, but the whole family was killed after the Zulus drove a herd of cattle among their wagons and got among them during the ensuing mêlée.

The Van Rensburgs lay to the south with eight or nine other families and they had a few minutes' warning of the onslaught. It allowed them to take refuge on a near-by sugar-loaf hill, and here fourteen men held out for several hours. Just when their ammunition was running short a commando which had been rapidly mustered by Cilliers and Gert Maritz came into view and one of its men, Marthinus Oosthuizen, rode ahead and succeeded in reaching them with powder and bullets. A little later a counter-attack dispersed their assailants.

Maritz had an hour's grace to prepare the defences of his camp. His people heard firing in the distance, and it is a measure of their confidence in the Zulus that at first they believed it signified Retief's men announcing their return with a *feu de joie* or possibly a treacherous attack by the British settlers at the port. The breathing space allowed the Boers in the camp to bring a small cannon into action and drive off the Zulus who had formed a human chain in their efforts to ford the flooded Bushman's river. It is said that a marksman among the Boers repeatedly shot down men in the centre of this chain so that it might fall apart, and many Zulus are believed to have drowned in the river. Maritz then pursued the impi with thirty-three men. A contemporary account has left us a brave vignette of Maritz rushing off with a musket to the fight followed by his wife and thirteen-year-old daughter, both carrying a bag of gunpowder in one hand and a bag of slugs in the other.

By day-break fugitives and wounded men were carrying news of the crisis to the main camp on Doornkop and here a strong laager was hastily formed. The Zulu offensive missed Sarel Cilliers' camp and he sallied forth courageously to assist his fellow trekkers. Cilliers led the counter-attack after admonishing his companions to 'Keep God before your eyes, and be not afraid, and follow me.' With five men,' he wrote afterwards, 'I first saved the laager of Gert Barends, which was on the point of surrendering to the greater strength of the enemy,' and he adds that in the running fight which followed, 'I fired so much that the barrel of my gun became so hot I was afraid when I put in the powder it might burst.' Then Cilliers joined with Maritz's men in bringing relief to the hard-pressed Van Rensburgs and other family groups near by. Later he remembered that 'Everything gave way to rage. There was no further resistance. We drove the kafirs into a confused heap and overwhelmed them until they were driven by us into the fastness of the mountains.'

At last night fell on the camps, a miserable night of fear and suffering. With the coming of morning the surviving trekkers were appalled by the magnitude of the disaster. Sorrowfully they counted the dead bodies of 41 men, 56 women and 185 children, besides those of 200 coloured servants. In a single bloody night nearly 500 members of the Great Trek had died, and the surviving camps were filling up with wounded stragglers. No mind can add up the sum of human anguish and anxiety which stemmed from Dingaan's work that night. Only two people were found alive among the wreckage of the Roussouw wagons: Daniel Bezuidenhout tells us that of them 'Elizabeth Roussouw had sixteen wounds, and died the next day. Adriaan had twenty-three spear wounds but escaped with his life.'[4] One catches the flavour of the horror too from the pen of Mrs Steenkamp who found it 'unbearable for flesh and blood to behold the frightful spectacle the following morning. In one wagon were found fifty dead, and blood flowed from the seam of the tent-sail down to the lowest part. . . . On all sides one saw tears flowing and heard people weeping by the plundered wagons, painted with blood; tents and beds were torn to shreds; pregnant women and little children had to walk for hours together, bearing the signs of their hasty flight.' Of another camp Cilliers writes, 'I was an eye-witness to the fact that little infants still in their swaddling clothes lay in their blood, murdered in the arms of their mothers.' Young Bezuidenhout when he got back to his camp found his wife lying dead and badly mutilated while her baby lay where her breast had been sliced off. It was even worse for Piet du Pré who returned from hunting to find his wife and seven children had all been murdered. An Englishman who later visited a survivor of the massacre tells us that when all her relations had been killed and 'lay in a heap of confusion weltering in their blood, this poor girl fainted among the dying and the dead at the sight, and being herself covered with the blood of her kindred escaped the destruction of her nearest and dearest relatives'.

The Zulus were pursued as far as the Tugela but the Boers only recovered a fraction of the stock that the impi was driving off. The trekkers estimated that in this single night they lost 35,000 cattle and sheep, but this is almost certainly an exaggeration: the true figure probably approximates to 25,000 head. Owen while still in Zululand saw the return of the impi with thousands of head of cattle, 'but', he adds, with 'only about 15 guns'.

The Zulu attack on the sleeping encampments had been brilliantly conceived but it fell far short of complete success. The Zulus believed they had killed most of the Boer men on Kwa Matiwane and were surprised by the resistance they encountered once the initial surprise had worn off. Nor had they appreciated that the trekkers' camps were scattered westwards as far as the mountains. Dingaan had hoped for total annihilation of the white trespassers into his dominions and he could not disguise his disappointment with the night's work: 'They told me,' he grumbled to Hulley, 'there was only one camp, Retief's, and that there were only about thirty-odd men left to defend it.' Looking back on it afterwards David Lindley, one of the American missionaries in Zululand, summed up the Zulu attack critically with the remark that, 'Considering the opportunity they had, the impi accomplished very little indeed.'

But the trekkers that February would not have agreed with this conclusion. They spoke of the night's deeds as 'The Great Murder'.[5]

134

On top of the seventy men lost on Kwa Matiwane they had suffered a second near-mortal blow. Their stock losses too had been disastrous. But their rapidly organised resistance had driven off the Zulus who had too easily surrendered the initiative to the Boers. The Great Murder, one sees now, was one of those events which mark off the past from the future and in themselves set off a new train of events. For from now on it would be war to the death between the Afrikaners and Dingaan's impis.

NOTES

1 It is rather curious that the document was drawn up in English; the handwriting suggests that it was written by Jan Gerrit Bantjes.
2 King was to gain fame later for his 600-mile ride from Durban to Grahamstown to summon help for the British beleaguered in the fort.
3 The Boers always spoke of leopards as tigers, and of hyenas as wolves.
4 The wounds never healed and the boy remained a medical curiosity until his death at the age of eighteen. A tantalising contemporary account tells us that an assegai had pierced his breast and penetrated the shoulder blade, and that 'The film of the stomach remained always exposed, and when he breathed one could see the film open.'
5 Nowadays 'The Great Murder' is usually referred to as 'The Bloukrans Massacre' and it is interesting to know that during the South African war of 1899–1902 Sir Winston Churchill was captured by the Boers close to where the old blood-bath had taken place.

9

Blood River

During the Great Trek many amazing episodes occurred, but I am willing to put high on the list of their achievements the fact that the emigrants stayed on in Natal after the Great Murder. Never was the faith, courage and endurance of the Afrikaners better demonstrated than during the weeks which followed the twin massacres of Kwa Matiwane and Bloukrans.

The trekkers, scattered in their bloody wagon-camps throughout upper Natal, were plunged into a situation filled with peril and uncertainty. They were left leaderless and dispirited. The number had been literally decimated. Everyone was hungry and half out of his mind with sorrow and apprehension. The encampments were filled with desperately wounded men, orphaned children and widows. The emigrants' fighting strength had suffered particularly severely. Of the 720 men capable of carrying a musket who had descended the Berg, 116 were dead. Ammunition was depleted. Provisions were running low and much of the stock looted. And no one knew when another Zulu attack might not descend on them and overwhelm the survivors in their camps.

This was Gert Maritz's great hour; it was now that this sickly man, who had always been thought of as something of a dilettante, showed his mettle. Maritz went from camp to camp consoling the bereaved, encouraging the remaining fighting men and telling them of his plans for vengeance. A few faint-hearted Afrikaners refused to be comforted; announcing that ever since they had entered Natal things had been going wrong, they trekked back to the high veld. But the vast majority of the trekkers simply refused to abandon the country; the womenfolk were particularly intransigent; Cilliers notes that it was 'those who were the most in distress, the widows and orphans, had the least inclination to return to the Colony'. To some extent no doubt they were influenced by the fact that to go back tamely to the safety of the Cape would condemn themselves to living on charity, whereas if the trekkers remained in Natal they might in the end defeat Dingaan and regain their stolen livestock. But what weighed far more with the women was a refusal to give up the absorbing dream of living in their own independent state; they were sustained still by a deep and mystic passion for personal freedom. And somehow despite all that had happened to the *Maatschappij* its people still felt themselves to be the special favourites of Heaven whose faith now was being tested. To return over the Berg, they believed, would be to fail their loved ones lying on the slopes of Kwa Matiwane and in scattered graves along the Bloukrans and Bushman's rivers.

The sheer danger of the Voortrekkers' situation has to be constantly borne in mind at this point: for the Zulu army was intact and Dingaan must now annihilate the trekkers or face destruction himself. It was clear that the emigrants' immediate necessity was to concentrate all their wagons in a few strong defensive positions. Three great camps were accordingly set up and turned into veritable fortresses with turfed walls and loop-holed palisades. Maritz himself occupied the largest of these laagers situated on bare dusty veld overlooking the Little Tugela river near the prominent hill named Loskop; he fortified the camp with a strong wall of sods and in consequence the Boers knew it as Sooilaer.[1] The remaining members of Retief's party consolidated their positions at Doornkop. And 290 wagons lay in another near-by laager on the Gatsrand.

Messengers were then dispatched for help to the overberg Boers. Uys at Winburg responded at once and came riding down the Drakensberg passes with welcome reinforcements of men and ammunition. His intense pugnacious spirit was not so much responding to the syren-song of Natalland, as pulled now by a very real concern for the safety of his fellow countrymen. Uys was followed, with noticeably less enthusiasm, by Hendrik Potgieter and his fighting men, muttering and fretful. Other far-riding couriers pleading for men, ammunition and provisions carried the news of disaster to Port Natal and the far corners of the Colony itself. The response was such that by April 1838 David Lindley could report that the trekkers 'have eleven hundred and about fifty men who are able to go on commando, besides old men and boys who would do good service in defending their encampment'. The overberg Boers poured provisions too down to their beleaguered kinsmen in Natal, and when Jacobus Boshof's well-laden wagon rolled into one of the camps, we read that 'Tears of gratitude were seen on every cheek, while others, weeping and sighing, said "Let our faith be in the Lord, for He will deliver us".'

All thoughts were now turned to revenge. But as so often among the Boers there was dissension over the leadership of the punitive expedition which it was proposed to mount. Maritz, the obvious choice, was ill (iller than he knew for he had a scant five months to live); the fighting men from Uitenhage would only follow Piet Uys; Potgieter's people refused to serve under anyone but their own leader. In the end Maritz wearily worked out a compromise which satisfied no one: the commando would operate in two separate contingents, one under Potgieter and the other under Uys. At the same time it was arranged through envoys to Port Natal that an entirely separate force made up of British settlers from Durban supported by a motley array of armed Bantu levies would cause a diversion by invading Zululand along the coast road. It was one of those plans which are so loosely tied together that the chance of its working smoothly is almost negligible, and this one was no exception.

The combined commando of Potgieter and Uys rode out of the encampments in two separate columns on 5 and 6 April 1838. Together they numbered 347 horsemen and thus constituted by far the largest force that the trekkers so far had been able to assemble. The Zulu commander, Ndlela,[2] allowed them to ride to within a few miles of Umgungundhlovu and only stood to fight on ground of his own choosing. 'The Zulus,' lamented Francis Owen, 'selected very advantageous ground for the fight within half an hour's ride, and in sight of Umgungundhlovu, my late residence.'

Here the road to the king's 'Great Place' entered a narrow defile commanded on both sides by steep rocky hills which provided excellent cover. At its end the defile led into a valley dominated on the right by a mountain known as Italeni. Below it three Zulu regiments could be seen, and after a short conversation with Potgieter, the impetuous Uys, shouting 'Comrades, the soldiers of the murderer are there. Let us fall upon them,' led his contingent towards them at a gallop. Immediately the hills on both sides came to life with hidden Zulus who swarmed down to block the exit of the defile. At the base of Italeni Uys's men dismounted to attack the Zulus on the right, while

Potgieter, more cautiously and with his men still on horseback, moved off on the other side to engage the enemy's right flank. Unfortunately the two attacks were utterly unco-ordinated.

Uys's charge scattered the Zulus opposed to him, but his fighting men then made the mistake of splitting into several small groups, and each one was quickly surrounded when the Zulus rallied and fought back among the boulders. A wild mêlée developed in which Piet Uys and his son Dirkie were tragically killed.

To understand the course of events we cannot do better than follow the account left by Jacobus Boshof.

'Uys gallantly rushed in among the enemy,' he writes, 'with a mere handful of men and drove a whole regiment before him; but, on returning to join the rest of his men, another large body of Zulus, who had concealed themselves in the gullies on each side of him, rushed upon him and his few brave followers, and killed seven of them. By this time Potgieter had begun to retreat, and Uys and his son, a youth of about fourteen years of age, had as yet escaped unhurt; but as the former stopped his horse to sharpen the flint of his gun the enemy approached and threw an assegai at him, which wounded him mortally in the loins. He, however, pulled out the weapon, and after this he even took up another man, whose horse was knocked up, behind him; but he soon fainted from loss of blood. Recovering again, he was held on his horse for some distance by a man on each side of him. At length he said he felt his end approaching, and desired to be laid on the ground. He then said to his son and the other men about him: "Here I must die. You cannot get me any further, and there is no use to try it. Save yourselves, but fight like brave fellows to the last, and hold God before your eyes." They here left him, but not before they saw that to remain longer on the spot would be certain death to them. After galloping for about a hundred yards, the younger Uys, looking round, saw the enemy closing round his dying father in numbers, and at the same time he perceived his father lifting up his head. This was too much for the feelings of the lad: he turned round his horse, and alone rushed upon the enemy, compelled them to retreat, and shot three Zulus, before he was hemmed in by overpowering numbers and dispatched.' Nine other Boers were killed before the party managed to withdraw to safety.

In this crisis Uys's men received no assistance from the other contingent of the commando which had drawn rein at a small spruit. Potgieter, who had always before been ready for a fight, now hung back. He refused either to press in an attack on the left flank or allow his horsemen to move over to cover the retreat of the Uitenhage men. (To their credit it must be noted that sixteen of Potgieter's followers disobeyed his orders and rode to their friends' assistance.) Potgieter himself, abandoning Uys's pack horses and ammunition, led the majority of his followers on to a high hill and then rode off with them in an ignominious retreat which did not halt until it had regained the safety of the trekker camps. It was no wonder that this foray was given the derisory name of the Vlug Commando – the Flight Commando.

'One whole division of 150 men were put to shameful flight,' wrote Francis Owen, forgetting his grammar for once in his indignation, and in sober truth the story of the vlug commando was a disgrace and a painful licking to boot. Nor could the trekkers afford to lose a man of Uys's fighting calibre. Accusations of cowardice and treachery were flung in Potgieter's face, and he was infuriated by the charges; had he gone over to the attack, he said, his men would never have escaped alive from Italeni and there was a good deal of substance in what he stated. But one suspects in fact that Potgieter had discharged what he believed to be his larger loyalty by refusing to endanger his own followers in an attempt to extricate Uys from his danger. One should perhaps not criticise his attitude too much. Potgieter's heart was not in the fight for Natal. He was a clan leader by nature; and the *Maatschappij* had only recently rejected him as leader of the trek and given its allegiance instead to Piet Retief. At all events he had come now to the final parting of the ways. He argued, grumbled and sulked, and then despite all Maritz's pleas that he should not leave his fellow-countrymen in the lurch, Potgieter withdrew with his followers over the Berg. Of a sudden the lion of the north had taken on the role of an anti-hero and to the majority of the trekkers his action was the classical *dolchstoss*, the legendary stab in the back; they watched him go with sullen resentment, and an erstwhile friend who met Potgieter on his way to the high veld was doing no more than express the general feeling when he fulminated against the man who had conquered at Vegkop, Mosega and Kapain as one 'to whose treacherous and cowardly conduct the farmers attribute their defeat and the death of Uys'.

The largest commando the Boers had been so far able to gather together had been vanquished in a straight fight. But if Italeni was a severe reverse, the attack by the Port settlers on the Zulus six days later was sheer disaster.

John Cane and Robert Biggar had mustered fifteen other Englishmen and 1,100 Bantu into an indisciplined rabble of armed men which nevertheless marched under a great banner inscribed with a Montrosian 'For justice we fight'. The British fighting men referred rather splendidly to the expeditionary force as 'The Grand Army of Natal'. On 2 April 1838 when Dingaan's soldiers were concentrated near Italeni the Grand Army triumphantly plundered and burned an isolated Zulu kraal near Krantzkop. The small success was only slightly marred by the loss of two men; one died of snake-bite and the other was shot by John Cane for stealing. A few days later the ramshackle army crossed the Tugela and carried war into the enemy's country. No doubt its leaders had some idea of co-operating with the trekkers in attacking Dingaan but they were probably more interested in carrying out some cattle rustling while the impis were engaged with the Boers. Certainly most of their Bantu followers regarded the foray as a cattle raid, and everyone who could joined in: 'Many of them,' notes Lindley gloomily, 'were so old they used walking sticks' to get along.

The mob of men crossed the Tugela close to its estuary and at once attacked a kraal named Ndondakusuka. An impi of 10,000 warriors which Tambuza had hurried across country from Italeni and which was still flushed with success, was waiting for them. While one Zulu regiment moved over to cut off retreat to the river, the remainder fell on the Grand Army like a thunderbolt.

Thirteen of the seventeen Englishmen were killed in the assault. The gigantic John Cane, his pipe still clenched between his teeth when he fell, was among the dead. Only a handful of the native levies escaped the butchery which followed and managed to cross the Tugela.

One refugee ran the seventy-six miles to Port Natal with news of this disaster. Hot on his heels came the Zulu impi, and it was only by the happy circumstance that a ship had just put into the bay that the British still at the port escaped with their lives. After spending an enjoyable nine days looting and destroying everything they could find in Durban the Zulus returned to Umgungundhlovu. They could now count four victories during the past three months –

Kwa Matiwane, Bloukrans, Italeni and Ndondakusuka – and Dingaan must have congratulated himself on having dealt a succession of near-mortal blows to the white intruders into his realm.

The Boers, it must be admitted, regarded the defeat of the English on the Tugela with mixed feelings. It had at least left a vacuum at Port Natal and despite their own grievous situation a party of trekkers led by Carel Landman moved at once to occupy the port. Landman conferred the post of Landdrost on the pro-Boer Englishman Alexander Biggar, who had returned to what remained of his house after the Zulus retired.

But in that winter season of 1838 the trekkers in Natal had reached the very nadir of their fortunes. They were herded together in unsanitary laagers; food was strictly rationed and no grain would grow until the summer rains fell; there was not even enough wine for the Communion service; the remaining cattle were starving because of the small amount of grazing that lay out of reach of prowling Zulus; saddle horses were in bad condition and only a few were fit enough to go out on commando; ammunition was perilously short; the response to requests for reinforcements had lately been disappointing; and worst of all the Zulu menace still hung like a doom over the camps. It was scarcely surprising that the men's morale had fallen to a dangerously low level.

The crisis came in August when an impi of 10,000 warriors was seen approaching the camp on Gatsrand; this time some of the Zulus were armed with muskets taken during the fights with the emigrants. One eye-witness found the 'kafir hordes terrible to see. I cannot describe their numbers; for one would think that all heathendom had assembled to destroy us.' For the next two days the Zulus encircled the laager, firing at it with their captured guns and skirmishing up to the wagons. Each day several serious attacks had to be driven off. The nights were even more terrifying. The warriors fired the surrounding veld and hurled burning assegais into the wagon tilts. The seventy-five white men fought back doing great execution with their *snaphaans* and a 3-lbr cannon, and we catch one vivid glimpse of conditions inside the laager from a description of the womenfolk who stood by with hatchets ready to cut off any black hands trying to untie the *riems* holding the wagons together. The Boers made several counter attacks on horseback, but the Zulus refused to give way; again and again they rallied and came back into the murderous fire from the laager, each charge becoming just a little feebler than the last; it was not until the third day, 15 August, that the impi finally moved off, carrying with it large cattle herds and leaving behind 'a thick bank of dead and dying'. Many of the defenders of Gatsrand had been wounded but only one of them lost his life.

Gatsrand after its defence was proudly renamed Veglaer – the fight laager. The action had proved again that from prepared positions the emigrants could withstand the entire Zulu army. But in some ways the trekkers' condition was now worse than ever. The stink of putrefaction made it essential to abandon Veglaer and its people moved across country to a site on the Little Tugela opposite Sooilaer. Then a different sort of disaster struck at the Voortrekkers of Natal; their leader Gert Maritz died at Sooilaer on 23 September, sighing with his last breath 'like Moses I have seen the promised land, but shall not dwell in it'.

The trekkers all this time had succeeded in keeping the road open to Port Natal, and it says a great deal for their courage and faith that at this time of universal gloom a venturesome party, that October in 1838, began to lay out a new settlement on the Umsindusi stream: they named it Pietermaritzburg to commemorate their two dead leaders. It was to become their capital.

That same month a ship put into Port Natal loaded with all sorts of provisions for the trekkers which had been sent by 'some liberal-minded countrymen of theirs at the Cape'. Now the emigrants luxuriated in ample supplies of sugar, rice, coffee, tea and spices which for so long had been denied to them. And as though this was a signal of better times to come gentle rain began to fall and green grass appeared by magic on the over-grazed veld around the camps. Finally on the morning of 22 November 1838[3] there was a great stir in the encampments as sixty burghers with a brass cannon rode into Sooilaer. They were led by a heavily-armed man who Erasmus Smit thought looked like a 'well-equipped, sabred and pistolled dragoon'. It was Andries Pretorius. The Great Trek had a happy knack of turning out new leaders at a critical time; Pretorius was one of them, and now with his arrival in Natal, the last leading actor of its cast had arrived on the stage.

From that morning until the day of his death fifteen years later Andries Pretorius no less than Potgieter dominates the trekkers' story. It is as well, therefore, if we pause here and take note of this man who brought the Afrikaner exodus to its successful conclusion.

Andries Pretorius at the time of his arrival in Natal was in his late thirties. Like Maritz he had grown up in Graaff Reinet, but he was a farmer at heart and as it turned out a successful one too so that he quickly became a man of wealth and consequence. For some years he had toyed with the idea of trekking from the Colony: in 1837 he paid a visit to the emigrant camps in Transorangia and served as a volunteer under Potgieter during the expedition to Kapain. Afterwards he rode into Natal with news of Potgieter's success, and he was greatly impressed by what he saw of the country.

Back at Graff Reinet Pretorius had received a deputation of Natalians during the April of 1838 which entreated him to lead reinforcements to Natal, but it was not until several months had passed that some inspiration of patriotism or ambition suggested to him that he might play a larger part in the Voortrekker drama, and he finally obeyed the summons. When in the October of 1838 he fitted out a convoy of sixty-eight wagons and headed north, a key piece of the Great Trek had dropped into its proper place. At the Modder river Pretorius learned how desperate were the straits of the beleaguered trekkers following the death of Maritz, and he hurried on ahead of his wagons with sixty horsemen. At the same time he was sure enough of his reception to send messengers to each of the trekker encampments asking for all possible fighting men to concentrate at Sooilaer armed and prepared to take the field.

He was received at Sooilaer with relief and something approaching rapture as well. Here was a man who had the gift of making fine phrases which perfectly expressed the trekkers' aspirations. He had not been involved in the bitter schisms of the past two years, and above all others he could replace the leaders that had been lost – Retief and Uys, Maritz and Potgieter, and unite the *Maatschappij* once more. And this ready-made hero proceeded to go about the task with efficiency and supreme self-confidence.

We know more about Pretorius than we do of the other trek leaders. In appearance he tended to an imposing portliness and carried a small paunch in a stately sort of way as though it was filled with securities and bank drafts. (A disrespectful English soldier, varying the simile, tells us that the Commandant-General 'is about six feet high and has a belly on him like a bass drum'.) Africans, however, who have an uncanny knack of picking out a man's most significant characteristics ignored his corporation and nick-named Pretorius 'Ngalonkulu' – brawny arms.

Pretorius's approach to the people he led was persuasive rather than self-assertive, that of a politician who knows how and when to use his charm; indeed he had about him something of the guile of men whom Afrikaners describe as being 'slim'. Sir Harry Smith who was no mean judge of character summed up Andries Pretorius as 'a shrewd and sensible man', but on occasion Pretorius could surprise everybody by bouts of unreasonable petulance which were all the more effective in getting his own way because they were so rarely exhibited. We have a portrait of Pretorius posing a little stiffly for the artist about this time; here his curious blend of phlegm and flame comes out very well in the expression on the clean-shaven, handsome face, and looking at it today one remains uncertain whether he is on the point of despair or fury.

Above everything else Pretorius was a hard worker, concerned with every detail of government (which the trek-leaders in the past had tended to ignore), a crisply efficient organiser, and, as he was about to demonstrate, a very competent military tactician.

Pretorius had been at Sooilaer no time at all before he began to get action: within a week of his arrival he had been elected Commandant-General of the trekkers and had set about the mustering of a commando which was to carry vengeance into Zululand. The previous attempts to deal with Dingaan had been bedevilled by the leaders' jealousies; now for the first time the burghers were to serve under a single commander. Late in November, after Erasmus Smit had preached to them from the appropriate text 'O Lord, defer not and do; defer not for Thy names Sake', Pretorius's commando pulled out of Sooilaer. When it had united with Landman's contingent from the Port his fighting force numbered nearly five hundred white men, and they were well supplied with stores and ammunition carried in more than sixty wagons. In addition over a hundred native levies under Alexander Biggar served with them. The Boers' fire power was enormously enhanced by three small muzzle-loading cannon of $2\frac{1}{2}$-inch bore which were mounted on crude undercarriages. The fighting men were divided into five separate divisions, each with its own commandant, and instead of the old dissensions Pretorius got on famously with them all. He established a proper chain of command to replace the old method in which groups of men only took orders from leaders of their own choice. Officers were distinguished by wearing pistols in their belts. Discipline was tightened up and although the men might grumble that their commander was something of a martinet, morale remained remarkably high.

It was now that the Boers really learned what it was to be commanded by Pretorius. Every evening during the approach march the wagons were pulled into a great circle, the gaps between them closed with ladders, and sentries were carefully posted. One man in the column noted with surprised approval the way in which the new Commandant-General 'ordered that the camp should be properly enclosed, and the gates well secured, after the cattle should be within the same, and that the night patrols should be properly set out; all of which was executed with the greatest activity and readiness'.

The strategy of Pretorius was simple enough. He intended to march directly on Umgungundhlovu until his patrols made contact with the Zulu army. Then he would seek a strong defensive position and invite attack from behind a wagon-laager; there was to be no repetition of the impetuous charge on the enemy like the one at Italeni which had run into ambush.

The commando passed the site of modern Ladysmith without incident, and a little farther on were entertained to a display of dancing by a friendly chief near the Sundays river at a place which accordingly was named Danskraal. On 9 December 1838 it camped on the banks of the Wasbank river, so called for the large flat stones on its banks which lent themselves to clothes washing. All during the march Sarel Cilliers had felt in his element. Erasmus Smit had been left behind, and if Andries Pretorius was the unrivalled secular leader of the commando there was no one to dispute its spiritual direction with Cilliers. Every evening it was he who conducted divine service, and rounded off the eloquent prayers and fervent psalm-singing with a lengthy sermon. His mind was filled with the risks and importance of the commando's tasks and he frequently discussed with Pretorius and the section commanders some way of commending their cause to God. He had in mind their collectively making a vow to God like those offered by the Bible saints and this led to an important event in Afrikaner history.

We can perhaps best follow what next occurred from a description left by one of the Boers on commando, J. G. Bantjes:

'On Sunday morning, before divine service commenced,' he writes, 'the Chief Commandant called together all those who were to perform that service, and requested them to propose to the congregation that they should all fervently, in spirit and in truth, pray to God for His relief and assistance in their struggle with the enemy; that he wanted to make a vow to God Almighty if they were all willing, that should the Lord be pleased to grant us the victory, we should raise a house to the memory of His great name, wherever it might please him, and that they should also supplicate the aid and assistance of God to enable them to fulfil their vow; and that we would note the day of the victory in a book, to make it known even to our latest posterity, in order that it might be celebrated to the honour of God: Cilliers, Landman, and Joubert were glad in their minds to hear it. They spoke to their congregations on the subject, and obtained their general concurrence. When after this divine service commenced, Mr Cilliers performed that which took place in the tent of the chief commandant. He commenced by singing from Psalm xxxviii, verses 12–16, then delivered a prayer, and preached about the twenty-four first verses of the book of Judges; and thereafter delivered the prayer in which the before-mentioned vow to God was made, with fervent supplication for the Lord's aid and assistance in the fulfilment thereof. The 12th and 21st verses of the said xxxviii Psalm were again sung, and the service was concluded with the singing of the cxxxiv Psalm. In the afternoon the congregations assembled again, and several appropriate verses were sung. Mr Cilliers again made a speech, and delivered prayers solemnly; and in the same manner the evening was also spent.'

It seems that the original vow was made at Danskraal and then repeated at services held on subsequent days, one of them being at Wasbank. We learn too that Cilliers conducted his services in the open air mounted on one of the cannons, and there with his congregation gathered before him and the mountains standing like a line of witnesses in the north, the trekkers daily entered into their solemn compact that if God granted them a victory over the Zulus they would build a church and keep the day of battle as one of thanksgiving for ever.

It is interesting to note that Alexander Biggar[4] and the other Englishmen in the commando joined in making the vow, but that five Boers abstained for fear of God's vengeance on their descendants if in years to come they broke the promise.

On 14 December the commando came up to a saddle-back hill named Gelato, and while the men rested their horses, Pretorius reconnoitred ahead, seeking a favourable site from which to offer battle to the Zulu army which was reported to be coming up. He found it just to the east of Gelato (soon to be renamed Vegkop) where a deep donga or sluyt, fourteen feet deep and fourteen feet across but yet

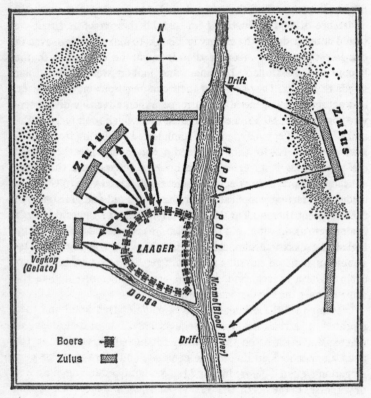

Diagram of the battle of Blood River

invisible from the plain, ran at an angle into the Ncome river and carried storm water into it. Just above this junction the river widened out into a long deep pool overgrown with weeds and a favourite haunt of hippopotami; the river here could only be forded at two drifts, one at either end of the pool. The angle between this hippo pool and the donga provided a perfect defensive position. It was so effectively protected on two sides that the Zulus could in practice only attack it directly from the north-west, and as they advanced they would of necessity be funnelled into a solid concentration which must be murderously exposed to the Boers' fire.

Cilliers saw the hand of God in the provision of such a stronghold, and later on he wrote, 'I must particularly mention how the Lord, in his watchfulness over us, brought us to the place where he had ordained the battle to be fought.'

Later that misty afternoon the Boers formed up their sixty-four wagons in the V made by the river and the donga. The laager was roughly triangular in shape, with two sides overlooking these natural obstacles and some seventy yards from them, while the third side arched out towards the north-west and stretched in a crescent-shape across the open tongue of land. The wagons were chained together securely, ladders were fastened across the spaces between them and skins stretched tightly over their wheels. Four openings were left in the laager's wall which could all be quickly closed by wagon-gates. The larger opening was intended, when the Zulu host drew near, to admit the horses and trek-oxen, numbering well over a thousand beasts, into the laager; the smaller 'gates' provided emplacements for the Afrikaners' cannons. The gun which Pretorius had brought to Natal was placed to the north-east; the second gun commanded the junction of the sluyt with the river; and the third, known affectionately as *ou Grietjie,* stood at the westerly end; today it occupies a place of honour near the Voortrekker monument at Pretoria. Next day, 15 December, after a brief skirmish with Zulu scouts, and satisfied that everything that should have been done to the laager had been done, Pretorius took out a strong patrol to make contact with the enemy. He encountered them, a menacing dark cloud of 15,000 men, in the Nqutu hills and watched the impi falling back in an attempt to draw him towards Italeni as though anxious to repeat the tactics which had defeated the Vlug Commando. It was a stimulating thing to see the Zulu main army at last, and Cilliers, who was always as ready to fall on his foes as to fall on his knees, was all for attacking it at once. But Pretorius was coolness itself: 'Do not let us go to them,' he said. 'Let them come to us.' Although annoyed at the time Cilliers later had the grace to admit that 'afterwards I saw that it was for the best that we had done nothing that day', and he adds

149

rather foggily, 'for the Lord hath said "My counsel shall remain. I will fulfil my desires".'

One can imagine Ndlela calling his commanders together once he had appreciated that Pretorius was refusing battle and that the well-tried Zulu plan for an ambuscade must be abandoned. The next few moments were in a sense the most significant in the whole course of the Great Trek. Ndlela knew perfectly well from his scouts that the Boers had set up a base laager on the banks of the Ncome, and with hindsight one can see now that in this situation which was as fluid as mercury a splendid opportunity lay open to him: he could throw his impi round the laager until hunger, thirst or even the boredom of sheer inaction drove the Boers to attempt a break out. But such thinking did not suit the Zulu way of fighting and Ndlela instead made a tactical error of the first magnitude: he decided that he would attack the laager directly and do so that very night. Orders went out for his regiments to make a forced march in the wake of the retreating Boers and storm their laager before dawn. The plan might have worked had the march not been so long, or the night so pitch dark and foggy that the regiments repeatedly lost themselves, or the Ncome unexpectedly in flood. As it was, during the dismal hours before dawn Ndlela was able to pass no more than 5,000 men across the river, and sunrise caught him with his army divided in two.

While the main body was coming up to the eastern banks of the Ncome the impi's forward elements spent the last hours of the night close to the Boer wagons and with some warriors huddled in the donga, all vastly awed by the eerie light shed by the lanterns which the Boers had strung up over the wagons, and even more by the deep-throated singing of psalms and hymns which arose a few hundred yards away from behind the wagon-wall. They had not the heart to make an assault in the darkness and the magnificent opportunity which was open to them fled with the morning's lightening skies.

The Boers had stood to their guns long before dawn, fearful that a ground mist would have formed as it had done during the past few days and allow the enemy to conceal their final approach. They were puzzled as they waited by a noise like a distant rain until someone called out that it was made by the warriors rattling their assegais against cow-hide shields to drum up courage before battle. For now when the advanced Zulus should have waited until the whole of their army was concentrated near the laager, those regiments which had crossed the river regained their courage with daybreak and impulsively decided to put in their attack at once. What this meant of course was that the Zulus were beginning the battle when the majority of their soldiers were still separated from the Boers by a flooded river which could only be crossed with difficulty at two widely separated drifts. Nothing could have been more likely to lead to disaster. As an example of martial courage the Zulu attack which followed on that Sunday morning could not have been excelled, but as an example of the employment of military tactics it was deplorable and suicidal.

As the air began to smell of morning the white men watched the pattern of flat-topped thorn-trees on the hills across the river starting to show against the eastern sky, and listened to the birds which began to give chorus before setting off on their daily quest for seeds and insects. Then the sun's rim broke free from the horizon, tinting the surrounding hills with red so that the entire landscape for a few moments seemed to be drenched in blood. And the Boers saw with relief that the weather had cleared. 'Sunday, the 16th,' one of them recalled afterwards, 'was a day as if ordained for us. The sky was open, the weather clear and bright.'

In the spreading light a solid mass of black humanity was seen only a few hundred yards away and racing towards the wagons. At once the Boer guns and cannons opened with a roar. It was impossible for a single shot to miss such a target. Never at any time was there a hope that this attack would succeed. The shock of the concentrated fire was devastating and almost at once the first wave of Zulus reeled back in disorder. Then for two mortal hours these regiments mounted a wild chain of doomed charges on the north and west faces of the laager and one after the other they were smashed and flattened. It was a strange and horrifying scene, and the painting which the artist W. H. Coetzer made of it is perhaps the most celebrated of all the pictures of the Voortrekker saga.

Commandant Visser remembered afterwards 'we fired chiefly slug shots. Although nearly every one of us had two or three guns, the barrels had then become hot from constant firing.' Because of the noise and the heat beating into their brains none of the Boers seemed afterwards to remember many details of the battle, and although in later years the action would be carefully chronicled, their accounts differ widely and it is still difficult for us to comprehend what really happened on the banks of the Ncome river that day in 1838. As one reads about it everything dissolves into a confused impression of a death-grapple that might go on for ever; each man is isolated within his own separate fight, lost in the blinding choking fog of blue powder, hammered down by the deafening noise, dazzled by the evil little spurts of fire around him. One eye-witness named Bezuidenhout recalled that 'Of that fight nothing remains in my memory except shouting and tumult and lamentation, and a sea of black faces; and a dense smoke that rose straight as a plumb line upwards from the ground.'

Each charge was followed by a lull with the battle smoke hanging in the thin morning air, during which the fighting regiments received a trickle of reinforcements from across the river, and the only noise was the rattling of spears on shields, the shuffling of naked feet on the ground as the warriors nerved themselves for another rush, and the moaning of the wounded.

The Boers' chief peril came from the hundreds of cattle and horses crowded inside the laager. The terrible and mounting clamour of battle maddened them; the beasts wheeled about in panic and threatened to break through the wagon-line towards the donga and river. Cilliers seems to have been the first to appreciate the danger; he promptly led some men to the southern flank of the laager and began firing into the dense mass of Zulus crowded within the donga. The din, as was intended, drove the cattle back into the centre of the laager, but the raking of the sluyt also did dreadful execution. Here indeed the worst killing of the entire action took place The very number of Zulus there was a disadvantage: they stood so tightly packed together that they were unable to climb the steep sides, unable even to throw their assegais, and when Cilliers called for volunteers to leave the shelter of the wagons and approach the donga every single warrior who stood there was shot dead.

As the initial Zulu attacks became weaker and weaker Ndlela's division on the eastern bank of the river was preparing to enter the battle. Now the guns were turned on this new target and the pounding they gave the Zulus seemed to act as a spur: it sent a mass of warriors racing through the drifts to join in the assault. The Boers coming out of the laager lined the river bank and drove them back with rapid fire. But even now Ndlela held back 3,000 of his crack soldiers, the White and Black shields, to make a final assault when the Boer fire showed signs of slackening.

He had good cause for being patient. Pretorius was sniffing trouble and becoming concerned that his ammunition would not hold out much longer. He decided he must resolve the issue by going over to the offensive. In risking a charge from the laager the Commandant-General was taking a calculated chance, but he reasoned that it was better to counter-attack now than wait until every bullet was spent. His anxiety is reflected in his dispatch. 'You will scarcely be able to form an idea of the sight presented around us,' he wrote, 'it was such as to require some nerve not to betray uneasiness in the countenance. Seeing that it was necessary to display the most desperate determination, I caused four gates of our enclosed encampment to be simultaneously thrown open, from whence some mounted men were to charge the enemy; at the same time keeping a heavy fire on them.'

So the wagons were wheeled back to provide the openings in the laager, and two successive cavalry charges went in a thundering yelling gallop across the open ground to the north. Both failed to break the Zulus. A third attack from the western face, however, was more successful. Three hundred horsemen drove a solid wedge into the Zulus on the left, riding them down, firing as they went, and they cut the impi into two. The warriors at last began to waver, and now the game was in Pretorius's hands. It was not yet mid-morning.

Led by the Commandant-General himself the greater part of his force now deployed north and south along both banks of the Ncome, shooting down the Zulus who approached or tried to hide among its reeds. These warriors could only cower helplessly in the water as the Boers came riding slowly down the banks, picking them off at leisure. The water was deeply stained that morning with their life-blood, and ever since the Ncome has gone by the name of Blood river. Some of the Boers believed that far more Zulus were drowned at Blood river than shot to death.

Only now did Ndlela fling his last reserves into battle. It was too late. The legendary 3,000 men of the Black shields and the White shields raced for the drifts; there was a final flare-up of firing from the Boers who by now were lining the river bank, and Dingaan's crack regiments were carried away by the mass of warriors escaping from the carnage; they were quite unable to affect the issue of the fight, and in a queer, slow stumbling flight, because they were simply too tired to run fast, an immense disorganised rabble of men streamed off in defeat in every direction with the Boer horsemen in pursuit.

The firing died away in the distance, and suddenly the drama of Blood river was over. Not a single warrior was to be seen on his feet: Jan Uys noted that 'In the space of about 400 yards square they counted 400 dead Caffirs' [sic] and one can imagine with what elation Cilliers stared around him at one of the most tragic and moving tableaux of the Great Trek and in a well-remembered remark noted that the dead lay around the laager as 'thick on the ground as pump-kins on a fertile piece of garden land'.

It had been a remarkable demonstration of fire-power over naked bravery. The number of Zulus killed at Blood river was estimated by Pretorius to have totalled '3,000 and some hundreds'. Yet not a single Boer had been killed, and only three wounded during the pursuit: one of them was Pretorius himself who had been pierced through the wrist by an assegai which had severed his radial artery.

The wheel of retribution had turned full-circle; Retief and the women and children of the Great Murder had been avenged. Curi-ously too the story of the struggle on the high veld had been almost faithfully repeated: as before, the trekkers' encounter with a Bantu military empire had begun with a massacre and now it had ended in signal revenge.

Pretorius allowed the pursuit to go on for most of what remained of the day and it was ten o'clock that night before the last weary horseman came back into the laager. Long before this Cilliers had conducted the mandatory service of thanksgiving. The Voortrekkers had good reason to be content with the day's work. It seemed now that Natal would be theirs after all. They had no inkling that already British red-coats had landed at Port Natal, and there on that very day would run up the Union Jack. No sooner had one enemy been dis-posed of (although they knew it not) than another one had appeared out of the sea.

For Pretorius the day of battle ended with his sending two cap-tured Zulus off to Dingaan carrying a white cloth on to which he had inscribed his name as a form of *laisser passer*, together with a verbal offer of peace on the terms of indemnity he had communicated before. It takes very little imagination for the mind's eye to visualise with what contentment then that night the Commandant-General climbed into his wagon and threw himself down to sleep.

The march to Umgungundhlovu was renewed after a day's rest during which the commando waited to see whether Ndlela would have another try. Then on 19 December its triumphant horsemen spattered across the Umhlatuzi river without opposition and came up towards the king's 'Great Place'. It was unfortunate that at this point one of the more high-spirited members of the party 'thoughtlessly shot at a crow', for we read from the account of one man on commando that 'not ten minutes afterwards the whole town and palace were in flames'. We know now that Dingaan had lingered in the town with his seraglio after the battle of Blood river, still hoping perhaps to come to terms with its victors. This chance shot frightened him and changed his mind. Waiting only to give orders for Umgungundhlovu to be fired, the king fled precipitately. Next day the commando rode into the deserted burnt-out town, and were drawn as though by invisible hands to the hill of Kwa Matiwane. They were appalled by what they saw there: from now on its name for Afrikaners would conjure up visions of death and deep shadows, a sinister name which carried a shudder with it: the corpses of the men who had died with Piet Retief lay mouldering on the rocky slopes together with hundreds of kerries which had been used to batter them to death. The bodies had been mummified by the sun, their faces burned to the colour of tanned leather, the bared teeth grinning fiendishly, fingers dried out into lacey claws which seemed to clutch at the polluted air. Most men had died from having their skulls shattered; many had been impaled after death. 'Their hands and feet,' Cilliers saw, 'were still bound fast with thongs of ox hide, and in nearly all the corpses a spike as thick as an arm had been forced into the anus so that the point of the spike was in the chest.' Retief's body was identified by a satin vest he had worn, and also by a leather pouch still hanging from a bony shoulder; inside it was the document by which Dingaan more than ten months before had ceded Natal to the trekkers. The way in which their title deed to the land had been preserved seemed like a sign to the Boers: 'The Papers were in as good a state of preservation,' gasped one of them, that they might have been 'left in a closed box'. Reverently the poor remains of their kinsmen and friends were gathered together and interred in a common grave.

The commando settled down that night close to the hill of Hlomo Amubuta, but after four days it moved a few miles to the south-east on to a high ridge overlooking the White Umfolozi, prepared there to celebrate Christmas and the New Year while waiting like Napoleon at Moscow, for a king's submission. If this was not forthcoming they proposed to gather in all the royal cattle before leaving. There was some concern expressed about the way armed Zulus were taking up positions on the neighbouring hills, and fearing that they would rally there and return to the attack, patrols were repeatedly sent out to keep an eye on the warriors; one of them brought back an ingratiating captive who said he would lead the Boers to a near-by ravine in which Dingaan's herds were hidden. Pretorius swallowed the tempting bait and issued orders for a mounted foray. He wanted nothing more complex than some cattle-booty and to stir up a good fight. He got his fight but failed to get the cattle. Two days after Christmas the Commandant-General led out this force of 300 white men supported by about 100 of Biggar's African levies. Almost at once his wounded wrist began hurting badly, and Pretorius turned over the command to Carel Landman with a warning against being ambushed: 'Landman,' Pretorius is reported to have said to his big shaggy companion before he rode off, 'place your scouts well forward on both sides of the patrol.' Whether Landman actually heard this admonition is a question; if he did he very quickly forgot about it.

So far everything during the Blood river expedition had worked out with a precision that is the rarest of all occurrences in military affairs. But now as the horsemen rode north-east they entered a winding defile leading towards a drift across the White Umfolozi; beyond it they could see open ground dominated by an isolated koppie. Large herds of cattle were grazing there and the men eagerly pressed forward. They were riding straight into a trap which bore an uncanny resemblance to the one prepared at Italeni.

As they cantered forward thousands of plumed warriors suddenly appeared along the hills on both sides of the defile, effectively cutting off their retreat; other regiments could be seen converging on the drift. Even the 'cattle' that had been seen on the open ground beyond turned out to be soldiers crouching under their ox-hide shields. Realising that they were in serious trouble, all Landman could think of was to take up a position on the conical hill in front and fight it out with the Zulus. But his second-in-command, Hans de Lange, had a better sense of tactics: 'Verdomp,' he shouted, 'look at the kafirs, how many do you think there are? How many can we kill, and for what length of time can our powder and lead last us against such an immense number? It is certain death for us to go on to that hill. Forward men, forward. He who loves me follows me.'

In a wild *sauve qui peut* de Lange led the commando off at a gallop, fighting off the Zulus as they crossed the drift and passed the koppie, and he only paused after a mile or two to consider the situation again.

It was an alarming one. The enemy was closing in and the commando had been weakened when sixty of its number had seen an opening in the Zulu ranks and cantered off to safety.[5] By now the remaining Boers were no longer a compact body of fighting men: they had separated into anxious little groups which were badly rattled by their narrow escape and concerned now that they were cut off from their base by an exultant army of savages. After holding a hasty council it was decided to cast out in a wide circle upstream to the north-west and only then search for a drift to recross the Umfolozi. There followed a terrifying ride of fifteen miles. The Zulus' pursuit was relentless; some of them were mounted on captured horses and in any case a running warrior could keep up with a horseman in this rough country. Even when they fell back the Boers would be harried all over again by fresh groups of Zulus. Time after time a gallant rearguard of twenty or thirty men would turn to beat off the enemy in wild flurries of hand-to-hand fighting. It was 3 p.m. before the disordered mob of horsemen found what looked like a drift across the river, and now they were daunted by the sight of hundreds of Zulus converging on them to contest the crossing. Hampered by quicksands in the river bed, six more white men were killed at this drift, among them Alexander Biggar who had ridden up to Zululand to avenge the death of his two sons. Biggar's levies suffered here far more severely: seventy are said to have died on the banks of the White Umfolozi.

Pretorius sent fresh men and horses out to assist the broken commando and that evening the survivors rode into camp grey-faced and stupid with fatigue; all in all they were lucky to come out of the affair alive. Had they been fifteen minutes later at the second drift not one of them would have escaped. The unhappy Landman was much

157

blamed for the débâcle; his companions rather unfairly dismissed him as 'a good old man who could never see danger'.

Following this setback the commando waited at the laager near Umgungundhlovu for a few more days to rest the knocked-up horses. Then, since there was no sign of the Zulus being enticed from their hilly strongholds, three great kraals near by were burned and the Boers withdrew. Despite the losses suffered during Landman's foray they could still congratulate themselves on the victory at Blood river, and felt justified in naming their expeditionary force the 'Wen Commando'. But they had failed to capture Dingaan, the Zulu army though badly mauled still lived and moved, and their haul of cattle was disappointing, certainly far less than the Zulus had swept away from them over the past year. 'One of the chief objects of the commando,' dryly commented a British spokesman, 'viz. the capture of cattle, was not effected, for a few horses and twenty-five muskets seem to have been the only spoils.' Landman was quite discredited; Andries Pretorius who had been spared involvement in the near disaster on the White Umfolozi was the only man on the expedition to carry a bigger reputation back into Sooilaer than he had taken out: from now on he was regarded by the trekkers as a lion-hearted soldier, wise beyond his years, and a hero in the mould of an Old Testament prophet.

Even as the commando rode slowly back towards the encampments on the Upper Tugela, it was disturbed by rumours that British soldiers had established themselves at Port Natal. A hundred redcoats had indeed been landed at the Port two weeks before Blood river and although so small a number could be swept into the sea without much difficulty, the Boers knew that the contingent was backed by the hated colonial Government at the Cape and, in the last resort, by the entire might of an Empire which only a generation before had defeated the great Napoleon. The home-coming of the Wen Commando ended then on a note of anti-climax, and one can sympathise with Sarel Cilliers when he reached his wagon at the end of all these stirring adventures and wrote angrily 'On arriving there we were very much put out by the receipt of a proclamation from the British Government in which we were told that if we went to Dingaan's country and took up arms against him, it would assist Dingaan against us.'

1 Throughout this book I have used the generic word laager for a fortified camp. The less familiar *laer* is closer to the trekkers' usage and has been retained in the names given to their various camps.

2 The trekkers had considerable respect for Ndlela's fighting reputation which was somehow enhanced by their knowledge that he was an ex-cannibal.

3 The date is disputed: some authorities place the arrival of Pretorius at the camps as early as 2 November 1838.

4 One day Biggar's wagon overturned while traversing a mountain range; the Boers immortalised the incident by naming the mountains the Biggarsberg.

5 These men had the grace to feel ashamed of their desertion and did not care to show their faces in the Boer camp until the following day.

Natalia

One cannot help feeling it to be extremely unfair that when after much anguish and grief the Voortrekkers had at last secured their position in Natal, it was immediately threatened by the *rooineks*.[1] For a new British governor at the Cape had resolved on a military occupation of Durban.

From the very beginning of the Great Trek the colonial authorities had shown concern about the way Cape Colony was being denuded of wealth and people. As Sir Benjamin D'Urban pointed out a little petulantly to Whitehall, 'It is a matter of deep regret that a large proportion of the farmers who have emigrated are of the oldest and most respectable of the districts to which they belonged, and are in themselves, as a brave, patient, industrious, orderly and religious people, an incalculable loss to the Colony in whatever way they may be regarded – whether as the cultivators, the defenders, or the tax-contributors of the country which they have quitted, and from which they have naturally carried away all their property and possessions, as well as such movables as of cattle, sheep and horses.'

But the counter-measures which had been taken were both timid and vacillating. Admittedly the promulgation of the Cape of Good Hope Punishment Act in 1836 had implied that the emigrants could not unilaterally dissolve their allegiance to the Crown and that Britain might still legally assert her authority over them below the 25th degree of latitude South, but no attempt had been made to apply these provisions. This was a law without teeth, and it certainly had done nothing to prevent the best type of settler from leaving the Colony.

But a more forward slant to government thinking became apparent in 1838 after Sir George Napier had replaced D'Urban at the Cape. He was concerned less with the weakening of the Colony by the massive Afrikaner emigration than with the treatment the trekkers might mete out to the Africans whose land they were in the process of appropriating, and he feared too that disturbances would follow which might involve the Cape's eastern frontier. He believed it to be in British interests to conclude a peace between the Boers and Dingaan, and, moved by humanitarian motives rather than political reasons, Napier on his own initiative made up his mind to occupy Durban. This step would provide him with a position of strength from which to act as mediator, and it would embarrass the Afrikaners. 'One of my principal motives in taking possession of Natal,' the Governor explained later, 'was to mark my disapproval of the emigrants' proceedings by throwing such impediments in their way as I could.' For by controlling their only supply port Napier believed he could bring effective pressure to bear on the trekkers, and persuade them against continuing the struggle with the Zulus.

Accordingly Napier sent a Major Samuel Charters with 100 Highlanders of the 72nd regiment by sea to Port Natal and they landed there without opposition on 4th December 1838. Twelve days later, after building a fort, and while the battle of Blood river was actually in progress, Charters ran up the Union Jack amid 'tremendous firing both of great guns and small arms'. Afterwards the British officer retired to the Mess tent to drink the Queen's health and toast absent friends. There was no question at the time of annexing Natal: Charters was careful to stress in a proclamation that his occupation of land was limited to two miles from the 'sinuosities of the bay'.

The news of this military occupation greeted the Wen Commando on its return from Umgungundhlovu at the close of 1838 and it was enough to set Cilliers writing sepulchrally that 'again another calamity was waiting for us'. For here again were the perfidious British dipping their fingers into the trekkers' affairs, and he could only console himself with the comforting thought that the Highlanders had arrived too late to prevent the Boer victory at Blood river. For Cilliers goes on to say that despite his people's concern 'We thanked our Lord God. The battle had been fought.'

It was noted too with relief that the British had refrained from outright annexation of Natal, and the Boers decided to ignore the soldiers drilling at the coast and draw up a constitution for their new republic as though they did not exist. They named the country Natalia and elected a Volksraad of twenty-four elected members to govern it. The unpopular Charters, the Boers were happy to see, did not stay long at the port: he very soon handed over his command to the placatory Captain Henry Jervis who made it plain that he was far more interested in acting as a mediator between the Boers and the Zulus than with contesting Afrikaner rule in Natalia. Dingaan, who by now had established himself on the Vuna river, turned out to be reasonably conciliatory too: he professed himself agreeable to return all the stock stolen from the trekkers and to recognise the Tugela as the boundary between Natalia and Zululand. At the same time the Natalians, despite Jervis's appeals, refused to renew their allegiance to the British Crown, and Pretorius declared that if necessary he would fight to protect their independence. Napier was getting precious little support at the time from the Imperial Government and in the face of such intransigence he had to give way. Orders were sent to Jervis instructing him to withdraw from the port, and at Christmas time in 1839 the red-coats sailed away.

The Natalians naturally regarded this evacuation as the final abandonment by Great Britain of any claim to Natal. Durban was reoccupied and the Bay resounded again to the noise of gunfire as the horsemen rode in from Pietermaritzburg, fired off a ragged volley and hoisted the flag of the Natalian republic. Its colours were described rather obscurely as being 'similar to the Dutch but placed transversely instead of horizontally'. In fact it was made up of red, white and blue triangles, with the white one on the outer edge.

Even during the time of the first British occupation of Durban the Natalian Boers had eagerly spread out through the country between the Tugela and the Umzinkulu (and, obeying their trekker instincts even beyond these, their republic's boundaries). Farms were marked out; townships were established at Pietermaritzburg which was nominated as the capital, at Congella close to the Bay of Natal, and at Weenen – Weeping – near the site of the Bloukrans massacre. For now with the British gone the Natalian Government began to act with more confidence. Pretorius, whose dream it was to reunite the trekker communities, rode up the Drakensburg to confer with the overberg Boers and he persuaded not only the settlers of Transorangia but even the reluctant Potgieter to agree to a loose form of political federation under the hegemony of Natalia. It was decided that local matters in Potgieter's fief, which was based on his twin 'capitals' of Winburg and Potchefstroom, should be dealt with by an 'adjunkraad' but that it should be represented too by delegates in the Natalian Volksraad. It seemed that the old dream of a united Afrikaner Empire with an outlet on the Indian Ocean had been realised, and throughout 1840 and 1841 there were high hopes that Great Britain would grant recognition to the United Voortrekker republic.

Pretorius presently even felt strong enough to retire the troublesome Erasmus Smit; the pastor and his mournful air disappear from now on into an abyss of intemperance, and his place as spiritual leader of the trekkers is taken by the more presentable David Lindley whose missionary work among the Zulus had proved to be unrewarding. Lindley held his services in the church built during 1841 in Pietermaritzburg (where eighty houses were now standing) in fulfilment of the vow made during the anxious days before Blood river.

There was a wonderful sense of achievement and spaciousness about Natalia during the first months of its existence, but it must be admitted that events did not go entirely smoothly in the new republic. The Volksraad went about its business slowly and with a delightful air of impromptu. Nor would the Boers have been true Boers had they not quarrelled bitterly over the allocation of their farms and the distribution of the cattle which were slowly extracted as an indemnity from Dingaan. Then there was the problem of their black labour. The country they had occupied had been swept almost bare of people by the *Mfecane* and they needed servants to run the farms. Admittedly now that they felt themselves safe from Zulu raids many Africans returned to their old homelands and were prepared to work for the white men; but their numbers at first were insufficient and the Boers tackled the problem by seeking opportunities of taking African children (who they said were orphans and rather euphemistically called 'apprentices') and put them to work as herders.

Then again there was trouble between the Volksraad and Pretorius; he had been confirmed in his position as Chief-Commandant, but even so he very frequently failed to see eye to eye with the legislative authority, and it need hardly be added that its members were always at loggerheads with each other. Jervis had been well aware of the dissensions which would inevitably rack the members of the Natalian Government. Before he sailed from Natal he had reported: 'In regard to their uniting under one head I see no probability of it; for even of their Volksraad, it is said, scarcely two of them

163

agree, and they are equally difficult to come to an agreement in the choice of their magistrates.' And he touched too on the Natalians' other harassing problem – the chastened but still formidable Zulu army – when he noted that 'Their greatest object was to make peace with Dingaan. But how to bring it about? They spoke of it as an impossibility; and even said he invariably put their messengers to death. The consequence is they have been kept in a most unsettled state, and which I have reason to believe they are determined to end by entering his country, and compelling him either to succumb and treat, or to destroy him.'

Jervis was of course perfectly right in stressing the Volksraad's overwhelming concern lest Dingaan rallied the Zulus and renewed the war; the snake had been scotched but it was not dead: the trek-kers in Natalia could never really feel secure until Dingaan's power had been utterly eliminated. The subject was never far away from their thoughts. Lindley wrote that the Boers 'are more afraid of his treachery than of all his warriors, and on this account are perhaps more uneasy now than when they were at open war with him'. For his part Pretorius confided in his journal that he was 'anxious to give the last death blow to the now humbled hound'.

The Boers' freedom of action had of course been made easier by Jervis's withdrawal and, in the casual way that things happen in Africa, only a few months earlier circumstances had further played into their hands when Mpande, half-brother to Dingaan, fled across the Tugela into Natalia together with 17,000 followers. The Volks-raad interrogated him at length. After making certain that he was willing to turn traitor on his half brother, it granted him land in the republic, embraced him as an ally, and in a queer little ceremony held in a marquee at Pietermaritzburg Mpande was proclaimed 'Reigning Prince of the emigrant Zulus'.

In fairness to Mpande, we should note that his treachery was forced upon him by Dingaan's all-too-obvious preparations to do away with him, but no one can doubt that he did very well for himself when he defected to the Boers. He was to succeed his brother as King of the Zulus and to reign over them until 1872. At the same time it is never easy to admire a renegade, especially when he is unaffectedly timid as well as being grossly fat. For Mpande could hardly walk because of obesity; the level-headed Henry Cloete who came to know Mpande well described him as 'an indolent pampered being, measuring nearly four feet six inches round his naked waist'.[2]

Once the alliance with Mpande had been concluded the Volksraad proceeded to pick a quarrel with Dingaan, and this was a matter of no great difficulty since the king was being uncommonly slack in fulfilling his treaty obligations to return looted cattle. And when no immediate satisfactions was forthcoming from its indignant protests the Commandant-General was instructed to proceed at once to Zulu-land and either negotiate the surrender of 40,000 cattle or seize them by force, which of course meant engaging Dingaan in a decisive battle.

Relishing again the pleasant flavour of a military campaign es-pecially as it was relatively free from risk (since he intended Mpande's Zulu emigrants to do most of the fighting) Pretorius on 14 January 1840 led a commando across the Tugela. With him travelled Mpande in the dual role of distinguished ally and hostage for the good behaviour of Nongalaza who led the allied Zulu army on a parallel course some way to the north. The Boers followed closely to the road which had taken them before to Blood river,[3] but they travelled this time in a vastly different mood from that of thirteen months before. There was no sense of danger now nor of urgency: the 500 beasts they drove with them alone limited the speed of the march. Everyone on commando seemed assured of their military su-periority, and they knew very well that Dingaan's hold over the Zulus was falling apart. And so the *Beeste Commando*'s[4] campaign bears something of the atmosphere of the last phase in the *corrida* when the bull is failing and the *torero* steps into the ring to finish it off with a single deft thrust of his sword.

March discipline may have been slacker this time, but there was of course no let-up in the religious observances which played so large a part in all the military adventures undertaken by the Voortrekkers. But the holiday atmosphere continued even when the expedition en-tered Zululand: Delegorgue who accompanied the commando tells us that during a two-day halt when they were not intoning psalms and hymns the men spent their time in roasting meat and indulging in meaningless games of wrestling without any artistic skill and seeking to shine by the rudest jokes'. He incidentally formed a very poor opinion of Pretorius's military prowess: the Commandant-General he says bluntly had 'his own system of tactics, and that was to have no tactics at all'.

On 29th January the commando reached the Blood river battlefield, and a strange episode now occurred. Pretorius threw down a gage to Dingaan by executing his chief councillor, Tanbuza who had fallen into the hands of the Boers. For when he heard that a punitive expedition was mustering, Dingaan had dispatched Tambuza to Pretorius with a *douceur* of 250 cattle and a request for more time to pay off the indemnity negotiated by Jervis. Tambuza was accompanied by his servant Kombesana. Pretorius, however, chose to regard the two men as spies rather than as envoys and when the commando rode off to begin the campaign, Tambuza and Kombesana accompanied it in chains. Mpande hated Tambuza; he insisted that it was he who had presented Dingaan to massacre Retief and his followers, and (what was worse) had recently incited the king to kill Mpande himself. So now, near the cairn which the victors of Blood river were to erect to commemorate the battle, Pretorious convened a court martial to consider Tambuza's guilt. Delegorgue was at his most scathing when describing the constitution of the Court. It was, he said, 'composed only of judges and reporters', and he compared 'this council of weak and cruel people' with a 'revolutionary tribunal . . . in the days of the Terror'. Reading his description of the trial it is not difficult to imagine the scene after all these years: the bearded Boers of the Court sitting stern and implacable, Tambuza and Kombesana standing opposite them and seeing only death in their eyes, the remainder of the commando crowding round to listen with gaping curiosity, all making a strange little tableau amid the strangely expectant hush which falls across all old battlefields. Tambuza obstinately refused to plead his case: he freely admitted all Mpande's charges and with quiet dignity accepted the inevitable sentence of death, asking only that the Boers might spare the life of his servant who, he pointed out, had committed no offence against them. Pretorius then spoke rather unctuously to the condemned man about his having to face the judgment of God besides his own, but one feels that Tambuza had the last word: according to one of the trekkers present, the *Induna* replied to Pretorius's moralizing by saying 'that he had but one master, Dingaan; that it was his duty to remain faithful to that master till the last, and that after having so acted the Master on high, if there was one, would not fail to approve his conduct'.

And so Tambuza and Kombesana, naked and manacled together,

were shot to death by a Boer firing party. There seems something very wrong here: Pretorius, usually compassionate and correct, is behaving quite out of character, and one's mind searches about for the reason. It may be that by this single act which seemingly disfigures his great career Pretorius was trying to grapple Mpande's loyalty to the trekkers; perhaps he had submitted to the mere seeking of vengeance for the deaths on Kwa Matiwane; possibly he was attempting to frighten Dingaan into submission without a fight.

Whatever the reason for it may have been, Tambuza's execution turned out to be unnecessary. By the time it had taken place the military issue with Dingaan had been resolved. For soon afterwards news reached the commando that Nongalaza had brought Dingaan's warriors to battle a little to the north of the Mkuze river and had won. The Boers learned that the remnants of the loyal Zulu impi had made off to the Pongola river in disorder. It had been a murderous fight: between six and nine thousand Zulus had been slain and according to Lindley the losses had been shared equally between the two sides. It was the end of Dingaan. The king fled to Swazi country and from there reports presently filtered south that he had been stabbed to death by hostile tribesmen in the wild country among the Lebombo hills, perhaps on the instructions of Pretorius.[5]

The trekkers had finally won the long struggle with Dingaan and at the end without firing a shot other than the bullets which had killed Tambuza and Kombesana. Mpande received his due reward. On 10 February 1840 Andries Pretorius pronounced his accession to the Zulu thone, and noted rather quaintly that his protégé was 'filled with excessive joy from head to heels' by the announcement. Four days later in a curious little ceremony Mpande was invested as King of the Zulus. The coronation must have made up an unlikely scene: the Natalian dignitaries in the frock coats which they had thoughtfully brought along on commando; Mpande, proud and corpulent, sitting on an old chair which did duty as a throne; his wounded impi strangely quiet and watchful in a great circle round him. The size of Mpande's kingdom had been drastically reduced for the Commandant-General had pronounced Natalia's annexation of all the country up to the Black Umfolozi as well as of Saint Lucia Bay, and the new monarch was to be subordinate to the Volksraad at Pietermaritzburg. He was poorer in cattle too, for Mpande was obliged to hand over 41,000 head of cattle to his kingmaker; they were duly driven back to the 'deel laager' outside Pietermaritzburg for division and distribution, but we may note in passing that not all the beasts reached this, their proper destination: a disappointed burgher recorded that many were spirited away 'in a riot of selfishness and greed', and another man on commando declared that in the end only 31,000 were available for distribution. Still Pretorius could look back on his latest expedition with the utmost satisfaction, and he was sure it would be usher in a new period of peace and promise for the trekker republic of Natalia.

And indeed prosperity now lapped over the republic. The mobile phase of the Great Trek appeared to be over; its burghers were united by federal bonds to the overberg Boers, some of the few British settlers remaining at Port Natal may have become discontented but they could now be safely ignored, the Zulu danger had been removed once and for all, many so-called after-trekkers were pouring into the republic whose white population soared to past 4,000, an impromptu land office worked overtime surveying farms for the settlers, and Whitehall was known to be considering the recognition of Natalia. And even the native problem which had arisen as more Africans entered the republic looked as though it could be solved by the enforcement of a policy of segregation.

It is of some interest at this point if we consider this solution of the Afrikaners to the Bantu problem because it reflects their contemporary attitude to matters racial.

Thousands of Africans had flocked into Natalia once the Zulu menace had been removed by the Wen Commando and the Beeste Commando. In a sense this was a tribute to the Boers who had replaced chaos in the country with security, and it allowed the Bantu to answer that primitive instinct which drives human beings to return to their old homes when conditions become more favourable.[6] But these people were unorganised, very few of them were under the control of a recognised chief, and as squatters they presented a serious problem to orderly government.

For the former kraals of many of the returning Africans now lay on farms marked out and worked by the Boers. To avoid overcrowding the farm lands the Afrikaners found it imperative to limit the number of squatters on their farms to five families, a figure which would satisfactorily provide for their labour requirements without being dangerously large. (Pretorius as Commandant-General was allowed ten families.) These Bantu were unenfranchised and subjected to numerous by-laws: thus those living on European farms were not allowed to ride a horse or carry a gun or drink intoxicating liquor without their master's permission. The problem of the 'surplus natives' on the other hand was solved by segregation in *ad hoc* reserves where they were stringently controlled by pass-laws. By an unfortunate mischance some of them were sent off to settle on land claimed by Faku, paramount chief of the Pondos, and this was to bring far-reaching consequences to the infant republic of Natalia.

Meanwhile another source of trouble was approaching like a thundercloud: for towards the end of 1840 the Natalian Volksraad had made a profound error of judgment whose effects were blown up into what we would nowadays call an international incident.

The circumstances were these: a Bhaca chief named Ncaphayi or Nkapi, who was a neighbour of Faku's Pondo tribe beyond the southern boundary of Natalia, was accused by the Boers of rustling some of their cattle. On the instructions of the Volksraad, Pretorius took the field once more with a punitive expedition. He crossed the Umzimvubu river on 19 December 1840 and attacked Ncaphayi's kraals. In Cilliers' words he there 'punished him well, and took so many cattle from him that whoever had suffered from his thieving was amply repaid'. The affair brought the missionaries of Pondoland out in full cry and the reports they circulated owed nothing to understatement. The Cape Government received them with particular anger for it regarded both Ncaphayi and Faku as living under its protection. In addition Sir George Napier learned that besides capturing cattle the commando had killed forty people during the foray and carried off seventeen children as 'apprentices'. All the Governor's humanitarian instincts were aroused afresh. Up to this time the emigrant Boers could fairly claim that they had fought with Africans only in self-defence but this raid on the Bhaca appeared at Cape Town to be an unprovoked aggression in which children had been carried off into virtual slavery. Episodes of this sort, moreover, Napier believed, would spark off all kinds of new tensions on the sensitive eastern border of the Colony and lead inevitably to serious trouble. He was still smarting over the abandonment of Port Natal a year before and his reaction was swift. During the January of 1841 he dispatched a Major Smith with 150 soldiers to Pondoland to reassure Faku and defend it from attack. And this little force of red-coats had another obvious function: it was poised to invade Natalia if after renewed representations from the Governor the Colonial Office decided after all on annexation.

Smith stayed in Pondoland for a whole year, while the Government at Whitehall pondered over the situation. There were strategic reasons in plenty to justify the occupation of Natal: it would deny the coast to any alien power which might use it as a base for threatening the sea lanes to India; the seizure of its only harbour would effectively control all imports into the trekker republic; and rich coal deposits had been reported in its hinterland. But in the end what swayed the British Cabinet was a humanitarian concern about the Volksraad's enforced resettlement of surplus Africans on land claimed by Faku between the Umtamvuma and Umzimvubu. In the December of 1841 Napier announced that the military occupation of Durban would be resumed and at the end of the following March Major Smith led his augmented force of 260 regulars northwards into Natalia.

Smith was a veteran who had been through the mill. At the age of nine he had joined the Royal Navy but soon transferred to the Army. An adventurous career followed. Smith was wounded three times during the course of the Peninsular War and once again at Waterloo. Now in 1842 Smith was a major and although he may have been a born scold and something of a fuss-pot, he was very much the soldier all the same and he commanded a military force which by contemporary South African standards was a powerful one. Its bulk was made up of riflemen from the Inniskilling Fusiliers; the remainder consisted of a handful of sappers and gunners together with fifty green-jacketed troopers of the Cape Mounted Rifles. With them marched a daunting number of women camp-followers, a clumsy train of sixty wagons, a howitzer and two small field pieces, as well as a herd of 600 ration-oxen. Accompanying the column too was the Reverend James Archbell (who four years before had been an indignant witness of Retief's shoddy seizure of Sekonyela) with his family. Smith's instructions were to occupy Port Natal but again the Government had not yet made up its mind about annexing the hinterland. Only that January Sir James Stephen at the Colonial Office had bleakly minuted that to do this 'would merely be to throw away so much money and to multiply our relations and responsibilities towards barbarous tribes, from which nothing could come, but the consumption of treasure, the waste of human life, and a warfare alike inglorious, unprofitable and afflicting'. It was not even considered that Smith would have to remain long at the Port: his presence was to be temporary and no more than a warning to the Boers against intrigues with foreign powers and any more adventures like the foray against Ncaphayi.

When he left his Umgazi camp in Pondoland Smith embarked on no mean task. With an unwieldy wagon column he had to cover 260 miles of rugged, uncharted and practically unknown ground which might well be disputed by hostile Boers. Every few miles the country was interesected by rivers swollen with summer rains. The first that had to be negotiated was the broad Umzimvubu and the troops, still in fine fettle, approached it with a lusty rendering of 'We fight to conquer'. Thereafter their troubles began. The bugler of the 27th Regiment, Joseph Brown, has fortunately left us a beguiling account of Smith's forgotten military expedition. He starts off by telling us that 'Two women were quickly delivered on the first night and next day'; then we find him complaining that the soldiers 'suffered much from marching in the sand, it got into our boots and cut our feet to pieces, and the sun reflecting the sand burned our faces. In like manner the men had many fatigues in repairing the roads every four or five miles they went along.' We learn from him that the expedition had to negotiate no less than 122 rivers, and Brown writes with feeling that 'the most of them we had to swim over'. But the soldiers had their compensations: there was a feeling of excitement about this march through virgin country and it was spiced by the dangerous possibility of running into a Boer ambush; the bathing off the lovely beaches they passed was a never-ending delight; everything about them was novel and the men gaped at all the wonders they saw – the tremendous skeletons of whales which had been cast ashore, the buck which they encircled and ran down, and the delicious oysters that could be gathered from the spume-sprayed rocks.

Near the Umkomaas river the column rested before undertaking the final lap of the journey; here they were greeted by a piratical party of British settlers from the Port who had ridden out to meet the column 'all armed with swords, pistols and double-barrelled guns' and delighted with the prospect of evicting the Boers. A few days later the soldiers marched into Port Natal without meeting any opposition. It was 3 May 1842. They tore down the Republican tricolour

171

and raised the Union Jack over their tents. Despite all difficulties the march had been brilliantly successful; the second occupation of Port Natal had begun, and this time as things turned out the red-coats had come to stay.

They established camp in the flat ground below the Berea ridge and settled down to watch the Natalian burghers who were mustered a mile away at the tiny hamlet of Congella. From his diary it would seem that Bugler Brown was more apprehensive of disease than of the Boers: the water at the camp, he grumbles, was 'as black as ink and full of different insects, and stinks in the bargain. I am very much afraid it will make away with the whole of us before long.'

The next three weeks passed in fruitless parleys between Smith and Pretorius. The Boers at Congella were well armed and truculent enough, although unwilling to open hostilities. But they succeeded in making it quite clear that they had no intention of submitting to a second British occupation of the port. Smith sought around for an opportunity of pulling off a coup by capturing the Boer leaders, but they were too well guarded for this to be attempted; 'I wish to God', grumbled Napier at the news 'that scoundrel Pretorious [sic] could be caught as well as Bosoff [sic], old Rose and Breda – but fear they are so cunning as they are cowardly, and will never show their faces in any place where there is a chance of catching them.'

And even as they waited, morale in the Boer camp was vastly stimulated by an unexpected event – the arrival in Natal from Amsterdam of Johan Arnold Smellekamp. It was the beginning of a strange little interlude in South African history.

News of the Voortrekkers' adventures in southern Africa had already reached Holland and aroused enormous interest there. In the hope of establishing trade relations with these kinsmen of the Dutch a public-spirited merchant, G. G. Ohrig, fitted out a schooner with all sorts of merchandise and the boat sailed into Port Natal towards the end of March only a few days before Major Smith started off from Faku's country. An agent acting for Ohrig named Smellekamp was on the schooner (he is always referred to in contemporary accounts as its 'supercargo'), and as soon as he had landed the 'supercargo' travelled up to interview the Volksraad in Pietermaritzburg. There he was received with enormous enthusiasm: the streets of the little town were so gaily decorated that, when all available flags and bunting had been strung up, even underclothes were pressed into

172

service. For the Natalians had jumped to the conclusion that Smelle-kamp's arrival signified full-scale intervention by the Dutch on their behalf. Overcome by his sudden importance, the excited agent did nothing to enlighten them as to his real role and, on 25 April 1842 when Smith was still a few days' march from Port Natal, the en-raptured Volksraad, in the hope of pre-empting the British, handed Smellekamp a document which offered Natalia as a colonial pos-session to King William II of Holland.

It is a little sad to note that before the year was out King William had apologised to Whitehall for the fuss that had been caused, and roundly denounced Smellekamp and all his works, but for the time being Pretorius and his men were convinced that they had a European ally and could afford to take a harder line with the British. Smellekamp once he had got over his delirious welcome departed with his precious document for Holland in a cloud of popularity and speculation. Unfortunately he had to travel by the Cape now that Smith was installed at the Port and he suffered the indignity of tem-porary detention at Swellendam before being allowed to proceed to Europe.

Pretorius had turned as well to the overberg Boers for assistance against the British; Hendrik Potgieter received his messengers with-out enthusiasm and excused himself from becoming involved in the trouble at Port Natal by explaining that Mzilikazi was on the war-path again: it seemed that the federal links between Pieter-maritzburg and Potchefstroom were not strong enough to with-stand the prospect of hostilities with Great Britain. Pretorius's envoys, however, had a better reception farther south when they visited Transorangia: for the fiery Johannes Mocke promised to raise the settlers around Bloemfontein and the Caledon river, and bring them to the aid of their fellow countrymen in Natalia.

But before their arrival Pretorius had become tired of waiting al-though still resolved not to fire off the first shot: on 22 May he reacted to some commandeering of provisions on Smith's part by suddenly ordering a raid to carry off the Britishers' cattle which were grazing peacefully around their camp. It was an overtly hostile act, an Afrikaner version of Caesar's crossing of the Rubicon.

Smith's response may have been quick but it must be counted the very extreme of incompetence. He decided to make a surprise attack on the Boer camp under cover of darkness. The idea might have been a good one if the assault had not been made on a bright moonlight night and so forfeited all element of surprise. This never stuck Smith, however, and just before midnight on 23 May 1842 he led 138 men round the shores of the bay trailing two field-pieces behind them and kicking up a tremendous din. As a master stroke Smith had trundled the howitzer into a boat and had it rowed parallel to the troops' march with the intention of using it to provide covering fire from the flank. Inevitably the attack ran into a chain of mishaps which are unrivalled even in the dolorous annals of British military affairs in South Africa. The Boers were thoroughly alert and were waiting for the soldiers from behind the tangled cover of mangrove trees which grew above the beach. They drove in a sudden hot fire which took the troops completely by surprise while still in column and it cut them to pieces; to make things worse the oxen drawing the field-guns stampeded at the first shot and got tangled up in their traces while the scow carrying the howitzer ran aground on a sandbank and the British secret weapon never came into action. Smith kept his head and ordered an immediate retreat but he left 49 men dead or wounded behind him as well as his precious field-guns. The Natalians had had things all their own way: they could rejoice in as easy a victory as any the Boers had gained against the Zulus and Matabele. 'We took two beautiful guns and their carriages,' boasted one of the burghers, and added with only a slight refraction of the truth, 'and not a single man of ours was wounded.'

Smith had floundered forward and got into a battle he could not handle. Now he had no option but to accept investment in his camp which was hurriedly fortified, and pray for relief. More useful than his prayers, one night Dick King slipped away from the fort with a single African companion, and made a remarkable ride to Grahamstown, 600 gruelling miles away. He accomplished the journey in ten days. The Cape authorities were overwhelmed with consternation at the news he carried, and indeed something very significant had occurred. The skirmish at Congella may have been a remarkably small battle as such things go, but it marked a landmark in South African history. British troops had met the Afrikaners in fair battle and had been defeated. Imperial prestige now must be restored, and suddenly everyone in the Colony began to envisage the annexation of the trekker republic. Strong reinforcements were started off at once for Port Natal by sea while Smith sweated out a 26-day siege. It was not hard pressed: his chief enemy was famine rather than the trekkers. All through their history the Boers have been averse to attacking a prepared position and although after Mocke's arrival their numbers amounted to 600 men, they were content to do no more than lob shells into Smith's camp after Pretorius had chivalrously allowed the British women and children to take refuge on a captured British vessel in the bay. Admittedly the Natalians snapped up an isolated fort which the soldiers had set up on the Bluff commanding the entrance to the harbour but no real effort was made to carry the main camp. By the third week in June the British counted 651 cannon balls which had fallen in their makeshift fort and the soldiers by now were in a pitiable condition. Twenty-six men had been wounded and the garrison was reduced to half rations of biscuit and ten ounces of horse flesh. On 25 June Major Smith counted himself lucky to break-fast on a dead crow.

But relief was at hand; a British frigate appeared off the bar that same day and discouraged the Boers who had taken up positions on the Bluff and the Point with a thunderous broadside. This allowed boats loaded with soldiers to run the gauntlet into the bay next day and Pretorius saw that the game was up. The siege was raised at once: eight soldiers and four burghers had been killed during its course.

The dragging pace of events which followed in Natal give the impression of a slowed-down movie, and one can only understand the protracted course of the consultations which now decided the fate of Natal by recalling that Napier was unable to negotiate a final settlement with the Natalian Boers until he had got definite instructions from Whitehall and that in the days of sail it took six full months for him to send off a proposal to London and receive a reply. But in fact there was no need for haste: all through the long months of waiting which followed the relief of Durban on 26 June 1842, the republic of Natalia was falling apart like a piece of soggy blotting paper.

The Volksraad in the capital, Pietermaritzburg, had lost its nerve. It knew that the Boer commandos would never stand up to the large number of troops now landed at Durban; its members were also well aware that their faithful ally Mpande, who having seen which way the wind was blowing, had suddenly begun to seek an accommodation with the British and was anxiously inquiring whether it would help if he attacked the Boers.

The trekker women were made of sterner stuff than their government. One of them, the redoubtable Mrs Erasmus Smit (long used to hectoring her husband), led a deputation to the British Commissioner and with some bluster announced her companions' determination to walk barefoot over the Drakensberg rather than submit to his terms. But such gestures failed to influence their menfolk and as early as 15 July 1842 the Natalian Volksraad formally tendered its submission to the British Crown. Yet for two more years the trekkers of Natalia continued to govern themselves from Pietermaritzburg while British sentries threw long shadows at Durban, and Whitehall perfunctorily considered the anguished appeals addressed to it by the penitent Voortrekkers.

At last on 12 December 1842 the British Cabinet did finally decide on the annexation of Natal, and in the following May, Napier proclaimed the country to be a British colony.[7] In size the new territory was to be considerably smaller than the republic of Natalia: to the south-west a large segment of land beyond the Umzimkulu was ceded to the Pondos, and suzerainty over the Zulus was abandoned so that Mpande was pleased to find himself ruling over an independent state beyond the Tugela and Buffalo rivers.

British troops were sent up to garrison Pietermaritzburg, and all the last-ditch Boers' vague thoughts of resistance died away when a delegation which had met Smellekamp at Lourenço Marques returned with the news that Holland had not the slightest intention of supporting them.

In December 1845 the republic of Natalia formally ceased to exist when a Lieutenant-Governer named Martin West arrived in Pietermaritzburg. It was a saddening moment. Long years after they had quit Cape Colony, Pharaoh in the shape of a British official had finally caught up with the Voortrekkers.

But many of them refused to be absorbed by the expanding British empire. For in the new colony there was to be no colour bar and conditions were in effect returning to those which had existed in the Colony before the Great Trek took shape. Slowly the Boers withdrew from contact with the British, concentrating at first in the Weenen district as though seeking moral sustenance from where they had known their greatest sufferings. Then they began trekking away to the still independent high veld, driving their creaking wagons up the Drakensberg passes which they had descended with such relish and visionary hopes five years earlier. 'The mass of the people,' Major Smith had warned Sir George Napier earlier, 'are determined not to submit to British authority, and will move farther inland to be out of reach.' He was perfectly right of course. The trekkers felt themselves more than ever to be burghers of a real nation now; the events of the Great Trek had developed a burning sense of Afrikaner nationalism; the martyrdom of Piet Retief, the horrors of Bloukrans, the heroism of Marthinus Oosthuizen, the death of Dirkie Uys when he had gone back to help his father at Italeni, the victories at Blood river and Congella, and the vow which they renewed each year, had all at last bound them together as a valid community. The events of the last decade had enthralled and entrapped the trekkers in a mystique of their own: they had become incorporated in a legend which stated their aspirations and expressed some obscure truth which could not otherwise be stated.

There were other reasons than their dislike of an alien government and a desire to live their own lives in liberty led to that Afrikaner exodus from Natal which has been termed the Second Trek. Natal. in the end had been something of a disappointment. Its lush grasslands had proved less productive than had been expected; cattle did not thrive as well on them as they did on the undulous pastures of the high veld, and sheep were apt to be affected by mystifying diseases. And so the Voortrekkers packed up their wagons again, the Great Trek regained its mobility, a trickle of Natalian emigrants grew into a steady stream, and the centre of trekker activity swung back to Potgieter's fief on the high veld.

Andries Pretorius stayed on in Natal longer than most of his countrymen. He was loth to leave his splendid farm near Weenen, he did not relish the idea of settling down in country dominated by his arch-rival Potgieter, and he hoped still to obtain better terms from the British. In September 1847 he rode 600 miles to Grahamstown to lay his people's complaints before the Cape Governor, Sir Henry Pottinger. There was still time he said, to find an accommodation in Natal which would prevent a final Boer exodus.

But Pottinger refused Pretorius an interview, and here one comes across an example of the petty action of a paper-shuffling bureaucrat which can alter the course of a nation's history. Pottinger instead insisted that Pretorius submit his suggestions in a memorandum, explaining that 'I cannot devote time to personal interviews; and besides, it has been a rule with me through a long public life, that written communications are to be preferred, as utterly obviating misunderstanding.' Pretorius flew into a rage at what he considered to be a calculated insult, and late in 1847 he decided to abandon Natal for the high veld. With him marched nearly all the Afrikaners who still remained in the new colony, and together they began climbing up the Berg passes.

It was at this point in time that Sir Harry Smith succeeded Pottinger as Governor at the Cape. He had known many of the Voortrekkers during his previous service in South Africa; they liked him and he had great sympathy for them. Smith accordingly hurried to the Drakensberg in a last-minute attempt to halt the Second Trek; there he met the Boers, promised reparations to them, and persuaded a few to turn back to Natal. But the large majority continued up the passes. Sir Harry was genuinely appalled by their situation and the description he has left of it better than anything else records the miserable conditions which were again gladly accepted if they were to lead to genuine independence: 'On my arrival at the foot of the Drakensberg mountains,' Smith writes, 'I was almost paralysed to witness the whole of the population, with few exceptions, trekking! These families were exposed to a state of misery which I never before saw equalled, except in Massena's invasion of Portugal, when the whole of the population of that part of the seat of war abandoned their homes and fled. The scene here was truly heart-rending. I assembled all the men near me, through the means of a Mr Pretorius, a shrewd sensible man, who had recently been into the colony to lay the subject of dissatisfaction of his countrymen before the Governor, where he was refused an audience, and returned after so long a journey expressing himself as the feelings of a proud and injured man would naturally prompt. At this meeting I was received as if among my own family. I heard the various causes of complaint – some I regard as well-grounded, others as imaginary, but all expressive of a want of confidence and liberality as to land on the part of the Government. I exerted my influence among them to induce them to remain for the moment where they were with their families, which they consented to do. The scene presented by about 300 or 400 fathers of large families assembled and shedding tears when presenting their position was more, I admit, than I could observe unmoved, each exclaiming "Our friend Colonel Smith, we were living quietly under a government which we were attached to; our loyalty has been suspected, our lands have been sparingly given or refused – we were not even allowed to purchase. Kafirs have been located on our lands and intermixed with us. These are the causes which have led us to abandon our houses, our crops standing, and the gardens which we planted with our own hands, abounding in fruit and produce. We are seeking a home in the wilderness."

All Hendrik Potgieter's old doubts about the suitability of Natal in the end had been vindicated. As for the Boers from Natal the best that could be said for their prospects was that farms in plenty were awaiting them beyond the mountains.

NOTES

1 Damned Rednecks – an Afrikaner expression for the British.

2 This was flattering compared with the most of our descriptions of Mpande's physical charms, but it is only fair to note that the French traveller Delegorgue held to a very different opinion. He was so taken by the Prince that with Gallic enthusiasm Delegorgue wrote of his 'brilliant black eye, deepset, well-guarded by an advanced frontal angle, a high forehead, straight at the sides on which the trace of wrinkles was beginning to be perceived, a nose of usual mould with gristles boldly shown, a large mouth often smiling with the smile which means "I understand", a square chin indicating resolution; in fact a large head, well formed, borne on a superb body shining with plumpness, but on which the carriage was so noble ... the gestures so precise that a Parisian might well have believed that Pande [sic] in his youth had frequented the palaces of kings'.

3 When the reminiscences of old Voortrekkers were recorded many years later it was suspected that the narrators' minds were confused by the two campaigns. Thus some authorities believe that the exhibition of dancing given before Pretorius at Danskraal took place during the 1840 expedition and not immediately before Blood river.

4 So called for the cattle loot it appropriated. It was also sometimes referred to as the *Straf Commando*.

5 The ubiquitous Carolus Tregardt, on his way back to Port Natal after his adventurous journey to Rhodesia and Ethiopia, maintained that he saw Dingaan's body only half an hour after his death.

6 The same phenomenon was seen in Poland during 1945. At the end of the Second World War only fifteen Poles were living in the mass of rubble that had been Warsaw; within a few months 300,000 of its old citizens had rebuilt make-shift homes in the gutted capital.

7 By a later proclamation Natal was annexed instead as a district of Cape Colony to be administered by a Lieutenant-Governor.

I I

The High Veld

During the years when the main trekker effort had been concentrated in Natal, the overberg Boers had enjoyed modest prosperity in a less spectacular fashion. Following the fights at Mosega and Kapain, Hendrik Potgieter had come to look upon the high veld almost as his personal property and after his brief appearance in Natal on the Vlug Commando he had thankfully returned over the Berg, humbled by the Zulus and condemned by a large section of his fellow Afrikaners as a traitor. Since then Potgieter had remained aloof from all the dramatic events which had led to the inauguration of the republic of Natalia and to its ultimate overthrow by the British.

It is as well if at this point we take a look at the situation on the high veld to which Potgieter returned after his unhappy experience with the Vlug Commando in 1838.

The country between the Orange and Vet rivers had long been settled by heterogeneous communities of Bantu, Bushmen, Griquas and trekboers as well as by Voortrekkers who had dropped out early from the mainstream of the Great Trek. On the other hand the country north of the Vet to as far as the Zoutpansberg was dominated by Potgieter's adherents. They lived at places which had been selected for their water, soil, pasture and timber. On and around these nuclear sites Potgieter now schemed to build the autocratic state of his dreams. With the instinct of a born dictator he proposed to set up a country governed by himself alone; the coloured inhabitants who wished to remain in contact with the whites there were to be segregated, but must give their services to the Boer farmers for a reasonable wage; they were also to be prohibited from vagrancy and among other strictures were not allowed to possess guns. Potgieter in short had been caught up in a pattern of government which a later generation of Afrikaners would label as apartheid.

Potgieter went about his task with expediency and skill. His men had taken their last look at Natal from the top of the Berg on 14 May 1838, after which he headed due west to his headquarters on the Sand river. Now that the Matabele had been driven away Potgieter could make his plans with complete confidence. He intended to live on amicable terms with the African tribesmen remaining in his domain, renew his search for a route to a Portuguese port which would be beyond British control, and gradually extend his influence over the whole of the high veld. To this end during the remainder of 1838 he made treaties of friendship with local African potentates including Sekwati who ruled the powerful Bapedi tribe. Then in June he entered into an arrangement with the Bataung chief Makwana by which for the bargain price of 38 head of cattle he bought the enormous tract of land between the Vet and the Vaal over which the chief asserted a rather dubious sovereignty. However implausible this may seem, the transaction[1] at least gave some semblance of legality to Potgieter's claim to have become lord and master of this first large section of the high veld.

For six months too Potgieter explored his domain, riding nearly to the Zoutpansberg in the hope of hearing news about Louis Tregardt who by now, however, had reached Lourenço Marques. And his people spread out, staking out their claims to attractive farmlands. Only at the end of 1838 did Potgieter break up his own camp at Sand river and move his wagons to a delectable site on the Mooi[2] river beyond the Vaal whose attractions he had noticed during his expeditions against the Matabele the year before. At first this settlement was called Moorivierdorp[2] but gradually it took on the name of Potchefstroom which on somewhat unlikely authority is said to be a reference to 'The stream of the chief Potgieter.'[3] At about the same time the village of Rustenburg took shape on the slopes of the Magaliesberg.

Potgieter ruled his trekker state from his twin 'capitals' of Winburg and Potchefstroom. Hartbees houses went up in its tiny hamlets together with store houses, and huts for carpenters, blacksmiths and wagon-makers, giving an air of permanence to these dozen or so little nuclei of European civilisation which dotted the veld. The great tented wagons stood motionless now beside these buildings and the rough stockades in which the cattle and sheep were herded and the small kraals near by where the Bantu servants lived.

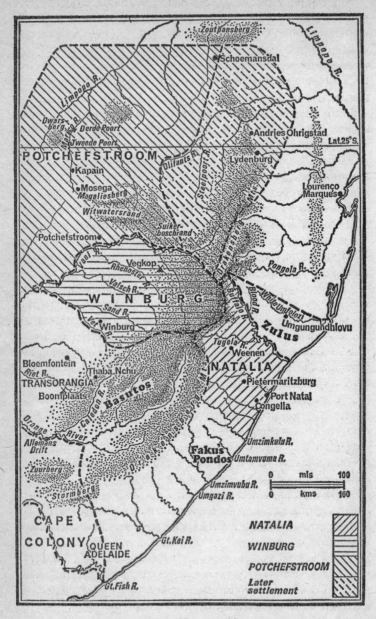

The Trekker Republics

After the proclamation of the republic of Natalia, Potgieter following a meeting held on 16 October 1840 somewhat reluctantly agreed to a loose form of federation between his own state on the high veld and the new trekker republic below the Berg. In return he was handed the sop of being appointed 'Commander and Ruler of Potchefstroom' with an *adjunkraad* to assist him in dealing with local problems.

By the April of 1842 when British troops were already marching from the Umgazi towards Port Natal relations between Potchefstroom and Pietermaritzburg were becoming strained, however, after the Volksraad withheld its approval of Potgieter's leading yet another expedition against Mzilikazi. In the crisis which followed when open conflict flared up between the Natalian trekkers and British troops Potgieter made no attempt to assist his fellow countrymen. After the British Government annexed Natal Potgieter detached Potchefstroom–Winburg from the Federal Republic and declared its independence on 9 April 1844. At the same time too he proclaimed a constitution of a sort. It was known as the Thirty-three Articles and in it Potgieter was recognised as sole ruler of a state whose boundaries he had extended in one direction from the Drakensberg to the Kalahari and in the other from the Limpopo to the Vet. Now that Pretorius had retired into the shades as a British subject and then vanished (finally it seemed) in the deeper shades of retirement at his farm near Weenen, Potgieter with some justice could regard himself as the unrivalled trekker leader, and in a moment of braggadocio he announced that his jurisdiction extended southwards as far as the Orange itself. On paper at least his high veld trekker republic now reached from the frontiers of the old Colony in the south to the farthest points which the emigrants had reached in the north.

But Potgieter's pretensions to control Transorangia, the land between the Vet and the Orange, were unrealistic. It had already a considerable white population which had lived there before the Great Trek; these people had no quarrel with the Imperial Government and even dissociated themselves from trekker politics. Their loyalties still lay with the Cape.

The position in Transorangia was further complicated by the heterogeneous character of its other people. Every sort of community that could be found in southern Africa was living here. Besides the white settlers, rival Sotho chiefs – Moshweshwe, Moletsane, and Sekonyela all claimed land on both sides of the Caledon and each of these potentates was supported by his own resident missionary. Adam Kok's Griquas in a rough and ready way had hammered out the rough outlines of their own state immediately to the north of the Orange and they were bolstered in their claims by the formidable John Philip after whom they had named their chief town, Philippolis. In Transorangia too, groups of Bushmen still eked out an existence which was heavily based on cattle-reiving from their neighbours. And now during the 1830s Great Britain was gradually sucked into this anarchic situation because of a wholly admirable anxiety to keep the peace in the country beyond the Orange river frontier.

Only the most diligent student of South African history would be able to find his way through the whole imbroglio of Transorangian political affairs at this time. All we need to know here is that they resulted in constant clashes between the Afrikaners and the Griquas, and between these two people and the Bantu. In an attempt to restore some sort of order the British warned the Boers not to interfere in the African chiefs' affairs, and when the fiery Johann Mocke announced in return that he intended to declare a trekker republic in Transorangia, a colonial judge who happened to be in Colesberg at the time equally impetuously proclaimed British sovereignty beyond the Orange as far as the 25th parallel.[4] Cape Town refused to ratify this annexation but in 1843 the Governor did intervene beyond the river by negotiation treaties with both Kok and Moshweshwe; they were to be paid annual salaries in return for an obligation to keep order within their respective territories. In a sense Kok and Moshweshwe had become Imperial allies and when renewed skirmishing broke out between Griquas and Boers, a small British force marched over the border to Kok's assistance and scattered an Afrikaner commando after a sharp action at Zwart Koppies during the May of 1845.

This support of coloured folk against white men overnight converted many of the Transorangian Boer loyalists into Republicans, and all of the whites disliked the compromise solution for the situation which the Cape Government now proposed. It pronounced that the land south of the Riet river belonged wholly to Adam Kok and was inalienable, while north of that line the Afrikaners could still lease land from the Griquas. To supervise these arrangements a British

Resident, Major Warden, was established at a farm named Bloemfontein in the alienable part of the country.

On the far side of the Vaal meanwhile Potgieter's old restlessness had returned. He had been badly shaken in 1842 by the peppery judge's announcement of the extension of British rule up to 25° south, and now his power was being threatened by the Natalians who were trekking over the Berg in increasing numbers after the red-coats had taken over at Durban. Natalian emigrants were even swaggering about in his own town of Potchefstroom and making his gorge rise with braying accusations about his behaviour on the Vlug Commando. The old stability of the trekker communities across the Vaal was being shaken, and after his pride had been solaced by his re-election as Chief Commandant and Ruler of the high veld republic, Potgieter thankfully resumed his old mantle of trek leader and, abandoning Potchefstroom, led his immediate followers to a new settlement below the western slopes of the Drakensberg. It was safely beyond the shadowy line of 25° south of latitude and the village was only two weeks' ride from Lourenço Marques. It was named Andries Ohrigstad, combining the rarely used first name of the Chief Commandant and the surname of the merchant who had hoped through Smellekamp to open trade between the Voortrekkers and the Netherlands.

Potgieter obtained the land for his new settlement by a verbal agreement with Sekwati, the Bapedi chief. The township stood where the deep valley of a tributary of the Blyde river running through the eastern slopes of the Drakensberg mountains suddenly opens out into a green and picturesque basin surrounded on three sides by an almost sheer wall of mountains. The land was fertile and ample enough for the trekkers. *Oom Hendrick* as the leader naturally took the pick of the farms and with unusual prescience named it Strydfontein – the Fountain of Strife. From now on Ohrigstad was to be the nation's capital while Potchefstroom and Winburg were regarded as satellite colonies. Here again at Ohrigstad the classical trekker policy was established: enough Bantu were allowed to live on the Afrikaner farms to provide them with labour; the remainder were either segregated in native reserves or continued to live under semi-independent chiefs.

But even in distant Ohrigstad Potgieter's new-found peace was not to last for long. Natalian trekkers flocked up to the new capital and under the leadership of 'Kootjie' Burger inevitably contested the Chief Commandant's authoritarian rule. It was hardly surprising. The passing years had rendered Potgieter increasingly intractable. Perhaps after the tremendous strain of his endeavours the dictator was growing weary. Certainly now he is even less patient with dissension than before and he reacts more harshly to opposition. Although his own followers remained always faithful to him, and canvassed the nomination of their leader as ruler of Ohrigstad for life, a party condemning Potgieter's monarchical establishment and advocating rule by an elected Volksraad made its voice increasingly heard. Relations between the two factions were just about as bad as they could be, short of actual physical combat; often indeed it seemed that this might break out and plunge the northern trekker republic into civil war.

Potgieter's claims to authority were bolstered by Sekwati's verbal cession of the land in his favour, but now the Volksraad party countered in 1846 by purchasing a large parcel of land north of 26° latitude from a Swazi princeling (though very little of it in fact belonged to him) for 100 head of cattle. The new bargain may have been no more binding than Potgieter's, but it was at least written out on paper, and besides this document Burger's party had a second trump card up their sleeves in the possession of the only cannon in Ohrigstad. It was all very disturbing and Potgieter after accusing the Volksraad of all sorts of sins, in Stuart fashion made an unsuccessful attempt to arrest its leader. Andries Pretorius added to the uproar at the time by settling in the Transvaal following his final disillusionment with British rule in Natal, and his untiring finger searching for a suitable pie promptly made him offer not only to reconquer Transorangia for the Boers but to mediate in the quarrelling at Ohrigstad.

It is not difficult to imagine 'Ou Blauberg's' discontent with the way things had turned out in Ohrigstad, and again in 1847 the familiar restlessness returns. Nothing it seems will ever stop Potgieter's slow persistent quest for the promised land; the more his plans miscarry the more determined he becomes to find the appointed place. To do so he will go on riding endlessly over the veld, deciding on another site, putting the plough to its rich alluvial soil, bulding a mud-walled fortress more for prestige than for protection, superintending the erection of his followers' houses, and laying a watercourse through the new settlement, hoping that at last he has found the security and independence he has craved so long. Thus in 1847 the *trekgees* in Potgieter is burning high again and we find him making another reconnaissance of the Zoutpansberg territory, happy to be removed from the bickering of his countrymen, and inaccessible to even the most persevering British imperialist. That same year he leads a large commando over the Olifants river again; while one section is detached to reconnoitre a route to Inhambane, he himself rides with 100 men far into the new empire which Mzilikazi has created across the Limpopo half expecting to find his new Canaan there. But it is the land lying below the Zoutpansberg which after all has exerted its old charm on him, and Potgieter impulsively decides to abandon Ohrigstad and settle his followers at a new site in its southern shadow; it was to be known first as Zoutpansbergdorp, and later (in deference to the name of the man who married the widow of 'Ou Blauberg's eldest son) as Schoemansdal.

It was not all that difficult to leave Ohrigstad: the factional strife had overtaxed the old warrior's mind, and the Steelpoort and Blyde valleys were so alive with malaria that their rich soil had been as fruitful of graves as crops. Then again the short route to Lourenço Marques on which so many hopes had been based was virtually closed by tsetse fly. So once more the wagons were refurbished, their great tilts were taken down from rafters in the huge barns of Ohrigstad where they had been stored out of reach of preying ants, the stock was mustered, and in January 1848 Potgieter led 600 of his people off towards the north. Ohrigstad looking now like a ghost town was left to its quarrels and the supporters of Kootjie Burger, and presently they too abandoned the place in favour of a healthier site thirty miles away which they called Lydenburg – the place of suffering – in memory of all the tribulations they had experienced.

Far away to the north, hardly affected by the tumult which threatened now to overwhelm their fellow countrymen in the Transvaal, Potgieter's clan set up their huts again beside a marshy stream on the southern slopes of the Zoutpansberg and drove their ploughs through the loamy earth. Elephants abounded in the area and for twenty years. Zoutpansbergdorp depended and boomed on the ivory trade. Here Hendrik Potgieter was to live until his death in 1852, and there in its deserted graveyard the first of the Voortrekkers slumbers today below the mountains he loved so well.

Meanwhile in the south, 1848, the year of revolution in Europe, opened on the high veld of Transorangia with the roar of an exploding meteor. A remarkably flamboyant actor had again stalked on to the stage, and for the next few months he was to dominate it – Harry George Wakelyn Smith.

Sir Harry Smith had been sent out as Governor to the Cape late in 1847 with additional powers as High Commissioner 'for the settling and adjustment of the affairs of the territories . . . adjacent and continuous to the . . . frontier', and he proceeded to go about these duties with the peculiar intensity which characterised all his actions.

He was sixty at the time of his appointment and he could look back on a splendid military career. Before he was twenty Smith had seen action in South America and he afterwards distinguished himself in the Peninsular campaign. He was the hero during its course of a romantic incident which caught the imagination of his fellow-countrymen. In 1812 at the end of the bloody assault on Badajoz, when Wellington's troops were allowed to sack the town for two days and nights, a Spanish girl sought safety with a group of British officers. She was fourteen years old, and even through her tears (for her ears had been hurt when some drunken soldier ripped off her ear-rings) Captain Harry Smith had seen that she was very beautiful. He stepped forward to ask her to accept his protection. With his usual impetuosity Smith very soon afterwards offered her his hand in marriage and within four days of their first meeting Juana Maria de los Dolores de Leon had changed her name to plain Mrs Smith. She was to be at her husband's side during most of what remained of his tumultuous career. Soon after his marriage Smith as a Brigade Major survived the holocaust at Waterloo. Then after service in England he was sent to South Africa in time to serve in the Kafir War of 1835. During its course he made a dramatic ride from Cape Town to Grahamstown and there won more renown by infusing his own courage into the colonists who had been demoralised by their losses. This and Smith's subsequent exploits in the fighting against the Xhosa made him the youthful hero of South Africa, the admired friend of English settlers and Boers alike. Harry went on to win new laurels in India, and it was a splendid victory over the Sikhs at Aliwal which really made him: he was rewarded with a baronetcy and promotion to Major-General. Soon afterwards, in December 1847, he came to Cape Colony again, this time as Governor.

A contemporary portrait of Sir Harry suggests that now he was the very incarnation of the regular army officer who has learned his soldiering under the great Duke. The patrician features topped by elegant waves of pewter-coloured hair, the determined chin, the long military moustache, the large aquiline nose and the nail-hard eyes all speak of a soldier of the up-and-at-'em school, and of a man accustomed to command and privilege. But one has to look hard to find evidence of another side to Harry Smith's character: for although he was very brave and very determined it cannot be denied that Smith was also conceited and pompous and the proud possessor of South Africa's largest ego. More than most men he was governed by his emotions; he boasted and bragged and was not ashamed on occasion to shed a tear; Smith was also happy to ignore everything which did not fit in with his preconceived ideas about the affairs of the sub-continent over which he had come to preside.

Although Harry Smith's energy and drive amounted to near-genius,[5] his unfortunate penchant for the dramatic often made his actions tremble on the brink of the ridiculous. His flamboyance no less than his girth had swelled with increasing years and he was a very different man in 1848 from the one the Colony had known ten years earlier. The new Governor now was for ever playing a part – an heroic part – of which he often seemed to be the most astonished spectator. It was typical of Smith that soon after his arrival at the Cape he should travel in state to its eastern frontier, and there regale an assembly of Xhosa chiefs with all sorts of threats and promises, after which each one was led in turn to kiss the gubernatorial boot in the manner of a Roman triumph. On another famous occasion Smith placed his foot on the prostrate figure of a defeated chieftain and brandished the sword of victory over him. Inevitably Sir Harry at this stage of his career inspired either admiration or loathing in all who met him: there was no in-between stage, and it was unfortunate that the Boers of Transorangia who had welcomed him as an old friend should very soon have learned to hate his very name.

For Sir Harry Smith, that disciple of British expansion, within a few weeks of his arrival in South Africa formally annexed all the land between the Orange and Vaal rivers under the name of the Orange River Sovereignty, and thus brought many of the Voortrekkers back within the Imperial fold. Pharaoh had struck again. First

Natal and now the central plains of the interior below the Vaal had been lost to them.

The annexation was the action of an impulsive man who was far too sure of himself; Smith had jumped to a wholly wrong conclusion; on the strength of a few messages of welcome from friends among the emigrant Boers beyond the Orange he had decided that they would welcome the imposition there of British rule.

The arrival at the Cape of Sir Harry Smith more or less coincided with the decision of Andries Pretorius to abandon his farm in Natal and seek a new home in the Transvaal. He settled in the Magaliesberg but almost immediately became caught up in the political agitation which followed Smith's proclamation of the Orange River Sovereignty. It fell now to Pretorius and not to the distant Potgieter to rally opposition to the annexation of Transorangia. In all fairness we must note that at first he attempted to work with Potgieter and made a genuine attempt to heal the old breach but his rival turned out to be more concerned with obtaining British recognition of his own independence than in offending Smith by supporting his fellow-countrymen on the other side of the Vaal. In any case Potgieter was preparing at the time for his move to the Zoutpansberg and this absorbed his interest, but of course the strained relations between the two men gave the situation a slant of its own and may have been at least partly responsible for 'Ou Blauberg's' unhelpful (and to Afrikaners, unpatriotic) attitude. Potgieter once again was discharging his larger loyalty at the expense of the majority of his countrymen. We must remember too that he regarded Pretorius as the man who had surrendered Natal and accepted British rule for years, yet who now wanted to improve his own political image by posing as the champion of an independent Transorangia; for his part Pretorius must have found it difficult to forget the way Potgieter had abandoned the Natalians after the Vlug Commando and now seemed more concerned with guarding the interests of Potchefstroom than with rescuing Winburg from the imperialists. The feud flared up again in the May of 1848 when Potgieter made his position plain at a public meeting held at Potchefstroom and then ostentatiously withdrew to the north. One can be certain that Pretorius was only too pleased to fill the gap. While he was itinerantly preaching opposition to British rule in the Orange River Sovereignty, Sir Harry Smith made a progress through the country in an attempt directed fire I had never seen maintained'. But he reacted quickly enough: he had sufficient time to deploy his troops and repel an initial attack which threatened to envelop his left flank. Then he charged the Boer centre and left, driving the burghers across a stream, through the farm buildings of Boomplaats and on to the adjoining ridge. The British guns were now unlimbered and opened up on this second position. Savage warfare had been an inadequate school for a cool reception of shell-fire and the Boers retired a little hastily to the next ridge. Here they broke and fled when the Griquas and the C.M.R. put in a cavalry charge. By 2 p.m. the battle of Boomplaats was won, and Smith was distributing staccato praise and blame. He had lost 25 men killed and 25 wounded; according to his dispatch the Boers left 49 dead on the field, but Pretorius later gave out his losses as being only 9 killed and 5 wounded.

Sir Harry was always a man to crowd a defeated enemy. His troops followed close behind as the disordered Boer rout went northwards; he swept into Bloemfontein and then into Winburg before the burghers could rally, shot an English deserter and a Boer prisoner named Dryer to show that he was in earnest, doubled the reward for the capture of Pretorius, and drove the remnants of his commando across the Vaal.

The rebellion had been effectively crushed in one swift campaign, and British authority was re-established in the Orange River Sovereignty. This was the second low ebb in the fortunes of the Great ...k. Of all their conquests only the Transvaal now remained to the ...igrant Boers, and this more than anything else had been due to ...gieter's conciliatory policy; but even the Transvaal was bitterly ...ded between hostile factions and it seemed only a matter of time ...re the British would take another step forward and occupy that ...try too. This would mark the final frustration of the Afrikaners' ...mpt to carve out new lives for themselves and the end of a whole ...le's dream of freedom. The Boers' oft-repeated joke that the ...est pests in southern Africa were drought, locusts and English-...seemed in one particular at least to be coming tragicall...

to calm its malcontents now teetering on the brink of revolt. The tone of the manifesto he addressed there to 'My friends, my half-lost friends and wavering Christians' perhaps better than anything else expresses the theatrical restlessness and the pious sentimentality which existed inside the uptight outward sheath of Smith's personality. It reads:

Oh! how I hate and detest the name of war and commotion! The many battle scenes I have witnessed arise like phantoms to my imagination. But as I abhor war, so will I terribly wield its power if you drive me from your affection. If you compel me to wield the fatal sword, after all I have attempted for you, the crime be upon your own heads; and while my troops shall exult in victory I will weep as you have seen me do over the fallen, the defeated, the deluded; your lands will be wrested from you, your houses destroyed, your herds swept off, your own hearts blackened by wicked ingratitude, and your faithful, your generous friend, who has exerted himself for your exclusive benefit, turned into the Avenger of Evil! There are limits to the extent of the most virtuous feelings in this worldly and uncertain trial of life. Aid me, as I desire you, to preserve them to us, and as in generous and uncorrupted minds the superiority of religion carries us through the calamities of this transient life, let us together thus pray: Lord of all power and might, disposer of all things, good and evil, deign to look upon us frail and sinful creatures; teach us *who* are our true friends – preserve and strengthen us in all the trials of temptation; defend us from all the evil practices of wicked men; teach us to worship Thee with our hearts, our minds, our souls, devoted unto Thee through Jesus Christ; direct our hearts and actions towards our neighbour; teach us to live that our course in life may lead us to life eternal; teach us to forgive our enemies and to love our friends; teach us after a peaceful life to look forward to that reunion in Heaven, the fountain of all our hopes on earth, the happy place of rest for our immortal souls. When we must put off the mortal garment, and lie down on the bed of death, let us be at peace with our own hearts!!! This grant us, O Lord, our God Almighty, through Jesus Christ. Amen – H. G. Smith.

Not since the days of Cromwell's victories has the Bible and the 'fatal sword' been brandished in this fashion, but it may be doubted whether in fact their 'generous friend's' rambling and impassioned manifesto did much to turn the discontented Boers away from revolt.

Instead a fresh wind of hope and determination began to blow among the Afrikaners as Pretorius continued his crusade. People's thoughts went back to Blood river and his very name seemed to guarantee success, and this in itself was remarkable since for the past six years Pretorius had quietly accepted British rule in Natal. Gradually his measured invective rose to a scream as he struck heroic attitudes before increasingly enthusiastic audiences from both sides of the Vaal, calling for Transorangian independence. Then he mustered the *Harde Emigranten*[6] of the Transvaal and marched them into the Sovereignty on a recruiting campaign. At first he said his assembling of the commando was no more than a peaceful demonstration to Sir Harry Smith, that he was mistaken in believing that the majority of the burghers south of the Vaal wished for British rule. But this was the year of revolutions. Revolt had swept through Europe during the early months of 1848. Within the space of a few weeks the sound of shattering glass and gun-fire had echoed in its capitals as revolts broke out in Sicily, France, Austria, Italy, Germany and Poland. And now even the Afrikaners took the contagion as they listened to Pretorius insisting that the English oligarchy too must soon be threatened by rebellion, and would then have to recall the red-coats from all the imperial outposts to defend it. Now, he insisted, was the time to liberate Transorangia by force of arms and proclaim it an independent trekker republic. The Great Trek for the second time had brought its children into open hostility against the British.

Everywhere Pretorius spoke the burghers flocked to join him. He was received with especial enthusiasm in Winburg and marched out of the place with 500 armed followers. By mid-July he was in Bloemfontein at the head of 1,000 men and gently shepherded the bewildered Major Warden and his few British assistants across the Orange with a fine collection of scare stories. By August he was commanding an army of 1,200 men and was in effective control of the country between the Orange and the Vaal. But now Sarel Cilliers once more had cause to lament, this time almost in falsetto, that 'again another woe befell us'.

For Pretorius was dealing with Sir Harry Smith and this was just the sort of situation which suited the Governor's undoubted talents. There was a sudden gleam of bayonets beyond the Orange as Sir Harry concentrated all his available troops at Colesberg to drive the invaders out of the Sovereignty. He was able to muster, four companies of the Cape Mounted Rifles, two companies each of the 45th Foot, the 91st Highlanders and the Rifle Brigade, together with

three field-guns. Now Smith had a compact little force of 800 regular soldiers which was supported by 250 mounted Griquas as well as by a handful of loyal farmers. It seemed more than enough to brush Pretorius aside and reoccupy Bloemfontein.

This evidently was the opinion of many of the Boers on command and they began to melt away when on 16 August 1848, after offering £1,000 reward for Pretorius's capture, Smith led the small British army across the Orange at Botha's drift. Smith was in Philippolis 27 August and he was no time waster. The following day he carried at Tauwfontein and resumed the march next morning. Pretorius now had decided to make a stand a few miles farther on with the burghers who still remained with him. He chose his ground care, placing his men along a ridge which straddled the main Bloemfontein, in front of a deserted farm named Boomplaats. lying pickets were strung out along spurs of high ground that the road on either side. It was a fine defensive position, near in length, and it would certainly have commended itself to Smith's old mentor, Wellington, for the burghers could retire cover 'on the other side of the hill' until the last moment series of parallel ridges lay behind it on to which the Boers back if necessary. Smith himself described the battlefield cession of ridges on either side of a stream covered with and bush'. From his headquarters at eleven o'clock

29 August 1848 Pretorius must have watched every British column advanced slowly along the road before the dead-flat plain, yellow with winter drought. separate splashes of green made by the C.M.R. and the scarlet of the 45th and the tartans of the behind them, shrouded in dust, came the wagons large group of Griqua horsemen. Even Sir tinguished, dressed a shade unsuitably in a bl breeches, all topped by a wide-brimmed whi they would march straight into the trap Pre them and his men would be able to shoot the column as in the action at Congella.

The Boers, however, disclosed their po long roll of fire when the troops were ba Smith, the veteran of many battles in the rally his command for he tells us that 'a

NOTES

1 In fairness to Potgieter we should note that the Wesleyan missionaries bought 250 square miles of land near Thabu Nchu for seven oxen, one heifer, two sheep and a single goat in 1833.

2 Beautiful River.

3 Six years after its foundation the settlement was moved to a new site where Potchefstroom stands today.

4 The area so proclaimed was that south of 25° of latitude and stretching from 22° of longitude as far as the Indian Ocean, but excluding Portuguese dominions and those of independent African chiefs.

5 They were recognised by the contemporary South Africans who named the towns of Smithfield, Harrismith, Ladysmith and Ladismith after the Governor or his lady; Aliwal North similarly commemorates his famous victory; Aliwal South subsequently resumed its previous name of Mossel Bay.

6 The die-hards.

7 Sir Harry wore civilian clothes because they were those in which he had previously met the Boers; he was still hoping to avoid bloodshed and believed that once he was recognised no one would have the heart to fire on him.

12

Fulfilment

One result of the Afrikaners' defeat at Boomplaats was their renewed attempt to find a way of binding themselves into some form of political union. The main obstacle of course remained the Potgieter–Pretorius feud. The two men were still at loggerheads, perhaps more so now than ever because their positions as regards the British differed: Potgieter's independence in the extreme north had been vaguely recognised by London, whereas Pretorius was a rebel with a reward on his head. In 1849 when a public meeting was called at Derdepoort in the hope of establishing a single government for the country, Potgieter refused to attend, and the Volksraad which was eventually elected there retaliated by abolishing his office as Chief Commandant.

But the increasingly hostile attitudes of the Bantu living inside the Transvaal made it essential to adopt some form of military organisation, and, in an attempt to appease all factions, the Transvaal Volksraad early in 1851 decided to appoint four separate Commandants-General. Potgieter was to serve in the Zoutpansberg and Andries Pretorius's son in the Magaliesberg, while two other burghers were appointed for the Lydenburg and Marico districts. It was an arrangement which made everyone unhappy: Potgieter remained aloof in the Zoutpansberg, the two officers at Lydenburg and Marico lacked prestige, while young Marthinus was but a shadow of his father. The end result was that the older Pretorius gradually gained the support of the majority of the Transvaalers and became their chief spokesman.

We must turn back at this point to examine the events which had occurred on the other side of the Vaal following the scrambling victory at Boomplaats.

The Orange River Sovereignty had again entered into troublous times. One cannot help feeling very sorry for Major Warden who had been re-established at Bloemfontein. He had hardly any funds at his disposal and only the backing of a handful of soldiers, yet Warden was expected to establish the fundamental institutions of government in an enormous territory, and his resources (and he) were simply not equal to the task. Warden was particularly plagued by boundary disputes with the Basutos, and when he dispatched a punitive expedition against Moshweshwe in 1851 it suffered a sharp defeat at Viervoet. The news was enough to turn the British Government's thoughts to ridding itself of the troublesome Sovereignty which Sir Harry Smith had so gaily annexed.

For a fundamental change had occurred in the political outlook at Whitehall. The early Victorians' thinking had been tinged with humanitarianism and there is no doubt that this had largely influenced their policy during the last two decades in southern Africa. But the old evangelical enthusiasm had burned itself out by now in Britain: the government had become dominated by materialism and obsessed with economy. At the Colonial Office it now seemed clear that the recent attempts to pacify the land beyond the Orange had brought only expense and military humiliation. Coincident with this feeling there had grown up a different attitude towards the emigrant farmers: during the first years of the Great Trek the British had held that the trekkers' 'allegiance was inalienable and their independence a dream', but already by 1848 Whitehall had acknowledged Potgieter's *de facto* control of the northern Transvaal and it was becoming heartily sick of spending money and lives in an effort to control the other high veld Boers. The idea was gaining ground that it would be far wiser to let the Afrikaners go their own way, though at the same time enrolling them as allies to protect Cape Colony's northern frontier. Accordingly two rather mysterious bureaucrats, William Hogge and Mostyn Owen, were sent out to South Africa with instructions to curb Sir Harry's expansionist policies, and to find a way of withdrawing gracefully from the high veld. Reading the history books of the period, we find their names appearing constantly in the text; but we never discover very much about Hogge and Owen, and they leave us with an impression of faceless men fumbling about with a problem which is much too big for them. But in fact, if their political and historical perspectives are at fault, Hogge and Owen in their own way were a very efficient and a very shrewd couple, and they acted throughout their stay in South Africa in what they considered their country's best interests, even if it did mean breaking faith with the considerable number of white loyalists in the Sovereignty as well as with the Griquas enjoying Her Majesty's protection.

Smith at this time had become fully engaged in fighting yet another Kafir war on the Cape's eastern frontier, and he rather casually sent the two commissioners up to Bloemfontein with a free hand to deal with the territory's many problems.

Owen and Hogge soon came to the conclusion that the most dangerous eventuality would be renewed intervention by Pretorius in the Sovereignty's affairs, and they recommended that something should be done at once to prevent it. At the same time the two commissioners advised that the Cape Government would find it impossible to control the 10,000 or more trekkers now living in the Transvaal. Taking these two facts together it seemed that the logical course would be to appease Pretorius by removing the reward on his head and to gain his friendship at the same time by recognising the Transvaal's independence.

Accordingly the offer of a reward for Pretorius's capture was hurriedly withdrawn, and a little later he travelled down to the Sovereignty with considerable dignity in order to meet the British Commissioners encamped at the Sand river. There they held a strange haphazard sort of conference: Owen and Hogge had no precise instructions to follow, while Pretorius only represented a section of the Transvaalers and certainly could not speak for those of the Zoutpansberg district. But there within a marquee that had been hastily erected on the banks of the Sand river the three gentlemen drew up rickety chairs together and began to discuss the situation. In these days when we have grown accustomed for negotiations over any international dispute to last for weeks and months at a time, one is constantly surprised at the speed with which the Victorians conducted their affairs. For now within a single day the future of the Transvaal was settled, and a binding document signed. On 17 January 1852 by the terms of the Sand River Convention, Great Britain formally recognised the independence of the Boers living beyond the Vaal. In return Pretorius promised that in the Transvaal slavery would be outlawed and that he would not interfere in the Sovereignty's affairs.

Without question the Convention was a triumph for Pretorius. He returned across the Vaal to find himself acknowledged as the leader of the Transvaal by the majority of its burghers. The only rift was the continued opposition to him by the Potgieter faction. For the old feud between Potgieter and Pretorius went on and on, and by 1852 it had come to wear a curious air of permanency; indeed it had been inflamed again rather than allayed by Pretorius's diplomatic success at Sand river. Yet at this late date, when the Volksraad was summoned to hear Pretorius's report on the Convention, the two men were induced to meet again. Potgieter rode to Pretorius's stronghold at Rustenburg, and as judicous intermediaries flitted up and down he was persuaded to enter his rival's tent. An anxious crowd waited patiently outside, and presently it broke into a cheer when the tent-flap was pulled back to reveal the two men standing with their hands clasped over a Bible. It was a tableau which has commended itself to all Transvaal artists. For the trek-leaders' ancient, almost visceral, dislike for each other had been publically shrugged off and at last the *Maatschappij* had found a semblance of unity. Joyous hymns and psalms were sung to mark the solemn reconciliation, and in the excitement hardly anyone noticed that Pretorius and Potgieter had prepared more trouble for the future by declaring that the two joint posts of Commandant-General which they had assumed would descend to their heirs. They had quietly agreed to a pact which would allow their families to rule the Transvaal as a condominium after their deaths.

And time for both men was running out. In the August of 1852 Hendrik Potgieter led out his last war-commando, this time against the Bapedi. The strain of the expedition told heavily on him; on his return the old man sickened and sat waiting for the end among the thatched cottages of Zoutpansbergdorp. A pleural effusion developed, and three days before his sixtieth birthday Andries Hendrik Potgieter died. It was the Day of the Covenant, 16 December 1852. Only eight months later Andries Pretorius followed him to the grave. Their passing left an odd gap in the trekker republic on the high veld and it soon widened.

For already the bullet which was to kill one of the co-heirs had been moulded: Commandant Pieter Johannes Potgieter was shot to death in 1854 during an attack on Makapan's tribesmen. Marthinus Wessel Pretorius, however, lived on into the new century and we may note in passing that he received the unique honour of becoming President of both the Transvaal and the Orange Free State.

The British mood for disengagement in southern Africa persisted after the signing of the Sand River Convention; the members of the Cabinet had now lost all their enthusiasm for costly adventures in a distant subcontinent especially as a Napoleon was sitting in the Tuileries again and the Tsar was becoming difficult. The Cabinet's defeatist sights were focused now on the Sovereignty. Late in 1851 Lord Grey in the Colonial Office had shown which way the wind was blowing by upsetting Sir Harry Smith with a dispatch stating that 'The ultimate abandonment of the Orange River Sovereignty must be a settled point in our policy.' A little later, and despite the Duke of Wellington's objections that Smith was one of the most illustrious officers in the British Army, the Government at London found that he had been 'equally deficient in foresight, energy and judgment' and brusquely dismissed him as Governor. He was replaced at the Cape by the gentler figure of Sir George Cathcart, but if the Cabinet looked forwards to a lessening of tension in South Africa it was in for a disappointment. For Cathcart got it into his head that British prestige among the Bantu must be restored before withdrawal from the Sovereignty could be contemplated and anyway he rather fancied himself as the commander of the local military forces which he described as being as 'perfect as he could desire and sufficient for all purposes'. He accordingly blundered into another war with the Basutos and his 'perfect' army only narrowly escaped complete disaster at the Battle of Berea.

The defeat came as the final straw. The British Government was determined now to disannex the Sovereignty as soon as time and the retention of a remnant of dignity allowed. Sir George Russell Clerk was sent out to effect the withdrawal and he took over from the thoroughly discredited Major Warden in Bloemfontein in August 1853. He had come at an unfortunate time. The country was drought-stricken; the clouds held no promise of rain, only of hot winds and dust, and the heat pressed down on Clerk's aching head. If we are to believe his reports the farmers in the Sovereignty were leading miserably squalid lives, and he wrote home to the Cabinet: 'The more I consider the position of the territory, the more I feel assured of its inutility as an acquisition. It unquestionably has some attractions; the herds of game are abundant; the Dutch settlers and their families rarely live on anything else whatever . . . But it is nevertheless a vast territory (that) . . . answers no really beneficial purpose; it imparts no strength to the British Government, no credit to its character, no lustre to its Crown.' In short Clerk assured Whitehall that retreat from the Sovereignty would be no loss. Somehow or other he then mustered a 'well-disposed' group of burghers who he sturdily announced represented the opinion of the farmers in the Sovereignty and by the Convention of Bloemfontein signed on 23 February 1854 half thrust and half bestowed independence upon them as a ruling Council of the Orange Free State. The Union Jack outside the little town's fort was solemnly lowered and the Batavian tricolour hoisted in its place. Great Britain for the first but by no means the last time in its history had pulled out from governing an African territory. Adam Kok and the Griquas had been abandoned to the Boers for the sake of expediency; British citizens, under protest, were deprived of their British citizenship; and as though to mark the sadness of the occasion at the flagpole outside Bloemfontein fort, a trooper on parade there collapsed and died.

The British had abdicated from all responsibility on the high veld; it now finally belonged to the Afrikaners. The trekkers after two decades had attained most of their aims. The wild impossible dream of Hendrik Potgieter all those years before had at last come true. The emigrants whom he had led over the Orange that February day in 1836, and the Boers who had followed them into the wilds now owned more land than they needed; their twin republics had been recognised as independent States and they were at liberty to go their own way, free to order their own constitution, and able to conduct the affairs of all the peoples who lived within their borders. By this time 18,000 Boers were scattered through the Transvaal and the Orange Free State; most of them lived on farms but there were 2,000 burghers now concentrated at Potchefstroom, 800 in Rustenburg, 400 in Lydenburg and 200 in the white cottages which clustered at Zoutpansbergdorp like a group of startled nuns. Two Afrikaner nations had been born from the pains of the Great Trek, and during their conception the two most powerful Bantu States in southern Africa had been utterly defeated.

In the twin Volksraads there was a strange exhilarating air of new beginnings. There were bound to be difficulties and disappointments in store to be sure, but on the whole there was great room for hope.

Natal it must be admitted seemed to be irrevocably lost now by the Afrikaners, and in a sense the two high veld republics were still dependent on British goodwill since England controlled the coast and was in a position at any moment to exert pressure on the interior.

And there were other awkwardnesses to be faced in the years ahead. The Afrikaners, as even the most sanguine among them would admit, had their short-comings. They were a wilfully quarrelsome lot and their feuds had been perpetuated by the continued rivalry of the Pretorius and Potgieter families. The two republics were economically poor and politically inexperienced. The Africans living inside their frontiers had been only temporarily subjugated, while the republics were surrounded by an ocean of independent tribesmen who were potentially hostile. In particular the old problem of the Basuto frontier, which had led to so many difficulties during the time of Smith and Cathcart, was still unresolved and it was bound to lead to difficulties with Moshweshwe in the future. And always in the background loomed the shadow of the Pharaonic Great Britain that at any time might resume its imperial aspirations.

Which indeed she did in 1877 when the British Cabinet reversed its policy and annexed the Transvaal. Although by the employment of brilliant military tactics during the First War of Liberation fought in 1880–81 the Transvaalers regained their independence, the noose around their country was tightened during the next decade after much of Bechanaland had been annexed to Cape Colony and the remainder declared a British protectorate, while Cecil Rhodes dashed all hope of expansion to the north by occupying Mashonaland and Matebeleland. And before the century was out the two high veld republics were to fight yet another war against Great Britain which ended in their defeat and annexation.

But these visitations were undreamed of in 1854. The trekkers deserved their ease. As they withdrew from the hubbub of past events and sat contentedly on the *stoeps* of their new farm houses, contemplating the herds and flocks which filled the veld to its distant horizons, a hush fell over the twin republics. Nothing moved now across the Orange river drifts. There was no dust stirring on the long road which led northwards to the Zoutpansberg. The air above the houses in the little village of Bloemfontein and Pretoria[1] danced in the silent heat. No horsemen clattered into Potchefstroom with news from the outside world, and the huts at Ohrigstad were fast becoming reclaimed by the bush. Birds were swinging high over the quiet battlefield of Boomplaats, and grass covered the wagon tracks Louis Tregardt had made over the Berg. Even the hill of Vegkop slumbered peacefully above its great plain forgetful of the tumult on its October day of greatness. The high veld lay quiet under the hand of its destined owners, the Afrikaners.

The Great Trek was ended, yet in a haunted way it was for ever unended; the farmers who had crossed the Orange twenty years before had wrought more than they had set out to do. They had gained most of their goals and they had also created the heroic period of Afrikaner history. The Voortrekkers had provided their descendants with a running current of cherished traditions and a whole pantheon of folk heroes. Strange new names – Veglaer, Blood river, Bloukrans and Weenen – had entered into the national consciousness. And the memory of the Voortrekker captains was to remain so tangible in South Africa that today they seem almost as quick as the living. The Afrikaners were manacled now for ever to the memories of Louis Tregardt who blazed the trail into the wilderness, to those of Gert Maritz who rallied the emigrants during the dark days of 1838, and Andries Pretorius who lost Natal but finally gained the high veld, and of 'Ou Blauberg' who year after year crisscrossed the high veld on horseback in his quest for the appointed place where his countrymen might live.

The tribulations of the Great Trek had created the intense unconquerable spirit of the Afrikaners which we know today; and these people are still bound together again each year as they repeat the vow made before Blood river. Because their forebears had won against all odds, the Afrikaners have come to believe that life will continue to go their way. They have been entrapped as it were in their own myth, but they have also been strengthened by it, for by a conscious return to the litanies and liturgies of their past, and especially to those of the Great Trek, the descendants of the Voortrekkers have been made acutely conscious of their own particularisms; they have been so enthralled by them that the Afrikaners now find it well-nigh impossible to escape from the dogmas of the past.

Of all the factors which had gone to fashion their ancestors' exodus, no two had been stronger than their fight to maintain racial purity and a wholly admirable anxiety to preserve those life-values which were being steadily eroded from without. Today because of the legend they created, the precepts of the Voortrekkers have taken on something of the force of Holy Writ. Yet as the years have passed and historical perspective has flattened out, it becomes obvious to on-lookers outside South Africa that the Voortrekkers' descendants harbour ideas which run counter to those of the modern world. Perhaps indeed one of the strangest aspects of the Afrikaners' struggle to exist during the last century has been Western liberalism's changed attitude towards them. In 1880 and again in 1899 the Boers were the darling heroes of most of Europe and America, a gallant little people staking their future on a lion-hearted struggle against imperialism; in more recent times if any man can be said to have been the chief architect of both the League of Nations and the United Nations it was General Smuts, the Afrikaner leader.

Yet today, because of the intense heat of partisanship between white and black aspirations in Africa, the Afrikaners who, through the ballot box, have succeeded in absorbing both Cape Colony and Natal into their system, are seen as the outcasts of the world. One marvels at the reversals of public opinion here. Yet, because history has the habit of repeating itself, one wonders too with what eyes the world will contemplate South Africa through the windows of the 1990s.

But for the present the Voortrekkers, in a way not entirely to be logically explained, have provided their descendants with the character and the strength on which their survival depends in a hostile continent. A brave past begets a brave future and whatever trials the Afrikaners may have to face in the future, of one thing we can be certain: they will face them with the courage and faith of Vegkop and of Blood river. For the Afrikaners are an indomitable people.

NOTES

1 Founded in 1855 as Pretoria Philadelphia to honour Marthinus Wessel Pretorius and not his father as is generally assumed.

Epilogue

The Thirstland Trekkers

The Afrikaners remained gripped by the *trekgees* even after the successful completion of the Great Trek.

In 1857 that innate restlessness drove ten Afrikaner families with fourteen wagons and 1,400 head of cattle to trek from the Transvaal through the Kalahari desert into the present-day South West Africa. One member of the party was an eighty-two-year-old Voortrekker named Johannes van der Merwe.

The expedition crossed the Kalahari – the thirstland of the Afrikaners – and established itself for the time being at Rietfontein just where the South West African border makes one of its dramatic right-angled bends, and the existence of a perennial stream allowed the growing of crops. When one of the trekkers was asked why he had emigrated he replied (with an unwitting definition of the *trekgees*) by saying that 'a drifting spirit was in our hearts, and we ourselves could not understand it. We just sold our farms and set out north-westwards to find a new home.'

The success of the Rietfontein venture encouraged another and much larger party to join the original thirstland trekkers: 500 men, women and children followed in their tracks with 128 wagons, 7,000 cattle, 500 horses, 1,000 sheep and (a surprising number) 200 dogs. But whereas the smaller caravan had crossed the Kalahari without undue loss the desert was unrelenting to larger numbers. Most of the stock died from thirst, the trekkers themselves were reduced to drinking sheep's blood and the contents of dead cows' stomachs, and it was a very ragged expedition which eventually staggered into Rietfontein.

The *trekgees* presently again impelled these Afrikaners to seek new land in the Okavango swamps of modern Botswana. Here there was water in plenty but also tsetse fly and mosquitoes. During the next

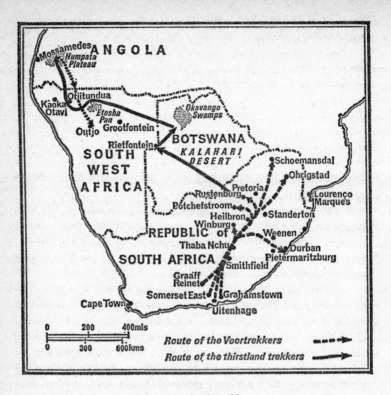

The Thirstland Trekkers

few months about half of the trekkers died from malaria and what remained of the stock perished from nagana.

Under a new leader the community now moved westwards to the Etosha Pan, and from here organised a *Comissie Trek* to reconnoitre the Kaokoveld lying to the west. Healthy country was discovered at Kaoka Otair and Otjitundua, and here the emigrants lived for several years. But again Pharaoh was on the march: the English appeared to be about to annex the Kaokoveld, and to escape them the trekkers loaded their wagons again, crossed the Kunene river into Angola, sought assistance from the Portuguese authorities, and settled down on the fertile Humpata plateau about 100 miles inland from Mossamedes.

By now the thirstland trekkers had travelled nearly twice as far

206

from their starting place as the Voortrekkers of 1838, but here in the magnificent Humpata country they believed they had found their new Canaan, and here they remained for fifty years as an Afrikaner enclave in Angola. The community was reinforced in 1893 and again in 1905 by new trekkers and eventually numbered 2,000. But there was friction with the Portuguese who pressed Catholicism on these brimstone Calvinists and insisted that their children attend government schools. All this led to fears that the emigrants' Afrikaner heritage would be lost. The *trekgees* too was still alive, and after 1928 nearly the entire community left Humpata with their wagons, Bibles, *riempie* furniture and guns. With help from the South African Government they settled in the Outjo district of South West Africa. There their descendants live today in such prosperity that at last the *trekgees* appears to be dormant.

Notes on Text

1. TREKBOERS

The free burghers who were granted land to farm on the banks of the Liesbeeck river (also known as the Amstel) can rightly be regarded as the forebears of the trekboers, and the founders of the Afrikaner nation. They would find difficulty today in recognising their pleasant stream; although part of it leaves the suburbs of Cape Town and flows through a golf course, even here it is more like a sewer than a river. Most of the granaries, mills, and forts the burghers built have of course long since been swept away; but three of the houses in which the pioneer farmers lived have lately been restored at Cornhoop in the suburb of Mowbray, and they stand there very much as their builders knew them. It is a strange feeling to enter these houses today and realise that from them the Boers began the long exploration of the South African interior, and that the track they followed at its outset has developed into part of the present Great North Road.

The coloured Buys folk still live in the Zoutpansberg district. They are concentrated round the village of Mara which means 'weeping', for it was here that they mourned for Coenraad Buys after he had trekked on alone to the north and disappeared. Residents in the area, however, say that his features have been unmistakably perpetuated in his descendants, and that the Buys folk can still be recognised by their everted eye-lids, short necks and wide shoulders.

2. THE AFRIKANER DEBATE

It is impossible to exaggerate the importance of the Slagters Nek affair in exacerbating the bad feeling between the British authorities in Cape Colony and its Dutch residents during the first decades of the nineteenth century. The five men who had been condemned to death after the abortive rebellion on the eastern frontier were taken to the place where it had been plotted and lined up under the scaffold on which they were to die. Rather pathetically they then asked if they might sing a hymn together before the hangman sprang the trap. Assent was readily given and their voices rang out, at first by themselves, but presently they were joined in the verses by the spectators who had been ordered to attend the execution. When the hymn came to its end and the last notes lingered over the mountain scene the hangman pulled his lever. Even as they fell four of the ropes snapped and only one man was left swinging from the beam: the other rebels lay trussed and crumpled on the ground, but very much alive. As soon as they realised that they had been granted an unexpected reprieve, three of these men rushed into the crowd seeking out their relations, while one made for the presiding officer to plead for clemency. But the officer was adamant about his duties: he insisted that the judicial sentences must still be carried out; the ropes were doubled and halters placed about the four men's necks, and at the second attempt their execution was effected. Despite the fact that all the authorities who had handled the sentences of the rebels were of Dutch origin, the manner in which they were done to death was ever afterwards regarded as a prime example of British repression.

The site of the executions can be reached along the Port Elizabeth–Cradock road, N.7. Fifteen miles to the north of Cookhouse a turn-off on the left directs the travellers to this place of doleful memories. But of greater interest to the connoisseur of historical sites and relics is the beam on which the executions were carried out. It has been preserved in the cellars of the Union Building in Pretoria. On request an official will conduct the visitor along a labyrinth of corridors lined with hundreds of bookcases overflowing with dusty volumes of correspondence to where the beam leans negligently across the corner of a shaded room. It is shrouded like a corpse in a long sail cloth. When this is undone the gallows beam is seen to be about twenty-five feet long, almost a foot across and two inches thick.

The great range of mountains which the Dutch called the Drakensberg because early travellers believed its shape resembled a dragon's back, stretches for over 600 miles from Stromberg in the Cape's east-

ern province to the Wolkberg in the eastern Transvaal. They owe their origin to a gigantic volcanic disturbance which more than 2 million years ago discharged a layer of basaltic lava, some 4,000 feet thick, over the central part of the older landscape of the sub-continent. The escarpment of the country's 'roof' presents a truly impressive appearance from Natal. It prompted the Africans living there to call the mountains 'Quathlamba' – a bundle of spears – because to them the succession of jagged peaks suggested a fistful of uplifted assegais.

In his journal Captain Garden notes that Shaka was known to his victims as 'I Fecani' – the marauder; the tribes he drove on to the high veld were similarly called the 'Amafecani' – the marauders. It is thus highly probable that the word 'mfecane' is derived from this source, and that 'marauding' is a better translation for it than the more generally accepted 'crushing'.

3. THE VOORSTE MENSE

Louis Tregardt does not seem very far away as one drives up the Great North Road and approaches the Zoutpansberg: the impressive line of the mountain wall has hardly altered since he saw it when his wagons made their laborious way northwards during the winter of 1836. Nor have the Bavenda people who made their homes on the mountain slopes much changed since Tregardt's time. They were the last Bantu tribe in the Transvaal to submit to the Afrikaners and only in 1898 were they finally subdued. Even today they seem as unresponsive to the dreary attractions of modern civilisation as they were when they drove the trekkers out of Schoemansdal a hundred years ago. Theirs is still a world of smoky fires and witchcraft, of involved traditional ceremonies and veneration for the Zimbabwe-like temples built by their ancestors, and at night the drums still sound over the mountains in a continuous beat as the Venda girls engage in some ancient fertility dance.

No trace remains in the district of Louis Tregardt's pioneer settlements but the salt pan at the western end of the Zoutpansberg where he encountered tsetse fly can be seen very much as it was when the trekkers camped there.

It is common for people to deride the naïvety of the Voortrekkers'

belief that during their northerly march they had traversed most of Africa and reached the Nile river. But there were several good reasons for their having done so: hereabouts they met a new people with a strange language, at the end of the annual rains the Transvaal Nyl floods in very much the same way as the river after which it was named, the sacred Ibis of Egypt is commonly seen here, and the great mass of near-by Kranzkop bears some resemblance to one of the pyramids which were so often illustrated in the trekkers' Bibles.

The exact route taken by Tregardt to Delagoa Bay has been the subject of considerable controversy. Bronze plaques have been put up at places which he is believed to have passed: they can be seen at Graafwater, Zebediela, Nico's halt close to Pietersburg, at Tshok-wane in the Kruger Game Park, and near Sikororo's location in the Berg. The road which runs from Ofcolaco to Trichardstdal follows closely to a section of the line taken by the *voorste mense* through the mountains. The fort at Lourenço Marques where Mrs Tregardt died is still in existence, and the Voortrekkers would have no difficulty in recognising it. The graveyard in which she and so many of the other members of the trek lie buried has been bought by public subscription in South Africa, and a suitable monument raised over it. The grave of Carolus Tregardt is to be found near his Transvaal farm in Middelburg cemetery.

4. POTGIETER

It is believed that Potgieter's party crossed the Orange river at Win-terhoekdrif near modern Bethulie, but it is difficult now to recapture the theatrical scene from the past since the building of the Hendrik Vervoerd dam has greatly altered the countryside's appearance.

5. VEGKOP

There are several curious features about the battle of Vegkop. One is the fact that we are uncertain of the exact date on which it was fought. General agreement exists that it took place during the October of 1836, but different authorities give the actual day as the 2nd, 16th, 19th and 29th of the month. To me the 16th seems to be the most likely of the four dates. Another perplexing point about the

battle is that although Potgieter commanded the laager, Cilliers in the account he gave of it many years later contrives to avoid mentioning his rival's name, and takes the entire credit for the laager's successful defence. Perhaps an old-standing grudge was responsible for the lapse, but it has been enough to puzzle several historians of the period.

Contemporary accounts of the battle give widely discrepant figures for the number of Matabele engaged. Lindley says 2,000, Moodie 5,000, and Cilliers 6,000. I am inclined to take the last figure as being most accurate. A similar disparity concerns the number of Matabele casualties: the figures range from 150 to 450. Cilliers gives the number as 430, while Potgieter says that 150 warriors were killed outright and over 200 mortally wounded.

The traveller can reach Vegkop from Heilbron some thirteen miles down the Lindley road: the hill is easily recognised, for not only does it dominate the surrounding plain but the letters VECHTKOP (an alternative spelling of the name) are picked out in large white letters on its scrubby slopes. For the *aficionados* of battlefields, Vegkop is something of a disappointment: the place has been badly disfigured by ugly corrugated sheds which were put up to give shelter to the pilgrims who visit the place on special occasions like the Day of the Covenant. In the presence of these monstrosities it is difficult to visualise in one's mind the place's day of greatness in 1836, or to catch a gleam of flung assegais between the stilted lines of Afrikaans on the three monuments which stand here, one of which incidentally gives the date of the action as 2 October 1836. Some trees have been planted among the sheds in memory of the battle, but they are sadly thin and straggly, and only owe their lives to the attentions of an African caretaker, whose face when I last visited Vegkop was snugly hidden behind an airman's helmet of First World War vintage to keep out the cold.

Two lonely graves are to be found just outside the huddle of sheds, memorials and trees. In them, where they were buried outside the wagon laager when Mkalipi's impi withdrew, rest Piet Botha and Nicholas Potgieter, brother of 'Ou Blauberg' himself.

Vegkop is perhaps a more satisfactory site for the archaeologist than the historian: a scramble to the top of the koppie will reveal some fine remains of the corbelled stone huts of an ancient Leghoya settlement.

Mosega is far more likely than Vegkop to release the springs of historical imagination. It can be reached from the road which links Mafeking and Zeerust. A large sign-board by the side of the road tells us most of what we should know about the place. It reads: 'West of this valley on 17 January 1837 Commandant Hendrik Potgieter broke the impis of Moselekatse. On the farm Sendlingspos, about one mile west of this place there are three small monuments, one for Mrs Wilson, the wife of an American missionary who died in 1836. The second monument shows the place where the French missionaries Lemue, Rolland and Pelleissier in 1832 erected the first houses for whites in the Transvaal. The third monument shows the place where the bodies of Mrs Wilson and Commandant J. G. Mocke were buried before the ground was ploughed up.' From the notice-board it is only a short drive to the basin of Mosega. A harp-like silence hangs there in the air as though all life in the basin was stilled by the sudden disaster of the Boer attack, and this despite the fact that six farmhouses are scattered in the valley below the mountain down which Potgieter's horsemen galloped to the attack, each one concealed by a screen of trees. The plough has cleared away all traces of the kraals in the basin, but hut remnants are to be seen in a ravine that cuts into the encircling heights on the west, and five or six years ago a prospector uncovered the remains of some of the Matabele killed during the fight.

A watercourse which irrigates the valley's fertile soil leads to the monument which marks the site of the house where David Lindley was aroused by Stephanus Erasmus desperately seeking news of his dead son. Less than fifty yards away is the memorial where the grave of fiery Johann Mocke, who declared the republican status of Transorangia, has been lost in the ploughland.

6. PILLAR OF SMOKE BY DAY

The trekkers travelled northwards in ox-wagons which were very similar to the Conestoga wagons of pioneer Americans heading towards the western prairies. For the trekkers each wagon represented a home, a fortress and a church. The Voortrekker Museum in Pietermaritzburg houses one of the wagons which was used during the Great Trek; another one stands in the museum situated beside the Voortrekker Monument in Pretoria but the best example of all is to be seen in the Potchefstroom museum.

It is easy to obtain a very good idea of the clothing worn by the Voortrekker by visiting the Pietermaritzburg museum. The dresses of the women exhibit a taste for daintiness which is at variance with one's usual sombre idea of the clothes associated with them. The long dresses exhibited are of floral, checked and striped cotton materials, with silk, satin, velvet and brocade reserved for Sunday best. Aprons of the waistband type reaching to about six inches above the skirts' hem were clearly popular: they were of print, silk and taffeta and many of them are richly embroidered. Fringed scarves were also commonly used to enhance the simple cut of the dresses; they were usually pinned in place by a brooch of gold, silver or ivory. Shawls were favoured by the older women. Bonnets or *kappies* were universally worn by the women and girls to protect their complexions from the sun, and great pains were taken to decorate them.

One is surprised too, in the museum, by the evident fondness of the Voortrekker men for fine clothes to be worn on special occasions. One sees there Sarel Cilliers' double-breasted wedding waistcoat of oyster-coloured silk, and that of Piet Uys in blue velvet corduroy, while Andries Pretorius favoured a waistcoat of blue satin brocade covered with red and white flowers, whose diminutive size shows him to have been an unexpectedly small man. The sheer physical stature which usually characterised the Voortrekkers, however, is exemplified by the enormous leather jacket and trousers seen here of one Coenraad Snyman.

Another collection of weapons and clothes worn during the Great Trek is exhibited in the museum at Pretoria.

The graveyard of the Dutch Reformed Church at Thaba Nchu contains the graves of several Voortrekker children who died of fever. Two of the bodies were discovered interred some miles away at Morokashoek on the southern flank of Blesberg, and this together with the find of many fragments of crockery enabled the site of the main trekker camp to be identified. The place can be reached over a rough track which runs in an easterly direction from the Morokashoek government farm. A considerable amount of 'foreign' bush grows here which obviously took root from the circular fences set up round their wagons by the trekkers when they rested at Blesberg. The place is a natural cattle camp, with open water, good grazing, and well sheltered by the encircling hills.

Two miles away a monument at the 'Nek of the jolting wheels' marks the only route the trekkers could have taken after leaving the Blesberg camp for the north. Maritz, Retief and Uys all came this way during the Great Trek, and proceeded through Hout Nek and Verkeerdervlei towards Winburg. But to my mind the most interesting memorial of the Trek in this area is Archbell's house which still stands at Thaba Nchu. It is solidly built of stone, though it has recently been plastered and painted a blueish green and a corrugated roof has replaced the original thatch. As soon as one enters this house it captures one completely. History comes alive here and it takes only a puny effort of the imagination to visualise Hendrik Potgieter striding again over its threshold as he did after Vegkop to thank the missionary for the help he gave in extricating the trekkers' wagons stranded on the battle-field.

7. SERPENT IN EDEN

Piet Retief gave the name of Blydevooritzicht – joyful prospect – to the place from which he obtained his first entrancing view of Natal. It can be reached along the crest of the Drakensberg after ascending Oliviershoek Pass along the Bergville–Harrismith road. Below it one can see the Steps Pass which Retief used to descend the Berg. It is always a little hard to leave Blydevooritzicht for it remains today a place of beauty, quiet with its memories.

A little farther along the main road and some eighteen miles short of Harrismith a side-road on the right leads to Kerkenberg. Its name can be seen from afar, written in large white letters on a grassy slope below a weathered sandstone cliff. This is the place where Retief's party rested under the mountain while he paid his first visit to Umgungundhlovu. Such a profusion of wild flowers grows now as it did then among the sweet grass that one can easily understand why the girls who accompanied the trek delighted in picking them to decorate their wagons. It was to this camp, whose site is marked by a stone cairn, that the two messengers brought good news from their leader to the trekkers on 11 November 1838 and sparked off their joyous celebrations. It is still possible to follow the winding path taken next day by Deborah Retief to the strangely shaped cave at its end where Erasmus Smit held his church services. A rocky chamber has been formed here by some ancient earthquake, and an immense rock rears itself up as though striving to embrace the parallel dome of its smaller sundered fellow. On the cave wall, and clearly to be seen behind its protecting glass, is the painting made by Deborah of her father's name in a mistaken spirit of gratitude and thanksgiving.

On my last visit to Kerkenberg I encountered some children who had found a spot near the Retief stone which gave a voice to the mountain above. 'Piet Retief' they yelled, facing towards Kerkenberg, and back echoed the name, reverberating far across the deserted veld until the whole air was filled with its fading repetition. But the echo seemed to be partisan: the children convinced me that when they called it out, by some curious trick of acoustics the Kerkenberg refused to repeat Dingaan's name.

Umgungundhlovu, now named Dingaanstat, is most easily reached from the Melmoth–Mahlabatani road. Little remains today of Dingaan's capital; old photographs show that a great deal of bush encroachment has taken place along the ridge where it stood, and the enormous oval parade ground is now a wilderness of *acacia tortilos* and *aloe marlothii*. All there is to see of the town itself today is a complex of hut floors which have been uncovered in the *isigodhlo*, the depressions which mark the kraal's grain storage bins, the mound of earth from which the king could overlook his subjects' activities, and a midden which for a long time was presumed to be Dingaan's bath. A monument has been erected at the spot where it is believed that the king put his mark to the deed of cession which gave the country south of the Tugela to the trekkers. It was here too that Dingaan entertained Retief's party on 6 February 1838, and where he stood up with his sudden shout of 'Bulalani abatagati' – 'kill the wizards'.

The Rev. Francis Owen's camping place near by on Hlomo Amabuto is marked by a giant euphorbia tree. It looks on to both the ridge where the great kraal stood, and on to Kwa Matiwane. Coming there today one sees the execution hill almost as with Owen's eyes and it is very easy to re-create the 'deed of blood' which is still remembered in South Africa with horror as though it had taken place only yesterday. The modern buildings of a mission of the Dutch Reformed Church surrounds Owen's camp. The church is an immense and impressive building. From it two cloister-like wings spread out as though to represent the horns of a Zulu impi, but they in fact symbolise a truly Christian concept and revenge of drawing men and women in to worship God where once the savage deities of Africa were propitiated and the trekkers treacherously slain.

The *pièce de résistance* among the exhibits of the Voortrekker Museum at Pietermaritzburg is a reproduction of part of Dingaan's 'palace' at Umgungundhlovu; it shows replicas of the beaded pillars which graced the interior of the great hut and also the figures on its floor of the snakes which, like his hideous vultures, the king chose to treat as pets.

8. THE GREAT MURDER

Kwa Matiwane, Dingaan's hill of execution, lies about half a mile from the entrance to the king's 'Great Place', and is joined to it today by a track which leads through the Umkumbane stream. This track follows the path along which Retief and his men were dragged to their deaths, and standing on it today it is very easy for the mind to visualise again the immense multitude of shouting Zulus which bore the white men along. I know of no place where the atmosphere is so stiff with dread and so oppresive as Kwa Matiwane, and where the dirty light is so frightening to the eye, and always one is glad to leave the place. Usually a few small African boys are hanging about the hill and with very little encouragement they will conduct the visitor over its slopes, excitedly indicating the place where Retief was killed and the round black boulders which were used to beat in the trekkers' skulls. They will point out too a round depression on the hillside which they assure you was made by men looking for the Pretorius stone. The story goes that the men of the Wen Commando engraved a large stone with the names of their officers and a short account of the success at Blood river. Then before they rode away they buried the stone on the slopes of Kwa Matiwane. However apocryphal the story may be, people are said to have been searching for this stone ever since.

At the foot of the hill stands a memorial erected in 1922 to the men who died here on 6 February 1838, and just below is the mass grave in which Pretorius buried the decayed remains of his countrymen on the Christmas day of the same year. The gravestone today wears a curiously modern appearance and before one goes away it is difficult not to think that it would feel far happier in Kensal Green than on the grim rocky slopes of Kwa Matiwane.

The chair carved from a single block of wood on which Dingaan was sitting when he gave the order for the murder of Retief's party is preserved in the museum at Pietermaritzburg, and it is, I think, one of the most melancholy relics of the Voortrekker saga.

The student will come across references to the suggestion that Gardiner and Owen instigated the trekkers' death in Gustav Preller's biography of Retief. There was in fact no basis for these allegations, and Helen Wilson in a rare book, *The Two Scapegoats*, has published an indignant refutal of them.

In 1895 the bodies of the Voortrekkers who died on the night of 'the Great Murder' were exhumed from their scattered graves along the course of the Moordspruits and the Bloukrans river, and they were re-interred during a solemn ceremony in a mass grave, near the Colenso–Durban road, where a monument was erected. The remains of Gert Maritz were also taken from Sooilaer and buried at this same site. The Bloukrans Monument is a spot especially revered by the Afrikaner nation. It can be reached down a sign-posted track some twelve miles from Estcourt.

The site of the laager from which Gert Maritz successfully resisted the Zulu attack on the night of 16/17 February 1838 is the most easily reached of all the contemporary Voortrekker laagers. It lies just outside Estcourt and what amounts to a bird's-eye view is obtained from Fort Durnford in the environs of the town. The horse-shoe bend of the river which gave the place its military strength is clearly visible. On the site itself remnants of the camp's clay walls are still to be seen, and the fields here are even now irrigated by the water furrow cut by Maritz in the happy days before the Zulu on-slaught.

At Willow Grange (a hamlet which incidentally was the high-watermark of the Boer invasion of Natal during 1899) on the road between Estcourt and Mooi River, a turn-off on the left indicates the way to Rensburgkoppie. A rough track leads to the hill on which the Rensburg party took refuge during the Zulu attack. But it is not of the Rensburgs that one thinks about here: instead the fragile ghost of Marthinus Oosthuizen hovers over the hill today, for here he entered into the pantheon of Afrikaner heroes by galloping through an impi and bringing ammunition to the hard-pressed trekkers.

The site of Doornkop where his family camped when Piet Retief made his second fatal visit to Umgungundhlovu is marked by a monument west of Chieveley along the Frere–Winterton road. The laager was a strong one but it lay beyond the Zulu advance and was not attacked. After 'the Great Murder' Doornkop acted as a rallying point for the mauled trekkers and from it was mounted the counter-attack which drove the Zulus back over the Tugela.

9. BLOOD RIVER

A number of controversies perplex the historical student who sits down to consider the Vlug Commando and Blood river campaigns. To begin with no one is quite sure where the Battle of Italeni took place. It is difficult to accept the Rev. Francis Owen's statement (which was given on hearsay information) that the action was fought 'within half-an-hour's ride and within sight of Umgungundhlovu'. A substantial amount of evidence on the other hand suggests in fact the battle was fought some distance from the 'Great Place', at a spot about ten miles south-west of Babanango and five miles west of Owen's Cutting; certainly this countryside fits very well with the descriptions of the battle-field left by the Voortrekkers, and to add substance to the suggestion the eminence there is known today as Taleni.

A national monument marks the site of the battle of Ndondaku-suka; it can be seen on a hill which stands on the northern bank of the Tugela where it is crossed by the James Ross bridge. Last time I visited the place, the plaque gave the date of the massacre as 1835 and not 1838. The names of the thirteen British who came to the aid of the Voortrekkers and were killed on this hill are commemorated on a tablet mounted in the Old Fort, Durban.

It is worth noting that the same site of Ndondakusuka saw more fighting in 1856 when Cetshawayo annihilated the army of his brother Mbuyasi during a dispute over their father's succession. No less than 23,000 men, including six of Mpande's sons and the only son of Dingaan, perished in this, the bloodiest battle of Zulu history.

A second dispute concerns the place where the Boers made their Covenant with the Lord during their approach march to Blood river. For many years it was accepted that this important event in Afrikaner history took place at Danskraal just outside modern Ladysmith, but some authorities have recently suggested that the Vow was made at the Wasbank laager. Curiously enough it would seem that neither opinion is entirely wrong, for the probability is that although the original Covenant was made at Danskraal, it was afterwards repeated every evening during the next week, and this included the overnight stop at Wasbank.

Since 1838 the Vow has each year been solemnly renewed in South Africa on the anniversary of the battle of Blood river. The 16th December is usually spoken of as the Day of the Covenant and is kept as a Sabbath holiday: sometimes, though less commonly now, one hears it being called 'Dingaan's Day'.

The exact site, shape and size of the Boer laager at Blood river have likewise been the subjects of argument. One would have supposed that at least there could have been no controversy about the site since at a meeting held at Blood river on 16 December 1866, survivors of the battle built a cairn 'about in the centre of the old laager', and when on the centenary of the battle a fine monument in the form of a granite ox-wagon was built it was placed directly over this old cairn. At the time of writing an even more ambitious monument in the shape of 64 life-size bronze-covered fibre-glass ox-wagons standing in a great D-shape is being erected round the traditional spot which for so long has been accepted as marking the centre of the laager.

Yet the cairn stands a considerable distance from the river and donga, and it is difficult to believe that a man of Pretorius's tactical ability would have deliberately placed his laager so far from such natural defensive obstacles. It seems more likely to me that the cairn was in fact raised in the main 'killing area', well outside the laager, and that the wagons stood nearer the river. It follows now that the outline of the laager would not be an oval but have had to conform to the wedge-shaped tongue of land lying between the donga and river, and that the front presented to the main Zulu assault was that of the arc of a circle. As regards the size of the laager it must have been dictated by the fact that it had to accommodate 500 horses and an even greater number of trek-oxen during the battle, for I cannot go along with the suggestion that Pretorius on the day of the battle concealed his oxen in the near-by hills, since by doing so he would have risked their being spotted and swept away by Zulu scouts, a loss which would have resulted in the commando's wagons being disastrously stranded.

The account of the battle of Blood river which I have given differs in other details from its generally accepted version. This is partly because, when considering this crucial event in the Voortrekker saga, I have relied to a considerable extent on the notes made on it by Captain Robert Garden. Garden during his service in South Africa, from 1843 to 1859, had an idea of publishing a book on the country and compiled copious reports of everything that interested him. Fortunately his manuscript has been preserved, and although the text dealing with Blood river was taken down more than ten years after the battle, it was clearly dictated by an eye-witness. Besides elucidating other puzzling aspects of the action, Garden's notes explain how it came about that Ndlela fought it with his army divided into two and so at a great tactical disadvantage.

Retief's water-bottle and prayer book which were found by the Wen Commando beside his corpse on Kwa Matiwane are both on display at the Voortrekker Museum in Pietermaritzburg.

The saddle-shaped hill overlooking the battlefield of Blood river was called Gelato by Pretorius, and afterwards renamed Vegkop. But one suspects that the Commandant-General, when he studied the terrain before battle and questioned his Zulu prisoners, became confused by the answers he received, for a hill called Hlatu (which sounds very similar to Gelato) stands some distance away to the east.

Six miles to the east of Umgungundhlovu, at a place on the map named Mtonjaneni, the traveller along the Melmoth–Mahlabatini road can see a long defile on the right leading down to a distant river and an isolated koppie beyond. This was the place where began the scrambling action which has been dignified by the name of the battle of the White Umfolozi river. The Boer commander, Hans de Lange, whose military reputation suffered as its result, escaped on this occasion with his life, but in his old age he came to a miserable end. De Lange stayed on in Natal after the British annexation and in 1860 was arrested for shooting an African servant. He was duly sentenced to death but when the time came for him to be hanged his sympathisers had seen to it that all the suitable rope in Natal had disappeared. Eventually some rope of poor quality was unearthed, but de Lange's heavy weight, in a gruesome reprise of Slagters Nek, broke it three times. In the end, and at the condemned man's suggestion, the British authorities finished him off with some *riems* taken from his own wagon which was standing near by.

Alexander Biggar was one of the Britishers in Natal who wholeheartedly threw in his lot with the Voortrekkers. He had his own reasons for compromising his English patriotism. For in 1817 Biggar was cashiered from the British Army after having embezzled regimental funds which he considered could be better employed in financing his daughter's education. Settling in South Africa Biggar became even more embittered against his countrymen by the failure of the Cape Government to recompense him for losses suffered during the 6th Kafir War. His change of allegiance, however, brought him little but sadness. One of his sons was shot dead by a Boer (who had jumped to the conclusion that the young man was pilfering his wagon) when he tried to warn the Bloukrans laagers of the coming Zulu attack; a second son fell at Ndondakusuka during Tambuza's attack on the 'Grand Army of Natal', while Alexander Biggar himself died with most of his levies that same year on the treacherous banks of the White Umfolozi.

Some way to the north of Umgungundhlovu the collector of historical sites will find the hill Isilala, where Dingaan sat and watched the burning of his 'Great Place' in a Zulu version of 'The Moor's last look'.

Early in 1839 lists were opened to erect a church in Pietermaritzburg in response to the vow taken by members of the Wen Commando. The building was completed in 1841 and is well preserved today although its gable and porch are new. It was used for worship until 1861 but after a new church had been built, the old building was used at first as a school, and then after being sold for £700 in 1874 served successively as a blacksmith's shop, a mineral water factory, a chemist's shop and a tea-room. The building was rescued for restoration by public subscription in 1910 and two years later was opened as a museum.

10. NATALIA

Close to the centre of bustling Durban, the park-like grounds of the Old Fort seem like an oasis of peace. In them one can still see a fragment of the earthern ramparts behind which Major Smith's men sheltered during their twenty-six day siege, and near by a plaque marks the spot from where Dick King set off on his epic ride to Grahamstown which resulted in the garrison's relief. A monument has been set up in Congella Park close to where Pretorius established his commando's camp in 1842. He chose a place where, twenty years before, Shaka had established a military post to keep an eye on the British Settlers at Port Natal (the Zulus had jokingly called the place *uKangel amaNkengane*, which can be translated as 'Watch the vaga-bonds', and the name had been simplified by the Boers). Today a wilderness of cranes and warehouses and all the other busy para-phernalia of a modern port have chased the ghosts away from the battlefield where Smith was so disastrously defeated during the night of 23/24 May 1842, and it is only possible to say that this one-sided skirmish took place somewhere along the sordid length of Maydon Wharf Road.

11. THE HIGH VELD

A good motor road traverses the long narrow winding valley of the Ohrig river to where it widens into a circular enclosed valley frowned over on the west by mountainous cliffs. This is the place where Hen-drik Potgieter founded Andries-Ohrigstad in 1845. Apart from one of the walls of the fort he built there, all signs of the trekker settlement have been swept away by time except for a small sad graveyard.

Time has also erased most of Potgieter's village of Zout-pansbergdorp which was renamed Schoemansdal after his death. The site can be reached from the modern town of Louis Trichardt after about ten miles along the Mara road. At one time Zout-pansbergdorp boasted 200 European inhabitants and after Pot-chefstroom was the largest white settlement in the Transvaal. But the place was surrounded by hostile Bavenda tribesmen and the area was malarial. In 1867 the townspeople accordingly abandoned it for the new village of Potgietersrust, named after the son and heir of 'Ou

Blauberg', who had been shot so soon after his father's mantle descended on him. Today only a few old fruit trees and a Voortrekker cemetery remain to remind the traveller of the old importance of Zoutpansbergdorp.

But the cemetery provides one of the most poignant memorials to the Voortrekkers. Their graves lie together in it dressed in rows like fallen soldiers, each one covered by a rather pathetic little heap of stones, and all of them imprisoned behind the least attractive walls it is possible to conceive. Only one tomb with a large grey gravestone disturbs their simple lines: it covers the remains of Andries Hendrik Potgieter; standing beside it today one somehow feels that his patriarchal spirit roams free, and yet broods over the length and breadth of the high veld.

The spirit of another person whom we have met in this chapter is said to be equally restless: the citizens of Grahamstown will assure a visitor that the ghost of Juana Maria de los Dolores de Leon who married Sir Harry Smith haunts the Botanic Gardens of the town, for there unaccountably in the evening one can still catch a whiff of Spanish perfume.

The farm near Rustenburg where Andries Pretorius settled after he abandoned Natal is covered now by the water of the great Hartebeespoort dam across the Crocodile river. The forgotten field of Boomplaats can be visited by taking a turn-off fourteen miles from Jagersfontein down the Trompsburg road. Nothing much has changed here since the day in 1848 when Pretorius suffered the only defeat of his career at the hands of Sir Harry Smith. Now the summer winds blow gently over the veld at Boomplaats, conjuring up memories of the two extraordinary men who were its chief contestants.

12. FULFILMENT

The place where Pretorius in 1852 met the British Commissioners Hogge and Owen, and with them signed a convention which recognised the independence of the Transvaal, is marked by a memorial overlooking the Sand river close to where a side road leads to the Willem Pretorius Game Park.

The grave of Andries Pretorius is to be found in the old cemetery at Pretoria, where so many of the paladins of South Africa have been buried that the plot has been named Heroes' Acre. The gravestone of Pretorius is exactly the same as that which commemorates Hendrik Potgieter's burial place at Schoemansdal. A third identical stone stands beside the one in Heroes' Acre. It was hoped that Potgieter's body could be brought to Pretoria so that the two greatest of the Voortrekker leaders might rest together, and a second grave was prepared to receive it. But the Potgieter family resolutely refused to allow the remains of 'Ou Blauberg' to be disturbed and the grave next to that of Pretorius is an empty one. It is as though, despite their ostentatious reconciliation at Rustenburg, even in death the two rivals cannot lie in peace together.

Most of the settlements founded by the Voorterkkers have prospered. Port Natal has grown into the city of Durban with a population of 670,000 (181,000 Europeans); Pietermaritzburg is a beautiful city of 120,000 inhabitants (50,000 Europeans); Bloemfontein is the judicial capital of the Republic with 160,000 inhabitants (71,000 Europeans); Potchefstroom was for a time capital of the Transvaal until it was replaced by Pretoria, and has 52,000 inhabitants (24,000 Europeans); Winburg, however, has been left behind by the twentieth-century progress and remains a sleepy little place with a population of 5,000 (1,500 Europeans). Weenen too has remained a small rural centre with an even smaller number of inhabitants.

To mark the centenary of the Great Trek a huge Voortrekker Monument was raised to dominate the southern approaches of Pretoria. After the pyramids this is the largest memorial in Africa.

The great edifice looks half fortress and half mausoleum. Basically it is a granite shell lined on the inside with marble. The main chamber is 100 feet square. Its floor is pierced rather in the manner of Napoleon's tomb at the Invalides, by a circular opening which reveals a cenotaph below commemorating those who died on Kwa Matiwane and during the Great Murder. A small hole in the blue domed ceiling above allows a ray of sunshine to fall on the cenotaph's inscription precisely at twelve noon on every 16 December, the anniversary of the battle of Blood river. Four huge granite figures representing Potgieter, Pretorius, Retief and an unknown trekker are mounted like sentries at each corner of the monument. The principal events of the Great Trek are depicted at the monument first in a series of tapestries housed near by which contains 3,400,000 stitches, and also on the marble frieze which surrounds the building's main chamber.

The very size and shape of the Voortrekker Monument has somehow exactly caught the spirit of the Afrikaners' grim determination to be free to go their own way, and symbolises the massive efforts they made to attain nationhood.

Glossary

Deel lager – sharing laager
Disselboom – axle tree
Donga – washed-out watercourse.
Hartbees house (more correctly *Hardbieshuis*) roughly thatched mud
    and/or daub house, whose name was originally derived from the *harde*
    biesies, stout reeds, which were used for covering the framework.
Isigodhlo – the harem section of a Zulu town
Kafir or Kaffir – derived from the Arabic word for an infidel
Kappie – bonnet which protects the neck
Kis – wagon kist
Laer – fortified camp
Landdrost – magistrate
Meester – teacher
Maatschappij – community
Predikant – Minister
Oom – Uncle
Ou – old
Riem – plaited or unplaited leather thongs
Riempies – thinly-cut rawhide thongs
Schiet-Hokken – loop-holed wooden strong points in a wagon laager
Sluyt or sluit – washed-out watercourse
Smouse – pedlars; many were ex-soldiers, ex-sailors or itinerant travellers
Snaphaan – flintlock muskets
Spruit – rivulet
Stoep – veranda
Touleier – see *voorloper*
Trekkie – a small band of travellers
Velskoens – shoes made from soft hide; copied from the Hottentots
vlei – valley, bog
Voorloper – a person, often a small African, who leads a team of oxen
Wen Commando – The Win or Victory Commando

Bibliography

Agar-Hamilton, J. A. I., *The Native Policy of the Voortrekkers*, C.T., Maskew Miller, 1928

Becker, P., *Rule of Fear*, Lond., Longmans, 1964

Becker, P., *Hill of Destiny*, Lond., Longmans, 1969

Bulpin, T. V., *Natal and Zulu Country*, C.T., Books of Africa, 1966

Bulpin, T. V., *The Great Trek*, C.T., Books of Africa, 1969

Cloete, H., *The History of the Great Boer Trek*, Lond., John Murray, 1899

Chase, J. C., *The Natal Papers* (reprint), S.T., Struik, 1968

Dickie, B. H., *The Northern Transvaal Voortrekkers*, Pretoria, Archives Year Book for South African History, 1941

Fisher, J., *The Afrikaners*, Lond., Cassell, 1969

Fuller, C., *Louis Trigardt's Trek*, C.T., Van Riebeeck Soc., 1932

Galbraith, J. S., *Reluctant Empire*, Berkeley Univ. Calif. Press, 1963

Harris, W. C., *Narrative of an Expedition into Southern Africa*, Bombay, The American Mission Press 1838

Kotzé. D. J., *Letters of the American Missionaries*, C.T., V.R.S., 1950

Lugg, H. C., *Historic Natal and Zululand*, Pietermaritzburg, Shuter and Shooter, 1948

Mackeurtan, G., *The Cradle Days of Natal*, Lond., Longmans Green, 1930

Macmillan, W. M., *Bantu, Boer and Briton*, Oxford, Clarendon Press, 1963

Molema, S. M., *Chief Moroka*, C.T., Methodist Publishing House, 1960

Moodie, D. R., *The History of the Battles and Adventures of the British, the Boers and the Zulus in Southern Africa* (2 vols.), Lond., Cass, 1888

Morris, D. R., *The Washing of the Spears*, Lond., Cape, 1966

Muller, C. F. J. (ed.), *Five Hundred Years*, Pretoria, Academica, 1969

Nathan, M., *The Voortrekkers of South Africa*, Lond., Gordon & Gotch, 1937

Noble, J., *South Africa, Past and Present*, Lond., Longmans, 1877

Nutting, A., *Scramble for Africa*, Lond., Constable, 1970

Oberholster, J. J., *The National Monuments of South Africa*, C.T., Historic Monuments Commission, 1963

Owen, F., *The Diary of the Rev. Francis Owen*, ed. Cory, Sir G. E., C.T., V.R.S., 1926

Pollock N. C. and Agnew, S., *An Historical Geography of South Africa*, Lond., Longmans, 1953

Patterson, S., *The Last Trek*, Lond., Routledge & Kegan Paul, 1957

Rooseboom. H. (ed)., *The Romance of the Great Trek*, Pretoria, Soc. Hist. Knowledge, 1949

Smail, J. L., *Monuments and Trails of the Voortrekkers*, C.T., H. Timmins, 1968

Smith, E. W., *The Life and Times of Daniel Lindley*, Lond., Epworth Press, 1949

Smith, G. C. M. (ed.), *The Autobiography of Sir Harry Smith* (2 vols.), Lond., John Murray, 1902

Thompson, L., *African Societies in Southern Africa*, Lond., Heinemann, 1969

Voigt, J. C., *Fifty Years of the History of the Republic of South Africa* (2 vols.), Lond., Fisher Unwin, 1899

Walker, E. A., *A History of Southern Africa*, Lond., Longmans Green, 3rd edn., 1957

Walker, E. A., *The Cambridge History of the British Empire*, Vol. VIII, Camb., Camb. Univ. Press, 1963

Walker, E. A., *The Great Trek*, Lond., Black, 5th edn., 1965

Wilson, H. E., *The Two Scapegoats*, Maritzburg, P. Davis, 1914

Wilson, M. and Thompson, L., *The Oxford History of South Africa*, Oxford, Clarendon Press, 1969

AFRIKAANS SOURCES

Fouché, L., *Die Evolutie van der Trekboer*, Pretoria, 1909

Kruger, D. W. *Geskiedenis van Suid-Africa*, Nosou, C.T., 1965

Ploeger, J. and Smith, Anna H., *Plate-Atlas van die Geskiedenis Van S.A.*, Pretoria, Van Schaik, 1949

Preller, G. S., *Andries Pretorius*, Jhbg., 1938

Preller, G. S., *Dagboek van Louis Trichardt*, Bloemfontein, 1917

Preller, G. S., *Piet Retief*, Pretoria, 1911

Preller, G. S. (ed.), *Voortrekkermense* (6 vols.), C.T., 1920

Van der Merwe, P. J., *Die Noordwaartse Beweging van die Boere voor die Groot Trek*, The Hague, 1937

Van der Merwe, P. J., *Die Trekboer in die Geskiedenis van die Kaap Kolonie*, C.T., 1938

Van der Merwe, P. J., *Nog Verder Noord*, C.T., 1962

Chronological Table
of the Great Trek

1806   Second British occupation of the Cape
1815   Slagters Nek Rebellion
1820   Influx of British missionaries
1822   Proclamation of gradual replacement of Dutch language by English
1824   Retief becomes bankrupt
        Lieutenant Farewell receives a grant of land round Port Natal from Shaka
1825   Reforms seriously affect lives of Cape burghers
1826   Cape Colony's boundary extended to Orange river
1828   Fiftieth Ordinance allows more freedom to the Hottentots
1834   Emancipation of Slaves
        Commissie Treks set out
        (Christmas) 4th Kafir War begins
1835   *(early): Tregardt crosses Orange river and remains near Caledon river*
        June: Dr Smith pays visit to Mzilikazi
        December: Potgieter begins to trek north from Tarka
        December: Rumours of Glenelg revocation of Queen Adelaide circulate
1836   *(early): Tregardt prepares to trek north*
        February: Potgieter party crosses Orange river
        March: Tredgardt crosses Vaal river
        May: Potgieter reaches Sand river and leaves to make contact with Tregardt
        May (end): Tregardt reaches Zoutpansberg
        June: Potgieter joins Tregardt at Zoutpansberg
        June 27: Potgieter reconnoitres over Limpopo river
        c. July 15: Van Rensburg massacre
        July (end): Potgieter returns to Tregardt's camp
        July (end): Tregardt leaves to search for the Van Rensburg party
        August: Maritz trek leaves for the north from Graaff Reinet
        August: Potgieter leaves Zoutpansberg

August 25: Matabele attack trekker parties which have crossed Vaal river

September 2: Potgieter rejoins his party at Sand river

October 16: Battle of Vegkop

November (early): Maritz reaches Blesberg

December 2: Maritz and Potgieter draw up a constitution for trekkers

1837 January 17: attack on Mosega

February: Retief's manifesto is published

March: Tregardt sends first message to Lourenço Marques

March: Potgieter moves to Winburg area

April 10: Tregardt sends off second message to Lourenço Marques

April 17: Retief elected Governor

Uys moves north from Uitenhage

May: Tregardt sends third message to Lourenço Marques

June: Meeting approves constitution of *Maatschappij*

June: Uys arrives at United Laagers

(end) Smit installed as Trekkers' Predikant

August 7: Buys arrived at Tregardt's camp on Doorn river to conduct his party to Lourenço Marques

August 23: Tregardt sets off for Lourenço Marques

September 9: Retief announces that passes over Berg have been found

September 13: Trekkers hold meeting at Sand river and split into two groups; one under Retief heading for Berg, while Potgieter and Maritz ride north and organise a second punitive expedition against Matabele

October 2: Retief camps at site of Bethlehem

October 7: Retief gets first view of Natal

Rev. Francis Owen arrives at Umgungundhlovu

October 10: Retief arrives Port Natal

October 19: Greyling camps at Kerkenberg

November 4–12: Running fight against Matabele at Kapain

November 7: Retief arrives at Umgungundhlovu

November 11: Retief's messengers arrive at Kerkenberg

November 13: Trekkers begin the descent of the Berg

November 27: Retief rejoins his followers

November 30: Tregardt arrives at summit of Berg

December 23: Tregardt completes descent of Berg

December 28: Retief sets off for Sekonyela's country

1838 January: Sir George Napier succeeds Sir Benjamin D'Urban as Governor of the Cape

January 25: Retief sets off on his second visit to Umgungundh-lovu

February 3: Retief arrives at Umgungundhlovu

February 6: Retief's party massacred on Kwa Matiwane

February 16/17: Bloukrans massacre

February 22: Tregardt reaches point west of Acornhoek and approaches low veld

March 13: Tregardt crosses Lebombo range

April 11: Vlug Commando ambushed at Italeni

April 13: Tregardt arrives Lourenço Marques

April 17: 'Grand Army of Natal' destroyed at Ndondakusuka

April 20: Peffer dies

May 1: Mrs Tregardt dies

May 16: Landman annexes Port Natal

       By this time Potgieter was two days west of the Berg

June (middle) Potgieter acquires land between Vaal and Vet

August 10: Tregardt closes his diary

August 13: successful Boer defence of Veglaer

September 23: Maritz dies in Sooilaer

October 25: Tregardt dies at Lourenço Marques

November: Potgieter settles at Potchefstroom

November 22: Pretorius reaches Sooilaer with reinforcements

November 28: Wen Commando moves out of Sooilaer

1838 December 4: British troops land at Port Natal

December 9: Oath of the Covenant

December 16: Battle of Blood river

December 16: Union Jack raised at Port Natal

December 27: Battle of the White Umfolozi

December 31: Pretorius burns the kraals round Umgungundhlovu prior to his departure

1839 *July: Twenty-five survivors of the Tregardt trek are evacuated from Lourenço Marques*

October: Mpande flees into Natal with his followers

December 24: Jervis evacuates Port Natal

1840 January 14: Pretorius leads *Beeste Commando* over the Tugela

January 29: Execution of Tambuza and Kombesana

January 30: Nongalaza defeats Dingaan's army north of the Mkuzi river

February 14: Mpande crowned King of the Zulus

October: Loose federation between Natalia and the high veld republics formed

December 19: Pretorius attacks Nkapi's kraals

1842 March (end): British troops under Major Smith begin march on
       Port Natal
      April 25: Natalian Volksraad under influence of J. A. Smellekamp
       offers Natalia to King of the Netherlands
      May 3: British troops reoccupy Port Natal
      May 23/24: Battle of Congella
      June 25: Boer siege of Port Natal raised
      December 12: British Cabinet decide on annexation of Natal
1844 April 9: Potgieter declared independence of Winburg–Potchef-
       stroom
1845 April 30: Battle of Zwartkoppies
      June: Potgieter treks to Ohrigstad
      December: Republic of Natalia formally ceased to exist
1846 June–September: Factional strife at Ohrigstad begins to reach its
       peak
1847 June: Potgieter leads reconnaissance across Limpopo and then
       revisits the Zoutpansberg district
      (end): Pretorius leads burghers from Natal to high veld
      December: Sir Harry Smith becomes Governor of the Cape
1848 (early): Potgeiter's people migrate to the Zoutpansberg
      February 3: Sir Harry Smith declares annexation of the Orange
       River Sovereignty
      August 29: Battle of Boomplaats
1852 February 17: Sand River Convention
      March 16: Reconciliation of Potgieter and Pretorius
      August: Potgieter leads his last commando in Sekwatiland
      December 16: Potgieter dies
1853 July 23: Pretorius dies
1854 February 23: British abandon the Orange River Sovereignty

INDEX

Abyssinia, 63, 179n
Acornhoek, 61
Afrikaans, origin of, 25
Afrikaners, nationalism of, 11, 12; origin, 17; life, 18–19; physique, 19; education, 19; love of the veld, 20; love of hunting, 20; form commandos, 20–21; religion, 21–2; attitude to coloured people, 22, 28, 32–3; character, 22–3; relations with British, 25–6, 27; execution at Slagters Nek of, 29; effect of Dingaan murders on, 129; Governor Napier's attitude to, 160–61, 169–70; empire of, 163; attitude to Bantus, 168–9; limitation of farmlands of, 168; battle with British, 173–5; exodus from Natal, 176–9; clashes with Griquas and Bantus, 184; opposition to annexations of Transorangia, 190–92; defeat at Boomplaats, 192–4; British policy towards, 196, 197–8, 200–201; feuds among, 202; traditions, 203; attitude of world to, 204; restlessness, 205–7; see also Boers; Voortrekkers
Albach, Isaac, 46, 47, 55
Algoa Bay, 30, 115
Aliwal North, 91, 195n
Aliwal South, 188, 195n

Alleman's Drift, 91
Allison, Rev. Mr, 121
Amsterdam, 13, 105n, 172
Angola, 206, 207
Antonie, Lascar guide, 57
Archbell, Rev. James, American missionary, 83, 96, 97, 170, 216
Atlantic Ocean, 23, 27
Austerlitz, battle of, 27
Austria, 192

Babanango, 220
Bantjes, J. G., 135n, 146–7
Bantu, 154, 211; effect of Voortrekkers' advance on, 11; migrations, 17, 37; fights with Boers, 25, 86, 184; language, 25; attitude of Boers to, 28, 168–9, 180, 185; characteristics, 36; as servants, 45, 181; attacked by Matabele, 73; levies, 138; settlements, 180; hostility to Boers, 196; fight with British, 141, 200; defeat of, 201
Bapedi tribe, 51, 181, 185, 199
Barends, Gert, 133
Baralong ribe, 71, 85, 86, 88n, 96, 104
Basuto tribe, 96, 197, 200, 202
Bataung tribe, 79, 181
Batavian Republic, 27

Batlokwa tribe, 'Wild Cat People', 38, 118, 119, 121, 124

Bavenda people, 211, 224

Beaufort, 91

Bechuanaland, 202

Bechwanas see Baralong tribe

Beersheba (Sevenfontein), 44, 65n

Berea, battle of, 200

Berg, Willem, 29

Bethlehem, 106

Bethulie, 212

Bezuidenhout, D. P., 122, 152

Bezuidenhout, Daniel, 132, 133

Bezuidenhout, Frederick, 29

Bezuidenhout, Johannes, 29

Bezuidenhout, family, 131, 132

Bezuidenhout's Pass, 123n

Bhaca tribe, 169

Bible, importance to trekkers of, 11, 21–2, 57, 94, 95, 199, 212

Biggar, Alexander, 109, 131, 141, 142, 145, 147, 156, 157, 159n, 223

Birchenough Bridge, 72

Blaauberg Strand, 27

Black Umfolozi river, 167

Blesberg mountain, 71, 76, 83, 84, 87, 96, 97, 100, 101, 102, 215, 216; see also Thaba Nchu

Bloemfontein, 173, 185, 192, 193, 194, 197, 198, 201, 202, 226

Blood river, battle of, 148–54, 155, 156, 158, 161, 163, 165, 166, 177, 191, 203, 218, 220–22, 226

Bloukrans monument, 219

Bloukrans river, 36, 131, 137, 142, 162, 177, 203, 219, 223

Blount, Edward, quoted, 20

Blyde river, 185, 187

Blydevooritzicht, 216

Boers, origins, 13–14; need to trek, 14–15, 16–17; contact with tribes 15; attitude to Dutch East India

Company, 17–18, 25; life, 16–20; physique, 19; religion, 21–2; directions of treks, 23–5; government, 27; relations with British, 25–6, 27, 31–2; attitude to missionaries, 28; execution at Slagters Nek of, 29, 209–10; emancipation of slaves, 32–3; plan migration, 32–4, 41; organise Commissie Treks, 33–4, 39, 40; voorste mense organised by, 41, 45; at Vegkop, 76–82; fight Matabele, 85–7, 103–4; quarrelling among, 87, 98–9, 104; at Zulu capital, 109–10, 117–19; Dingaan to cede land, 119, 155; attacked by Zulus, 130–35; effect of massacres on, 136–7; mutual aid among, 137; at battle of Italeni, 138–41; occupation of Port Natal, 142; attacked at Gatsrand, 142–3; vow to build church (Day of Covenant), 147; at battle of Blood river, 148–54; at Kwa Matiwane, 155; battle at Umfolozi, 156–8; relations with Dingaan, 162; draw up constitution for new republic, 161–2; settle in Natalia, 162–3; federation of, 162–3; problem of black labour, 163; make peace with Mpande, 164–5; final campaign against Dingaan, 165–7; offer Natalia to Holland, 173; attack on British, 173–5; exodus from Natal, 176–9; opposition to annexation of Transorangia, 190–92; defeat at Boomplaats, 192–4; appointment of Commandants-General, 196; British policy towards, 197–8; independence of, 198, 201; settlements, 201; see also Afrikaners; Voortrekkers

Boomplaats, battle of, 193–4, 196, 203, 225
Boschberg, 43
Boshof, J. N., 99, 139, 172
Botha, Hendrik, 46, 47, 55
Botha, Piet, 213
Botha, family, 41, 67, 131, 132
Botha's Drift, 193
Botswana, 104, 205
Brak river, 23
Breed family, 131
British, attitude to Boers, 27; settlers, 90, 168; redcoats, 26, 154, 158, 162, 169–70; in Durban, 98, 108–9, 129, 138; defeat of Grand Army, 141–2; occupation of Durban by, 160, 161–2; battle with Boers, 173–5; submission of Natalia, 176–7, 183; *see also* Great Britain
British Empire, 32, 176
British Government, occupies Cape, 12, 25–6, 27; ordinance against discrimination, 28; policy towards Boers, 29–30, 68, 98, 108, 168, 197–8; Hintsa's war, 30–31; attitude to trekkers, 89–90, 158, 160–61; treaties with tribes, 184; compromise solution of land dispute, 184–5; Orange River Sovereignty annexed, 189–90; gives up Orange River Sovereignty, 198–9, 200–201; annexes Transvaal, 202
Bronkhorst, J. G. S., 71–2, 73, 79, 83
Brown, Joseph, 171, 172
Bruintjes, Hoogte, 23
Buffalo river, 25, 34, 176
Burger, 'Kootjie', 185, 186, 187
Bushman's river, 36, 131, 132, 137
Bushmen, 36, 45, 184; settlements, 15, 180; attitude to Boers, 15, 91; fights with Boers, 21, 24, 70; thefts by, 67
Buys, Coenraad, 33, 57, 209, 234
Buys folk, the, 33, 52, 209
Buys, Gabriel, 57

Cabrobasa Falls, 63
Caledon river, 33, 44, 102, 173, 184
Calf river, 95
Calvin, John, Calvinism, 21, 22, 70
Cane, John, 109, 125, 129, 141
Cape Colony, 112, 178, 179n, 202; Boers in, 11, 33, 39, 41, 43, 69, 89, 176, 204; British in, 12, 90, 160–61, 209–10; harbours of, 98
Cape of Good Hope, 13
Cape of Good Hope Punishment Act, 90, 98, 160
Cape Mounted Rifles, 170, 192
Cape Town, 23, 24, 30, 100, 129, 169, 188, 209
Cathcart, Sir George, Governor of the Cape, 200, 202
Cetshawayo, 220
Champion, Rev. George, American missionary, 114, 121
Charters, Major Samuel, 161, 162
Cherokees, 11
Chieveley, 121, 220
Churchill, Sir Winston, 135n
Cilliers, Sarel, 134, 192, character and appearance, 70–71; fights Matabele, 77, 80, 81, 82, 83, 104, 213; musters commando, 132; fights Zulus, 133; in Natal, 135; in camp on Wasbank, 146–7; at Blood river, 149–50, 152, 154; at Kwa Matiwane, 155; on British, 158, 161; attacks Pondo tribe, 169; clothes worn by, 215
Ciskei, 30

Clapham Sect, 31

Clerk, Sir George Russell, 200–201

Cloete, Henry, 164–5

Coetzee, Jacobus, 23

Coetzer, W. H., artist, 151

Colenso, 130

Colesberg, 70, 184, 192

Colonial Office, 170, 197, 200

Commando drift, 85

Commissie Treks, 33–4, 39, 40, 113, 118, 206

Congella, 162, 172, 174, 177, 193, 224

Congo, the, 36

Convention of Bloemfontein, 201

Council of Seventeen, 13, 16

Cowan, Dr, 36

Crocodile river, 73, 225

Danskraal, 146, 147, 179n, 221

Davids, David, a Griqua, 85

Day of the Covenant, 221, 235

De Beer family, 131

De Beer's Pass, 123n

De Doorns, 56, 57, 60

Deerdepoort, 104, 196

De Kaap, 13, 14, 15, 17, 24

Delagoa Bay, 41, 45, 46, 47, 53, 54, 56, 57, 59, 63, 64, 72, 88, 99, 212

Delegorgue, French traveller, 165, 166, 179n

Dewetsdorp, 65n

Dingaan, king of the Zulus, 51, 123n, 137, 145, 154, 158, 163, 179n; army, 38; relations with Europeans, 40, 108, 109; Retief seeks interview with, 105, 106; Retief's letters to, 109, 112, 121, 122, 124; palace, 110–11, 218; cattle, 111, 114; cruelty, 111–12, 113–14, 115; awaits Retief, 112–13; harem, 110, 114; appearance, 114–15; Owen's attempt to convert, 116–17, 118; reception of Retief, 117–19; cession of land to Boers, 119, 126; unpredictability, 122; fear of Boers, 124; decides to murder Retief, 124–6; murder of Retief and party, 126–8, 129, 218–20; plans massacre of trekkers, 128–9; army attacks trekkers, 130–35, 138–41; flight, 155; British attitude to, 158, 161; is conciliatory, 162; Boers wish to reduce powers of, 164; final campaign against, 165–7, 223; his capital today, 217, 218

Dingiswayo, chief of the Mthethwa tribe, 36–7

Djindi river, 54

Doornkop, 121, 122, 132, 133, 137, 220

Dopper sect, 70, 75n

Drakensberg mountains, 37, 53, 57, 65n, 98, 102, 103, 105, 106, 107 112, 119, 120, 124, 125, 130, 162, 176, 178, 183, 185, 216; description, 34, 35–6, 58, 210–11; difficulty of, 40, 59–61, 64, 107

Dryer, English deserter, 194

D'Urban, Sir Benjamin, Governor of the Cape, 91, 160, 234

Durban, 40, 98, 108, 123n, 135n, 138, 160, 161, 162, 175, 185, 224, 226; *see also* Port Natal

Dutch, 11–12

Dutch East India Company, 13–14, 16, 17–18, 21, 23, 25, 26, 27, 43, 215

Dutch Reformed Church, 22, 70, 75n, 90–91, 215, 217–18

Eastern province, 45, 67

Edict of Nantes, 13
Egypt, 13
Elim Hospital, 52
English language, 32, *see also* British
Erasmus, Stephanus, 73, 74, 86, 214
Estcourt, 131, 219
Ethiopia *see* Abyssinia
Etosha pan, 206
Europe, 14, 15–16, 25, 35, 37

Faku, paramount chief of the Pondos, 169, 170, 172
Ficksburg, 121
Fish river *see* Great Fish river
Fort Durnford, 219
France, 19, 26, 192
Froude, James Anthony, quoted, 11

Gabarone, 104
Gaika, chief of Xhosa clan, 30
Gamtoos river, 23, 24
Garden, Captain Robert, 123n, 211, 222
Gardiner, missionary, 125–6, 129, 219
Garnett, settler, 129
Gatsrand, 137, 142–3
Gelato, hill renamed Vegkop, 148, 222
Germans, 13, 25
Germany, 19, 192
Gewonden, a farm, 52
Glenelg, Lord, Colonial Secretary, 31
Graaff Reinet, 25, 29, 84, 85, 144
Graafwater, 212
Grahamstown, 90, 135n, 174, 177, 188, 224, 225
Grahamstown Journal, 100, 109
Great Britain, occupies Cape, 25–6;
relations with Boers, 162, 173, 198; imperial aspirations, 202; *see also* British; British Government
Great Fish river, 24, 25, 29, 36, 43
Great Karoo, 15, 18, 23
Great Letaba river, 57
Grey, Lord, 200
Greyling, Abraham, stepson of Piet Retief, 106, 107
Greyling family, 132, 234
Griquas, 'Bastards', 33, 74, 85, 91, 102, 180, 184, 201; fight on British side, 67, 192, 193, 194
Gumpies river, 59

Harar, 63
Harris, Cornwallis, quoted, 32, 66, 80–81, 84, 85, 95–6
Harrismith, 195n, 216
Hartebeespoort dam, 225
Heart-water, cattle disease, 52, 65n
Heidelberg, 72, 76
Heilbron, 76, 213
Hendrik Vervoerd dam, 212
Herodotus, 49
Hintsa, paramount chief of the Xhosa, 30–31, 43, 44
'Hintsa's War', 30–31
Hlomo Amabuto, soldiers' hill, 111, 156, 217
Hlubi tribe, 37
Hogge, William, British Commissioner, 197–8, 225
Holland, 13, 19, 77, 97, 172–3, 176, 185
Holstead, Thomas, interpreter to Retief, 123
Hottentots, 16, 29, 75; labour of, 14, 18; settlements, 15, 24; relations with Boers, 15, 21, 28, 91; ordinance affecting, 28, 235

Huguenots, 13
Hulley, interpreter to Rev. F. Owen, 116, 129, 134
Humpata plateau, 206, 207

Imperani mountains, 121
India, 26, 27, 170, 188
Indian Ocean, 36, 163, 195n
Inhambane, 35, 41, 52, 53, 54, 63, 187
Inniskilling Fusiliers, 170
Isaacs, Nathaniel, 38–9, 114
Italeni, battle of, 69, 138–40, 141, 142, 149, 156, 177, 220
Italy, 192

Jacobs, Pieter, 91
Jervis, Captain Henry, 162, 163–4, 166, 235

Kafir Wars, 30, 77, 129, 188, 198, 223, 233
Kalahari Desert, 34, 38, 183, 205
Kaoka Otari, 206
Kaokoveld, 206
Kapain, capital of Mzilikazi, 68, 73, 74, 75, 87, 103–4, 117, 121, 124, 140, 180
Karoo, the, 43
Kei river, 25, 30, 31, 43
Keiskama river, 25
Kerkenberg mountains, 108, 109, 119, 216, 217
Keyser, Bushman slave, 45
King, Richard, driver to Rev. F. Owen, 116, 131, 135n, 174, 224
Kirkman, interpreter, 129
Klein Letaba river, 54
Knysna, 25
Kok, Adam, 184, 201

Kombesana, servant to Tambuza, 166–7, 235
Krantzkop, 141, 212
Kruger, Paul, 78
Kruger family, 41, 67
Kruger National Park, 54, 61, 212
Kunene river, 206
Kurrichane mountains, 85
Kuruman, 38, 73
Kwa Matiwane, Dingaan's execution place, 111–12, 113–14, 116, 123n, 127–8, 129, 130, 134, 135 136, 137, 142, 155, 167, 217, 218–19, 222, 226

Ladismith, 195n
Ladysmith, 146, 195n, 221
Landman, Carol, 142, 145, 147, 156–8, 235
Lange, Hans de, 156–7, 222–3
Langebergen, 23
Langekloof, 23
Lebombo hills, 54, 61, 167
Lemue, French missionary, 214
Lesotho, 38
Liebenberg family, 41, 67, 73, 74, 131, 132
Liesbeeck river, 14, 24, 209
Limpopo river, 34, 36, 48, 54, 64, 72, 73, 104, 183, 187
Lindley, Rev. David, American missionary, 86, 87, 88n, 134, 137, 141, 163, 167, 213, 214
Little Karoo, 15, 23
Little Tulega river, 137, 143
Livingstone, David, 58
London Missionary Society, 98
Loskop, a hill, 137
Louis Trichart, 52, 56, 224
Lourenço Marques, 35, 41, 45, 46, 51, 52, 53, 54, 57, 62, 63, 176, 181, 185, 187, 212

Lourins, Lascar guide, 57
Lydenberg, 54, 187, 196, 201

Macdonald, a schoolmaster, 73
Madagascar, 63
Mafeking, 214
Magaliesberg, 34, 181, 190, 196
Makwana, chief of Bataung tribe, 71, 118, 181
Malan family, 122, 131
Malitel, 54
Manthatisi, woman leader of Batlokwa tribe, 38
Mara village, 209
Marico river, 38, 73, 83, 103, 104, 196
Maritz, Gert, 89, 106, 144, 216; arrives Thaba Nchu, 84; appointed President, 84; description, 84–5; relations with Potgieter, 85, 87, 99, 104; sets out for the north, 85; attack Matabele, 85–6; at Blesberg, 97; meets Retief, 101; sets out for Natal, 105; goes to Kerkenberg, 119; warns Retief, 122, 123; attacked by Zulus, 131–3; effect of massacre on, 135; prepares defences, 137, 138; falls ill, 138; tries to help Potgieter, 140; death, 143, 144; memories of, 143, 219; remains transferred, 219.
Mashonaland, 202
Matabele tribe, 40, 52, 69, 88, 99, 102; relations with other tribes, 38, 71, 73, 96, 109, 181; and relations with Boers, 39, 45, 51, 57, 94, 103; boundary, 72, 74; attacks trekkers, 57, 73, 74–5, 76; at battle of Vegkop, 77–84; 213; attacked by Boers, 85–7,

103–4, 112, 117, 214
Matabeleland, 202
Matiwane, chief of Ngwaneni tribe, 37, 38, 111–12
Matlaba, a Barolong chief, 85
Mbuyasi, 220
Merwe, Johannes van der, 205
Mfecane (crushing or marauding), 36, 72, 163, 211
Middleburg, 65n, 212
Middledale Pass, 123n
Missionaries, 27–8, 67, 74, 75, 83, 86, 87, 96, 97, 109, 113–14, 121, 169
Mkalipi, Matabele induna, 74, 75, 79, 82, 84, 87, 213
Mkuze river, 167
Moche, Johannes, 173, 175, 184, 214
Modder river, 34, 144
Moffat, Dr Robert, 28, 38, 73
Moletsane, Sotho chief, 183
Molopo river, 73
Mooi river, 219
Mooiriviersdorp, 181
Moroka, chief of Barolong tribe, 71, 83, 96, 102
Morokashoek, 215
Mosega, 68, 73, 74, 83, 103; battle of, 85–7, 89, 99, 104, 112, 140, 180, 214
Moshweshwe, Sotho chief, 38, 102, 183, 184, 197, 202
Mossamedes, 206
Mossel Bay, 195n
Mpande, half brother to Dingaan, 220; granted land by Boers, 164; succeeds brother as king, 164, 167; physique, 164–5, 179n; at campaign against Dingaan, 165–7; seeks understanding with British, 175; rules over independent state, 176
Mthethwa tribe, 36

Mtonjaneni, 222

Mzilikasi, chief of Matabele tribe, 51, 88, 95, 103, 124, 173, 183; army of, 38; relations with Potgieter, 69, 98; attitude to Europeans, 73–4; sends impi to attack trekkers, 74–5, 79, 84; trekkers attack, 85–6, 87, 104; territory annexed, 104; empire of, 187

Nagana, cattle disease, 54, 56, 57, 65n

Namaqua Desert, 14

Namaqualand, 24

Napier, Sir George, Governor of the Cape, 160–61, 162, 169, 170, 172, 175, 176, 177, 234

Natal, 34, 41, 102, 105, 119, 202, 216; struggle for, 12, 98, 99, 129, 140, 144, 154, 158, 161; description, 36, 39–40, 106–7; Zulus in, 37, 38; Boers in, 39, 63, 108–9, 124, 136–8, 142; British annexation, 170–72, 176, 179n, 183; Afrikaner exodus from 176–9; Afrikaners absorb, 204; see also Natalia

Natalia, made a republic, 161–2; federation of Boers under, 162–3; area, 167; British march into, 170–72; offered by Boers to Holland, 173; submits to British, 176; republic ceases to exist, 176; see also Natal

Nathan, M., 11

Ncaphayi, or Nkapi, a Bhaca chief, 169, 171

Ncome river, 148, 150; renamed Blood river, 153

Ndlela, a Zulu commander, 117, 128, 138, 150, 152–3, 155, 159n, 222

Ndondakusaka, 141, 142, 220, 223

New York, 105n

Ngqika, chief of Xhosa clan, 30

Nguni tribes, 36, 38, 80

Ngwaneni tribe, 37

Nieuwveld mountains, 23

Nongalaza, a Zulu commander, 165, 167, 235

Nqutu hills, 149

Nyl river, 51, 212

Ofcalco, 212

Ogle, a settler, 129

Ohrig, G. G., 172

Ohrig river, 224

Ohrigstad, 60, 185, 186, 187, 202, 224, 236

Okavango swamps, 205

Olifants river, 34, 51, 59, 72, 187

Oosthuizen, Marthinus, 132, 177, 219–20

Orange Free State, 34, 104, 200, 201

Orange river, 18, 23, 37, 38, 58, 64, 95, 102, 183, 184, 189, 192, 193, 197, 203; as a frontier, 25; land to north of, 33–4, 39, 41; Tregardt crosses, 44; Potgieter crosses, 53, 66–8, 201, 212; description, 66; Maritz crosses, 84; thousands of Afrikaners cross, 89, 91; Pretorius crosses, 192

Orange River Sovereignty, 189–94, 196–8, 200–201, 236

Otjitundua, 206

Oudtshorn, village in the Karoo, 43

Outjo district, South West Africa, 207

Owen, Mostyn, British Commissioner, 197–8, 225

Owen, Rev. Francis, 111, 124, 131; arrives at Zulu capital, 109, 115–16; relations with Dingaan,

109, 115; conveys messages from Retief, 109; on Dingaan's cruelty, 113–14; attempts to convert Dingaan, 116–17, 118; writes letters for Dingaan, 125, 129; witnesses murder of Retief and party, 127–8; leaves Zulu capital, 128; suspected of prompting Dingaan to murders, 129; sees return of impi from massacre of trekkers, 134; account of battle of Italeni, 138, 140, 220; memories of, 217, 219

Owen's Cutting, 220

Paarl, 15
Paris Evangelical Society, 44
Parys, 74
Peace of Amiens, 27
Peffer, Daniel, 45, 47, 56, 62
Pelleissier, French missionary, 214
Philip, John, missionary, 28, 98
Philippolis, 91, 184, 193
Pietermaritzburg, 143, 162, 163, 164, 167, 168, 172–3, 175, 176, 183, 214, 223, 226
Pietermaritzburg museum, 215, 219, 222, 223
Pietersburg, 59, 212
Plettenberg, Governor van, 23
Plettenberg Bay, 25
Poland, 179n, 192
Pondo tribe, 169, 176
Pondoland, 169–70, 171
Pongola river, 37, 167
Port Natal, 63, 107, 108, 117, 123n, 125, 142, 183; harbour at, 40; English settlers at, 106, 108–9, 119, 129, 141, 168, 224; Rev. F. Owen in, 116–17; British soldiers at, 119, 154, 158, 161, 162; news of Dingaan murders reaches,

129, 130–31, 137; trekkers keep road open to, 143; British occupation of, 161; and abandonment of, 162, 169; reoccupation of, 170–72; population, 226; see also Durban

Potchefstroom, 162, 173, 181, 183, 185, 190, 195n, 201, 202, 224, 226
Potchefstroom museum, 215
Potgieter, Andries Hendrik ('Ou Blauberg'), 89, 143, 144, 212; prepares to trek, 41; assists Tregardt, 44, 45; his stock, 65n; Tregardt waits for, 52, 56, 57; reaches Tregardt's camp, 53; rides to Sand river, 55; reaches Orange river, 66–7; his party, 67–8; character and appearance, 68–9; treks towards Blesberg, 71; relations with tribes, 71, 75, 96; crosses Limpopo, 72; returns to Sand river, 72; fights Matabele at Vegkop, 76–82, 217; chosen laager commandant, 84; rivalry with Maritz, 85, 99; attacks Matabele, 85–6; quarrels with Maritz, 87, 104; returns to Vet river, 87–8; attitude to Erasmus Smit, 97–8, 99; ideas on destinations of Great Trek, 98, 99, 103, 105; deprived of office, 101; success at Kapain, 103–4, 117, 121, 124; battle at Italeni, 137, 138–40; agrees to federate, 162–3; reluctant to be involved against British, 173; centre of trekker activity, 177; doubts about Natal, 179; builds up a state, 180–83; announces jurisdiction over Transorangia, 183; abandons Potchefstroom, 185; quarrels with opposition, 185–6;

Potgieter, Andries Hendrik—*contd.*
treks to Zoutpansberg, 187;
death, 187, 199; feud with Pretorius, 190, 196, 199; appointed
Commandant General of Zoutpansberg, 196; leads last war
commando, 199; memories of,
203, 214, 216, 224–5, 226; grave,
225, 226

Potgieter, Hermanus, brother of
Andries, 83

Potgieter, Nicholas, brother of
Andries, 82, 213

Potgieter, Pieter Johannes, 199

Potgietersrust, 224–5

Pottinger, Sir Henry, Governor of
the Cape, 177–8

Pré, Piet du, 134

Preller, Gustav, 219

Pretoria, 85, 149, 202, 204n, 225,
226

Pretoria Museum, 215

Pretorius, Andries, 168, 224;
admired, 69, 158; at the Berg,
122; arrives at Sooilaer, 143,
144, 159n; life, 144; appearance
and character, 144–5; elected
Commandant General, 145; prepares for battle, 145–6; commands at Blood river, 148–55,
221, 222; wounded, 154; sends
out foray, 156; prepared to fight
British, 162; arranges federation,
162; retires Erasmus Smit, 163;
quarrels with Volksraad, 163;
final campaign against Dingaan,
165–7; has Zulus shot, 166–7;
pronounces Mpande's succession,
167; leads punitive expedition,
169; parleys with Major Smith,
172; fights British, 173–5; sees
Governor, 177–8; retires to high
veld, 178; settles in Transvaal,

186, 190; feud with Potgieter,
190, 196, 199; opposes annexation of Transorangia, 190–92;
occupies Bloemfontein, 192; defeat at Boomplaats, 192–4; reward on head, 193, 194, 196;
offer of reward withdrawn, 198;
meets British Commissioners,
198; agrees to Sand River Convention, 198–9; meets Potgieter,
199; death, 199; memories of,
203, 218–19, 225, 226; clothes
worn by, 215; grave, 225–6

Pretorius, Jan, 46, 47, 48, 55–6,
60–61

Pretorius, Martinus, son of Andries,
196, 199–200, 204n

Prinsloo, W., 120

Punt, Dr W. H. J., 46, 54

Quagga Pad, 123n

Queen Adelaide, province of, 30, 31,
32, 41, 100

Rabe, clan of Xhosa, 30

Rachel, a Bushman slave, 45

Rensburg, Van, family, 131, 132,
133, 219

Rensburg, Johannes Van, 52, 69, 71,
72, 74; a leader of the *voorste
mense*, 41; travels with Tregardt,
44, 45, 48; his party, 46, 48–9;
route taken by, 50 (map), 65n;
quarrels with Tregardt, 51;
anxiety for, 53; murder of, 53–5,
57, 64, 75

Retief, Deborah, daughter of Piet,
120, 217

Retief, Piet, 104, 130, 140, 166,
170, 177, 216; drives off raiders,

30; affection for, 69; arrives at Blesberg, 100; character, 100, 102; reasons for emigrating, 100–101; elected Governor, 101; attitude to Smit, 102; ideas on destination of trek, 102, 103; makes treaties with tribes, 102–3; interviews with Dingaan, 105, 106; sets out for Natal, 106–8; arrives Port Natal, 108–9; messages to Dingaan, 109, 112, 121; at Zulu capital, 117–19; at Doornkop, 121, 122; into Wild Cat country, 121; arrests Sekonyela, 121–2; Dingaan plans to murder, 124–6; murder of, 126–8, 129, 130–31, 222; murder avenged, 154; burial, 155; memories, 216, 217, 220, 222, 226

Retief family, 132
Rhenoster river, 34
Rhodes, Cecil, 202
Rhodesia, 53, 54, 63, 71, 104, 179n
Riet river, 34, 184
Rietfontein, 205
Robberts family, 41, 67
Robert's Drift, 51
Roedolf, Barnard, 97
Rolland, French missionary, 214
Roussouw family, 132, 133
Rustenberg, 181, 201, 225, 226

Sabi river, 72
Sagana (Soshangane), Zulu chief, 54, 55, 57, 65n, 75
Saint Lucia Bay, 167
Sand river, 53, 70, 71, 72, 73, 76, 102, 104–5, 106, 181, 225
Sand River Convention, 198–9, 225
Scheepers, Anna, 56
Scheepers, Gert, 46, 55
Schoemansdal, 187, 211, 224, 226

Scholtz, a burgher, 39, 40
Sekonyela, chief of Batlokwa tribe, 38, 118, 119, 121, 123n, 129, 170, 183–4; Retief makes treaty with, 103; arrest of, 117, 121–2; release of, 124
Sekwati, chief of Bapedi tribe, 181, 185, 186
Seminoles, 11
Shaka, chief of Zulu tribe, 37, 38, 112, 123n, 211, 224
Sicily, 192
Sikororo tribe, 60
Sioux, 11
Slagters Nek, 29, 33, 68, 209–10, 223
Slaves, Malay, 19; emancipation, 32, 70–71, 198
Smellekamp, John Arnold, 172–3, 185, 236
Smit, Erasmus, 105n, 120, 146; appearance, 97; attitude of trekkers towards, 97–8, 99; installed as Predikant, 102, 234; christens Kerkenberg, 108; journal, 120; describes Pretorius, 143; sermons, 145; retired by Pretorius, 163
Smit, Mrs Erasmus, 176
Smith, Major T. C., sent to Pondoland, 169–70; marches into Natalia, 170–72, 173; life, 170; parleys with Pretorius, 172; attacked by Pretorius, 173–5; on Afrikaners, 177; memories of, 224
Smith, Dr Alexander, 113
Smith, Dr Andrew, 39, 40, 233
Smith, Juana Maria de los Dolores de Leon, Lady, 188, 225
Smith, Sir Harry, 195n, 202, 224, 225; death of Hintsa and, 30–31; on abandonment of Queen Adelaide province, 31; offers reward

Smith, Sir Harry—*contd.*
for Tregardt, 44; on Pretorius, 145, 178; appointed Governor of Cape, 178, 188; on Voortrekkers, 178–9; marriage, 188; life, 188; appearance and character, 188–9; sets up Orange River Sovereignty, 189–90, 197; opposition from Pretorius, 190–92; crushes rebellion, 192–4; fights Kafir war, 198; dismissed, 200
Smithfield, 70, 195n
Smuts, General, 204
Sneeuwbergen mountains, 23, 24, 35
Snyman, Coenraad, 215
Sofala, 35, 41, 52, 53, 63, 72
Somerset East, 24, 30, 43
Sooilaer, 137, 143, 144, 158, 219
Soshangange *see* Sagana
Sotho tribe, 37, 38, 183
South Africa, white occupation in 11; trekboers in, 13; houses, 18; animals of, 20, 35, droughts, 32; scenery, 34–6, 49, 59, 106–7
South West Africa, 34, 39, 207
Spelonken country, 54, 57
Standerton, 65n
Steelpoort, 187
Steenkamp, Anna Elizabeth, quoted, 32–3, 133–4
Stellenbosch, 48
Stephen, Sir James, 170–71
Steps Pass, 107, 123n, 216
Steyn family, 41, 67
Stormberg mountains, 23, 35, 210
Strydom, Alidu, 56
Strydom, Hans, 46
Strydpoort, the Pass of the Quarrel, 51, 52, 59
Stubbs, visits Zulu capital, 129
Suikerboschrand, 51, 72
Sundays river, 23
Swart family, 131

Swazi tribe, 186
Swellendam, 25, 173

Table Bay, 14
Tafaltop, 103
Tambuza, Zulu commander, 117, 128, 141, 166–7, 223, 235
Tarka district, 44, 45, 68, 233
Tauwfontein, 193
Thaba Nchu, 51, 65n, 71, 83, 84, 85, 87, 96, 195, 216; graveyard at, 215; *see also* Blesberg
Theal, Dr George McCall, quoted, 22
Toit, Johannes du, 73
Trafalgar, battle of, 27
Transorangia, 33, 45, 92, 144, 162, 173, 183–4, 186, 189, 190–94, 214
Transvaal, 34, 38, 104, 187, 192, 194, 196, 198, 200, 201, 202, 211, 212, 225, 226
Tregardt, Mrs Johannes, 43
Tregardt, Karel or Carolus, eldest son of Louis Johannes, 46, 48, 63–4, 179n, 212
Tregardt, Louis Johannes, 66, 69, 71, 72, 74, 87–8, 105n, 181, 203; birth and early life, 43; leaves farm, 43–4; leads *voorste mense*, 41, 44–64; journal, 45, 56, 58–9; relations with Pretorius, 46, 55, 60–61; character, 48; quarrels with Van Rensburg, 51; searches for Van Rensburg, 53, 55, 72, 233; death of children, 56, 59; his route to Delagoa Bay, 59, 65n, 212; death of wife, 62–3; death, 63; memory of, 64, 211
Tregardt, Mrs Louis Johannes, 57, 62, 212, 235
Tregardt, Petrus Frederick or Pieta, younger son of Louis Johannes, 46

Trekboers *see* Afrikaners; Boers;
  Voortrekkers
Trichardstal, 212
Tromp, A. H., 54
Tropic of Capricorn, 35
Tsetse fly, 52–3, 54, 56, 57, 59, 72,
  187, 205, 211
Tshokwane, 212
Tswana tribe, 38
Tswapong mountains, 104
Tugela river, 36, 37, 105, 108, 113,
  118, 119, 120, 123, 126, 130, 134,
  141, 142, 158, 162, 164, 165,
  220
Two Scapegoats, The, 219

Uitenhage, 39, 91, 138, 140
Umgazi river, 171, 183
Umgungundhlovu, Zulu capital, 109,
  115, 116, 125, 138, 141, 158, 161,
  220; execution place at, 111,
  113–14; Retief's party at, 117–19,
  216; meaning of name, 123n;
  tribal ritual at, 124; rumours
  about disaster, 129, 130; Pre-
  torius marches on, 146, 155;
  change of name, 217
Umhlatuzi river, 155
Umkomaas river, 171
Umkumbane river, 110, 111, 218
Umsindusi river, 143
Umtamvuna river, 170
Umzimkulu river, 105, 162, 176
Umzimvubu river, 119, 126, 169,
  170, 171
Union Building, Pretoria, 210
United Laagers, 96, 99, 102, 103
United Voortrekker republic, 163
Uys, Dirkie, son of Piet, 139, 177
Uys, Jan, 154
Uys, Piet, one of leaders of Great
  Trek, 29, 90, 91, 102, 103, 118,
  121, 144, 177, 216; sets out for
  Natal, 39–40, 105; pledges alle-
  giance to United Laagers, 122; at
  battle of Italeni, 137, 138–9;
  killed, 139–40; clothes worn by,
  215

Vaal river, 34, 37, 38, 40, 45, 51,
  57, 71, 72, 73, 74, 75, 76, 77,
  84, 85, 87, 95, 98, 102, 181, 185,
  189, 190, 192, 194, 196, 198, 199
Valsch river, 34, 70
Van Rensburg *see* Rensburg
Vasco da Gama, 36
Vegkop, battle of, 68, 76–83, 85,
  87, 88n, 89, 96, 104, 109, 140,
  203; modern site of, 212–14
Veglaer, 143, 203
Vet river, 70, 71, 76, 87, 88, 102,
  106, 180, 181, 183
Victoria Falls, 63
Viervoet, British defeat at, 197
Visser, Commandant, 151
Voortrekker museum, Pietermaritzburg, 214–15, 218, 219, 222
Voortrekkers, 35, 36, 45; histories
  of, 11; first waves of, 45, 58, 66,
  68; clashes with Matabele, 74–5,
  103–4; start of Great Trek, 84,
  89–91; wagons, 92–3, 214–15;
  dress, 94, 215; religion, 94; life,
  94–5; camp at Blesberg, 96–7;
  dangers, 137; establish Pietermaritzburg, 143; monuments to,
  149, 214, 219, 220, 226–7; give
  thanks after Blood river, 154;
  threatened by British, 160; effect
  in Holland of adventures of,
  172; exodus from Natal, 176–9;
  settlements, 180–81, 201, 226;
  traditions, 203; graveyard, 225;
  see also Afrikaners; Boers

Vuna river, 162

Wolkberg, 211
Wood, William, 126

Walker, E. W., 11
Warden, Major, 185, 192, 197, 200
Wasbank river, 146, 147
Washbank, 221
Waterberg mountains, 34
Weenen, 162, 176, 177, 183, 203, 226
Wellington, Duke of, 188, 189, 193, 200
Wen Commando, 110, 158, 161, 168, 218, 222, 223
West, Martin, Lieut-Governor of Natal, 176
West Africa, 105n
White Umfolozi river, 156–7, 158, 222, 223, 235
Wild Cat People see Batlokwa tribe
Wilge river, 34
Wilhelm Pretorius Game Park, 225
William II, King of Holland, 173
William, Jane, maid to Rev. Francis Owen, 128
Willow Grange, village, 130, 131, 219
Wilson, Dr, American missionary, 75, 83–4, 86
Wilson, Helen, author of The Two Scapegoats, 219
Winburg, 53, 162, 181, 183, 185, 192, 194, 216, 226
Winterberg district, 30, 100
Winterhoekdrif, 212
Wintervogel, Bushman slave, 45
Witwatersrand, 34, 35

Xhosa tribe, 24, 25, 29–30, 31, 43, 44, 60, 129, 188, 189

Zambesi river, 63
Zastron, 33
Zebediela river, 59, 88, 212
Zeekoe river, 23
Zeerust, 73, 214
Zevenfontein, 44
Zoutpansberg mountains, 33, 34, 39, 41, 45, 46, 51, 52, 53, 54, 55, 56, 57, 59, 71, 72, 73, 88, 180, 181, 187, 196, 198, 202, 209, 211
Zoutpansbergdorp, 187, 199, 201, 224, 225
Zulu tribe, 37, 38–9, 40, 74, 98, 109, 137, 146; characteristics, appearance, 39; kill Retief and his party, 126–8; attack trekkers, 130–35, 142–3; at battle of Italeni, 138–40; attacked by English, 141, 142; loot Durban, 141; attack Gatsrand, 142–3; battles at Blood river, 148–54; at Umfolozi, 156–8; Mpande's accession to throne, 164, 167; at Mkuze river, 167; at Ndondakusuka, 220
Zululand, 38, 54, 105, 112, 113, 123, 124, 138, 144, 157, 162, 165
Zwart Koppies, action at, 184
Zwartbergen mountains, 23

THE WASHING OF THE SPEARS

The Rise and Fall of the Zulu Nation

DONALD R. MORRIS

A brilliant account of the life of the Zulu nations under the great ruler Shaka, and its tragic fall under Cetshwayo in the Zulu war of 1870. The Great Trek by the Boers in the 1820s brought them face to face with the expanding power of the Zulus – then the most formidable nation in Black Africa. This confrontation brought about a prolonged struggle culminating in the Zulu war, when, armed only with their assegais, the Zulus challenged the might of Victorian England. Their startling success at the battle of Isandhlwana carried with it the seeds of their ultimate and humiliating destruction.

'The author's style is quiet and unobtrusive, well suited to his torrid material; he knows how to tell a good story; and his numerous character-sketches of Bantus and Britons alike are always sympathetic and often perceptive. Particularly well done is his account of Shaka, the ruthless giant whose powerful will united the Zulu tribes into a ferociously disciplined nation, and whose grotesque disregard of human life and suffering resulted in his own murder in 1828. . . . Commander Morris's thorough and understanding book provides a sad commentary on the enduring attitudes of mind that have made the solution of such problems so intractable' *Christopher Hibbert, The Spectator*

£1·00

HUMBOLDT AND THE COSMOS

DOUGLAS BOTTING

Alexander von Humboldt was born in 1769 into a Prussia where science was considered an unworthy subject for a person of his social standing. In 1799, after a short but brilliant career as a Prussian mining official, he set out to explore the little-known world of South America. The formidable mass of scientific data he collected during his five-year expedition laid the foundations for modern physical geography, and his investigations as a naturalist established the concept of plant geography.

The world of Humboldt, the last truly Universal Man, is vividly recalled in this biography by Douglas Botting. He describes Humboldt's expeditions all over the world, his investigations as a naturalist, his political activities which made him the idol of the German revolution of 1848, and, in the last years of his life, the completion of his greatest work – *The Cosmos* – his vision of the nature of the world.

For this book, Douglas Botting followed Humboldt's route on the Orinoco and Casiquiare. The book contains many of the engravings which illustrated Humboldt's own work, together with other contemporary prints and paintings of the places he visited and the people he met.

£1·75 Illustrated

THE VOYAGE OF THE CHALLENGER

ERIC LINKLATER

In 1872 HMS *Challenger* sailed from Portsmouth on a journey that was to circumnavigate the world, covering over 68,000 nautical miles and lasting a thousand days. She was a three-masted corvette with auxiliary steam, and as well as a crew of over two hundred she carried a team of scientists led by Professor Wyville Thomson.

The voyage of the *Challenger* was a pioneer expedition of immense importance. Sponsored by the British Government and organised by the Royal Society in collaboration with the University of Edinburgh, its ambitious aim was to chart the depths, movement and contents of the seas, to scour the oceans for marine life, minerals, and clues to climatic phenomena. The naturalists on board, Henry Moseley and John Murray, were observant recorders of life ashore as well as at sea, and their personal journals provide a vivid picture of their remote ports of call – the bleak penguin rookeries in the Antarctic, East Indian coral and spice islands, the hostile tribes in New Guinea, and a meeting with the Mikado in Japan.

'Much information of a technical and specialist order made the voyage of the *Challenger* an unqualified success from the scientific point of view. What Linklater has done is to go back beyond the facts to the men who found them, and in recreating that company of personalities on board that packed little ship . . . he has made the voyage of the *Challenger* an equally unqualified success from the point of view of an ordinary human being.'
The Scotsman

£2·50 Illustrated

HISTORY OF CIVILISATION

THE AGE OF RECONNAISSANCE

Discovery, Exploration and Settlement 1450 to 1650

J. H. PARRY

The Age of Reconnaissance was the period during which Europe discovered the rest of the world. It began with Henry the Navigator and the Portuguese voyages in the mid-fifteenth century and ended 250 years later when the 'Reconnaissance' was all but complete.

Dr Parry is concerned with an analysis of the factors which made the voyages possible. These factors include the rapidly developing technical devices used by seamen – the ships, the charts, the instruments and the weapons – but they also include new pressures and inducements, political, economic and psychological, which favoured overseas enterprise. The first part of the book is devoted to analysis and description, the second part to a narrative of events. The third part summarises the geographical knowledge which the discoverers accumulated; describes the various types of commercial and colonial settlement established by different European nations in the lands which the discoverers revealed; and comments on the legal and moral problems with which the European governments of the time were confronted in dealing with wars of conquest, competitive claims to colonial territory, the government of weaker peoples, slavery and the trade in slaves.

'A major work of historical synthesis and an important contribution to our knowledge of the society, economy, and historical geography of the sixteenth and seventeenth centuries.'
The Guardian

£1·00 Illustrated

HISTORY OF CIVILISATION

EUROPE IN THE EIGHTEENTH CENTURY
Aristocracy and the Bourgeois Challenge
GEORGE RUDÉ

A description of Europe during the three quarters of a century between the death of Louis XIV and the industrial revolution in England and the social and political revolution in France. George Rudé has organised his material into three main parts: population, land and peasants, industry, urban growth and society; government, administration, religion, the arts, ideas; tensions and conflict within nations and in their external relations. Particular attention is paid to why these factors contributed to the overthrow of the established order in some countries – notably in France in 1789 – but not in others, and how the growth of social classes and their subsequent conflicts acted as agents of historical change.

'This is a book that really can be recommended to beginners, not because it over-simplifies but because it provides them with all the basic information.'
Times Literary Supplement

£1·40 Illustrated

JANE AUSTEN

ELIZABETH JENKINS

Elizabeth Jenkins has written the classic biography of Jane Austen, whose life mirrors so many of the characters, events and settings of her perenially popular novels.

'One of the best literary biographies published in England for many years. Everything that a biography should be: beautifully written, full of atmosphere, lively in humour and wisely critical.' Hugh Walpole

'An ease and a lucidity in Miss Jenkins' descriptions of Jane Austen's different homes, the atmosphere of her family, and the subtleties of her own character ... her comments are just, crisp and original.'
London Mercury (when the book appeared in an earlier edition)

£1·25 Illustrated

LADY CAROLINE LAMB

ELIZABETH JENKINS

Of all the affairs that shook an epoch notorious for its scandals, there was none more tempestuous than the liaison between Lady Caroline Lamb and Lord Byron. Even as the wife of William Lamb, Viscount Melbourne and later Prime Minister, Lady Caroline's wayward disregard for convention made her the topic of conversation in fashionable salons throughout England. The affair ended in tragedy: she was ostracised by society; her long-suffering husband left her; and her romantic hero grew tired of her demands. Her life had become overshadowed by isolation and despair and she died in 1828 from 'complete exhaustion'.

In this biography, Elizabeth Jenkins has produced a sensitive and colourful portrait of Lady Caroline and of the Regency era.

45p